LAS VEGAS

Wilbur S. Shepperson Series in Nevada History

LAS VEGAS

A CENTENNIAL HISTORY

EUGENE P. MOEHRING AND MICHAEL S. GREEN

UNIVERSITY OF NEVADA PRESS ▲▲ RENO & LAS VEGAS

Series: Wilbur S. Shepperson Series in Nevada History
Series Editor: Michael Green

University of Nevada Press, Reno, Nevada 89557 USA
www.unpress.nevada.edu
Copyright © 2005 by University of Nevada Press
All rights reserved
Manufactured in the United States of America
Design by Omega Clay

Library of Congress Cataloging-in-Publication Data
Moehring, Eugene P.

   Las Vegas : a centennial history / Eugene P. Moehring and Michael S. Green.
     p. cm.—(Wilbur S. Shepperson series in Nevada history)
   Includes bibliographical references and index.
   ISBN 0-87417-611-5 (hardcover : alk. paper) / 0-87417-615-8 (pbk : alk. paper)
   1. Las Vegas (Nev.)—History. 2. Las Vegas (Nev.)—Economic conditions. 3. Las
Vegas Region (Nev.)—History. I. Green, Michael S. II. Title. III. Series.
   F849.L35M638 2005
   979.3'135—dc22   2004017239

The paper used in this book meets the requirements of American National Standard
for Information Sciences—Permanence of Paper for Printed Library Materials, ANSI
z.48-1984. Binding materials were selected for strength and durability.

This book has been reproduced as a digital reprint.

FRONTISPIECE: The Strip at night. Photograph by Clint Karlsen
and copyright by *Las Vegas Review-Journal.*

 Winner of the Wilbur S. Shepperson Humanities Book Award for 2005

This book is the recipient of the Wilbur S. Shepperson Humanities Book Award,
which is given annually in his memory by the Nevada Humanities and the University
of Nevada Press. One of Nevada's most distinguished historians, Wilbur S. Shepperson was a founding member and longtime supporter of both organizations.

Publication of this book was supported in part by a grant from the Las Vegas
Centennial Celebration.

For Frank Wright,

Gary Elliott, and

Ralph Roske,

who did so much

to promote Las Vegas

and Nevada history

CONTENTS

ILLUSTRATIONS

FIGURES

PREFACE

LAS VEGAS IS MANY THINGS TO MANY PEOPLE.
During the past half century, Las Vegas has become an icon of gambling and leisure. It attracts more than 35 million visitors annually, more than Orlando, more even than Mecca in Saudi Arabia. To most of these visitors, it is "Sin City," the "City without Clocks," where "what happens in Vegas stays in Vegas."

But to the people who live here, the better word to describe Las Vegas is "home." To these people—over 1.7 million of them according to the 2000 census, and more arriving every day—the metropolitan Las Vegas area is where they work, raise families, go to school, play ball or go jogging, and dream the same dreams and live the same lives as their fellow Americans all over the country. That the city's major industry involves a sometimes forbidden activity—gambling—and an attitude unappreciated by puritans of all stripes—the pursuit of pleasure in all its forms—does not contradict the fact that the majority of Las Vegans earn their living in ordinary workplaces like offices, shops, and construction sites, and in the same vast range of occupations and professions that other Americans pursue.

Las Vegas began its existence as a rest stop for travelers on the Old Spanish Trail (the city draws its name from a group of springs that once offered a welcome oasis in the blazing Mojave Desert). Less than a century ago, the town was little more than a sleepy whistle-stop servicing a railroad. Many consider Las Vegas's date of birth May 15, 1905, the day when representatives of Senator William A. Clark of Montana and the Union Pacific Railroad auctioned off blocks and lots of dusty desert land on an unseasonably hot day. But a town plat does not ensure the growth of a city—by 1910, fewer than 1,000 people lived in the town and its environs.

This book describes how, in this most unlikely of settings, the world's leading tourist center was born and grew. It commemorates the centen-

nial of that auction—and of the establishment of Las Vegas—by chroni-
cling, analyzing, and celebrating the city in all its diversity and paradox,
and by describing how the city's residents effected this dramatic transformation in less than a century. We shall be looking at far more than the
Strip, which is a much more recent phenomenon—its first hotel, the El
Rancho Vegas, only opened on April 3, 1941—and technically is not even
in the City of Las Vegas, which stops at Sahara Avenue, where the Strip
begins. Nor is our purview limited to the official Las Vegas city limits.
When commentators point out that nearly 2 million people reside in Las
Vegas, they mean in the Standard Metropolitan Statistical Area, which
incorporates not just the city of Las Vegas but the neighboring cities of
North Las Vegas, Henderson, and Boulder City, the unincorporated townships of Paradise, Winchester, and Spring Valley, and county land. The
population of the City of Las Vegas actually accounts for no more than
one-third of the metropolitan population.

Las Vegas's destiny was never assured. The little town limped along
until World War I sparked a brief boom in the transshipment of local minerals, food, and horses. Then, in the 1920s, a slowdown in commerce and a
bitter strike against the Union Pacific Railroad cost Las Vegas its valuable
railroad repair shops, left the place in limbo, and prompted residents to
take steps to attract tourists. Federal intervention in the 1930s, along with
the happy combination of geology, geography, and technology, made Las
Vegas the national gateway to Boulder Dam. This project, with its infu-
sion of federal money, supplies, and workers from all over the country, plus
the interest the project created, began to shift the little town's economy
slowly toward tourism—helped by Nevada's legalization of wide-open
gambling in 1931.

World War II completed the process. Federal spending was again
crucial to the city. The construction of a giant magnesium plant and the
instant suburb of Henderson, the establishment of an army gunnery
school near what later became North Las Vegas, and the creation of numerous military bases and defense plants in neighboring California and Arizona began to flood the growing casino center on Fremont Street with visitors. During the war, Las Vegans increasingly realized that tourism and
gambling, not railroading, would be their salvation. Additional stimulus
for growth came from federal defense spending during the cold war, especially at Nellis and the Nevada Test Site.

This book looks at how Las Vegas evolved from a nineteenth-century Mormon outpost and ranch area into a railroad town, then a dam town, and then into something far grander. The key to this evolution was not just the development of the central city, as it was in New York, Philadelphia, and Boston, but of the suburbs as well. Indeed, gambling was remarkably energized when it was liberated from cramped hotels on the central city's narrow lots and placed in spacious resorts in the suburbs. In 1940–1941, when Thomas Hull built his El Rancho Vegas just south of the city line (across from the front of today's Sahara Hotel), he recognized that Clark County's cheap desert land provided the best sites for the casino-resorts that came to typify Las Vegas's principal industry. With the help of electricity (which could be transmitted anywhere in the metropolitan zone) and the internal-combustion engine, decentralization became the key to Las Vegas's development, just as it was in the Los Angeles Basin.

In this book, we trace the development of Las Vegas's twin gambling centers on the Strip and downtown. We also explain why the Strip never joined the city, and why the Strip eventually grew larger than the city that inspired it. We cover all the major events in the city's history, including the more recent ones like the housing boom in master-planned communities, the Disneyfied architecture of the Strip's newest resorts, and Mayor Oscar Goodman's plans to diversify downtown's economy. We also offer material with which many are less familiar, such as a discussion of the Ku Klux Klan's presence in Las Vegas during the 1920s and 1930s, and we provide a frank and detailed account of the battle for civil rights in both the community and the gaming industry, in a city whose rigid and restrictive racial policies made it known for many years as "the Mississippi of the West."

However, our purpose is not just to provide an account of metropolitan development. We also engage in some policy analysis to show that many of the issues that residents grapple with today have deep historical roots in the community. For example, we show that growth has always been expensive in Las Vegas. In every decade after 1930, residents recognized that population growth was welcome, but it was also expensive, requiring frequent bond issues to finance new streets, sewers, water lines, schools, libraries, and other infrastructural improvements. We examine the political fragmentation of the metropolitan area into three cities (four, if you count Boulder City) and one county with multiple police and fire departments, and we explain why, for good historical reasons, this wasteful situation will probably never change.

We want to tell both stories—the story of the flamboyant people, shrewd businessmen-gamblers, and colorful industry that built the Strip and its worldwide reputation as "Sin City," and the story of the metropolitan area around it that grew parallel to and partly because of the success of gambling and entertainment. As the city enters its centennial year in 2005 and celebrates its prodigious growth in the breathtakingly brief span of a single century, our objective is to explain why and how Las Vegas accomplished this growth and how it got to be the way it is today.

ACKNOWLEDGMENTS

THE AUTHORS WELCOME THIS OPPORTUNITY to thank those who have aided this project. First, those associated with the planning of the Las Vegas Centennial have encouraged us over the years in ways related and unrelated to this book. The list is lengthy. But we are especially indebted to Bob Stoldal, a longtime Las Vegas broadcast journalist with an insatiable interest in our city's history. He worked with the committee of historians and with civic leaders to encourage us in this effort.

The staff of the Department of Special Collections in UNLV's Lied Library aided with photographs and research. We especially thank Kathy War and Su Kim Chung for their help with the photographs. Also helpful were Dave Millman of the Nevada State Museum and Historical Society in Las Vegas and Nate Stout who expertly prepared the maps for publication. We would also like to acknowledge the *Las Vegas Review-Journal* for supplying some of the photographs, and especially to Jerry Henkle and Jeff Scheid for their assistance. Joanne O'Hare and the staff of the University of Nevada Press are marvelous professionals, and we appreciate all they have done to bring this book to fruition.

Our colleagues at the University of Nevada, Las Vegas, and the Community College of Southern Nevada have been sounding boards, friends, and teachers. Some of them have done significant research and writing on Las Vegas, while others have aided us with administrative and teaching tasks. We would like to acknowledge, in particular, Tom Wright, Andy Fry, Sue Fawn Chung, Hal Rothman, Joanne Goodwin, and David Tanenhaus of UNLV and Alan Balboni, DeAnna Beachley, Fran Campbell, and Candace Kant of CCSN.

Fellow Las Vegans have also provided us with ideas, sometimes unwittingly. To try to name all of them is to leave out too many of them. They are fewer than the population that lives here, but large in number. We are grateful to them and to our doctoral advisers and other graduate professors, who had nothing to do with Las Vegas but taught us much about researching, teaching, writing, and thinking about history in these pages. We are grateful for the example set by Richard C. Wade, Arthur M. Schlesinger Jr., Eric Foner, and Eric McKitrick.

Authors generally thank their wives for love, sustenance, and occasionally for helping with the technology. When it comes to Christine Wiatrowski and Deborah Young, all of that is true and so much more.

Finally, the book's dedication reflects another debt. Ralph J. Roske wrote a fine history of Las Vegas and played a large role in hiring one of the authors and mentoring the other. Frank Wright spent two decades as curator at the Nevada State Museum and Historical Society, dispensing facts and wisdom to anyone who asked—and we often did—and all of us profited just from knowing him. Gary Elliott not only wrote a history of Las Vegas, but was also a student of one of the authors, largely responsible for the hiring of the other, and a dear friend to both. Their families are in our thoughts, especially Rosemary Roske, Dorothy Wright, and Debbie Elliott. We miss our three friends and colleagues and wish they had been here—to join in the celebration, and to make this a better book.

Eugene P. Moehring
Michael S. Green

LAS VEGAS

BEFORE THE CITY

LAS VEGAS CELEBRATES ITS CENTENNIAL in 2005 as a typical city—and a totally unique one. No other American city founded in the twentieth century has grown into an urban area of more than one million by the twenty-first century. Although outside the city limits, the Strip—Las Vegas Boulevard South—is one of the world's most famous and recognizable streets, with the neon that continues into the city's downtown Glitter Gulch area visible from outer space. The city and its cash cow, gaming, have evolved from a "green felt jungle" and "sin city" into a respected industry run by executives with national and international corporations.

Each year, millions of tourists visit the city, including the downtown and Summerlin areas. They also frequent surrounding locales like the Strip, North Las Vegas, Henderson, Boulder City, Red Rock Canyon, and the Valley of Fire, to name only a few. Tourism obviously affects the economy greatly, but the city also depends upon such typical industries as construction, municipal services, and health care. Politically, Las Vegas leans toward the Democratic Party, due partly to the presence of powerful unions, yet it tends to be fiscally conservative and slow to deal with social problems. The area increasingly resembles the sprawl, smog, and rush-hour traffic of southern California. Culturally, Las Vegas offers much of what residents of comparatively sized cities might find, yet it still lags behind them in its offerings of museums and music, and in the support they receive. Growth has been and will continue to be an all-important issue: how to deal with more traffic, more use of water, more students attending more schools, and, always, more growth.

Las Vegans of 2005 are familiar with these issues, but not always with their history. It turns out that what they find today in their desert oasis is similar to what has come before: encounters with travelers, connections to southern California, and the combination of a typical community merged with guilty pleasures. Las Vegans do not live in the past—but the past remains very much alive.

Long before today's large population of residents and tourists arrived, people lived in the Las Vegas Valley. Archaeologists have found evidence of Native Americans living in southern Nevada more than ten thousand years ago from baskets, petroglyphs, pictographs, and other materials in locations as diverse as Gypsum Cave to the east and Tule Springs to the northwest. Perhaps as early as A.D. 700, Paiutes moved into southern Nevada, spending summers in the nearby mountains and winters in the valley, often by the Big Springs. They survived mainly by gathering plants and berries, occasionally farming on small plots of land, and hunting for small animals such as desert tortoises, rabbits, snakes, and lizards.

The Las Vegas Paiutes probably encountered Spanish traders in the eighteenth and early nineteenth centuries, but no conclusive evidence exists to prove this. At the end of 1829, Rafael Rivera apparently became the first non–Native American known to have set foot in the Las Vegas Valley. A scout for New Mexico merchant Antonio Armijo, Rivera diverted from the group, then rejoined the traders when they camped in Las Vegas that January 7 before going on to California. Armijo and Rivera established Las Vegas as the northern branch of the Old Spanish Trail, which travelers between New Mexico and southern California used for the next two decades.

Even then, though, Las Vegas had competition and a reputation. George Yount and William Wolfskill laid out a branch of the Old Spanish Trail to the south, through what is now Needles, California. Many travelers preferred Needles because of the abundant water and grass in the Las Vegas Valley. That might seem to make no sense, but the water and grass also attracted horse thieves and traders in Indian slaves. Indeed, in 1840, mountain man Bill Williams and Ute chief Wakara led a raid on California ranches that netted perhaps one thousand horses that galloped through Las Vegas.

Americans soon learned about the Las Vegas Valley's attractions through the work of federal explorers. On May 3, 1844, Captain John C. Frémont and his fellow mapmakers from the U.S. Army Topographical Corps arrived at the Big Springs, part of today's Las Vegas Springs Pre-

This 1877 photo shows Southern Paiutes outside their wickiups, shelters built of branches and other resources. When the Armijo trading party from New Mexico came through in the winter of 1829–1830, these were the valley's only residents, and had been for centuries. Their number has dwindled, but Southern Paiutes still reside downtown on land donated to them by Helen Stewart, on the Moapa Reservation northeast of town, and throughout the valley. Special Collections, UNLV Libraries

serve near U.S. 95 and Valley View. "After a day's journey of 18 miles, in a northeasterly direction," he wrote, "we encamped in the midst of another very large basin, at a camping ground called Las Vegas—a term which the Spanish use to signify fertile or marshy plains." Frémont found the springs too warm to drink—about seventy-two degrees—but excellent for bathing. He became the first to list Las Vegas on an official government map and named the large mountain to the west for Charleston, South Carolina.

Raised in the Palmetto State, Frémont had married the daughter of Thomas Hart Benton, a longtime senator from Missouri and firm believer in Manifest Destiny. Like many at the time, Benton considered it the nation's destiny to expand its borders beyond the Rockies and all the way to the Pacific Ocean. The official report of Frémont's trip—which benefited from his wife Jessie's editing and rewriting—described a vast and beautiful territory occupied by a few Native Americans and Mexicans, whom Frémont disdained. This encouraged American interest in acquiring the West.

Not only did the federal government look to the West, so did members of the Church of Jesus Christ of Latter-day Saints, founded in New York in 1830. The Mormons had moved westward in an unsuccessful effort to escape oppression. In 1844, a mob, upset mainly with the Mormons' sanctioning plural marriage for men, murdered their leader, Joseph Smith. Brigham Young succeeded him and decided to take his community west, beyond U.S. borders. Early in 1847, Mormons arrived in the Salt Lake Valley. After building a community there, they erected other towns, missions, and forts to provide rest stops and seek additional resources.

The Mormon quest to escape the United States failed. The United States declared war on Mexico in 1846 and, negotiating the fruits of victory in the Treaty of Guadalupe Hidalgo, obtained nearly five hundred thousand square miles of land, including not only California but all or part of six other states as well. In 1850, Congress passed and President Millard Fillmore signed legislation creating the state of California and two new territories: Utah, which included all of that present-day state and virtually all of Nevada north of present-day Clark County, and New Mexico, consisting of that state, Arizona, and the rest of Nevada, including the Las Vegas Valley. With Brigham Young as territorial governor, Mormons prepared to build a corridor of fort missions stretching from Salt Lake to San Bernardino, California.

In 1855, Young issued an order for thirty Mormons to head southwest to Las Vegas. Their duties included building a fort mission, spreading the word about their church to the local Indians, and possibly creating a military alliance with them. As the mission's leader, he chose William Bringhurst. The first group of Mormons arrived in the valley on June 14. When they reached the Big Springs that Frémont had described in his report, they found some of the Paiutes there. Unsure of how friendly they would be, the Mormons looked about four miles northeast. They chose a natural bench or hill from which they could guard against attack from above or below. Better still, the Las Vegas Creek flowed nearby.

The men almost immediately began building a fort. Made of adobe brick with stone foundations, the fort's fourteen-foot-high walls and two blockhouses offered protection against attackers, white or Indian. The men shared small houses until, the next year, some of their families arrived from Utah. They planted crops and received help from the thousand or so local Paiutes. They set up an experimental farm a mile and a half north of the fort for the natives, who learned about new crops to add to those they had grown for centuries.

But troubles afflicted the mission. Growing crops proved difficult in the arid desert and hard ground. Rainfall declined thanks to a mild drought. Viewing private property differently than the whites, Paiutes helped themselves to the crops. In 1856, a lead discovery at nearby Mount Potosi (near today's Blue Diamond) divided the missionaries between those, like Bringhurst, who saw mining as secondary and those who supported Nathaniel Jones, whom Young sent from Salt Lake to run the mining operations. When Bringhurst challenged Jones's authority, Young replaced the mission leader with the more agreeable Samuel Thompson. But the lead contained too much silver and unwanted compounds to be valuable. After Jones gave up, the Paiutes stole the 1858 harvest from the fields, and Young soon allowed the mission to disband.

While the mission failed, the fort survived. Two Mormon brothers, Albert and William Knapp, ran a general store at the fort for the next few years, serving miners at Mount Potosi and south at Eldorado Canyon. One of the miners, Octavius Decatur Gass, became the next important influence on Las Vegas. An Ohio native who had worked on the Gold Rush and later pursued tin mining in southern California, Gass arrived in Eldorado Canyon in 1863—about the time that Congress created Arizona Territory, which included most of southern Nevada. Within two years, he began obtaining and farming the land until he controlled nearly one thousand acres.

Gass, for whom a downtown street is named, proved successful—for a while. He eventually employed more than thirty workers. He ran fifteen hundred cattle and grew various fruits and vegetables. He found markets in California and Arizona, and along the Colorado in Callville, a Colorado River port the Mormons founded. He became speaker of Arizona's territorial assembly. He married and started a family. If anyone proved that a ranch could prosper in the Mojave Desert, it was Gass.

But trouble loomed. In 1867, he lived in what became part of the state of Nevada, and since most of the population and political power resided in the Virginia City area, he lost his influence. He questioned whether he

In 1876, Frederic Dellenbaugh of John Wesley Powell's exploration party painted a portrait of the Las Vegas Ranch, then owned by Octavius Decatur Gass. Today, the area is part of the Las Vegas Mormon Fort State Park. While Las Vegas celebrates its centennial, the fort celebrates its sesquicentennial. Special Collections, UNLV Libraries

actually resided in Nevada and refused to pay taxes, leaving him with a large bill. Nearby army posts claimed that he overcharged them. His wife and growing family wanted to live somewhere with more amenities—and more neighbors than just the Wilsons, who lived at the Las Vegas Spring Ranch and Spring Mountain Ranch, and Conrad Kiel, a fellow Ohioan whom Gass had encouraged to move to southern Nevada and take over the old Paiute experimental farm in what later became North Las Vegas. Gass kept mortgaging the ranch to pay for lawsuits over the tin mines he claimed to own south of Los Angeles—and his financial problems caught up with him.

In 1879, Gass mortgaged the ranch for five thousand dollars in gold to Archibald Stewart, a businessman in Pioche, the Lincoln County seat, about 150 miles north of Las Vegas. Unable to repay him, Gass and his family left their Las Vegas Ranch in 1881. Stewart then persuaded his wife, Helen, to move south with their three children. The ranch prospered, and their family life appeared happy: they added a fourth child, and by the summer of 1884, Helen was pregnant with a fifth. But Kiel feuded with Stewart, believing that he had swindled his friend Gass out of his land.

In 1884, ranch hand Schuyler Henry left Stewart's ranch to work for the Kiels. Apparently, Henry spread gossip about Mrs. Stewart. When Archibald returned from his trip on June 13 and Helen told him what had happened, he rode away with his gun. A couple of hours later, she received a note from Kiel, informing her that her husband was dead. She buried Archibald on a hill just west of the original fort in a coffin fashioned from two wooden doors of the ranch house.

At age thirty, Helen Stewart was a widow awaiting the birth of a son she would name for the father he would never see. She blamed her nearest neighbors for her husband's death; while a coroner's jury found no proof, she remained convinced that Kiel and the gunslingers with whom he associated had ambushed Archibald. She had inherited a ranch and nearly one thousand acres of land that had to be managed. Despite the bleakness that obviously would await her, she chose to remain in Las Vegas, declining low offers to sell the ranch. She ran a roadside rest stop for travelers, raised her children, hired tutors to educate them, and served as local postmistress. She hired foremen to help her run her ranch until she married one of them.

But her life remained difficult. She refused to speak to Conrad Kiel or his heirs, Edwin and William. In 1899, while home from boarding school, her son Archibald died of injuries sustained from falling off a horse. She apparently never wrote about her husband, but her son's death devastated her. The next year, her soon-to-be husband, Frank, and son William went to the Kiel Ranch to report the arrival of some wagon wheels and found the two brothers dead of gunshot wounds. A coroner's jury ruled it a murder-suicide, although anthropologists who examined the bodies more than seventy years later called it a double murder for which no one ever came forward to claim responsibility.

Meanwhile, Helen Stewart waited and hoped to sell her land. Reports often appeared that various entrepreneurs wanted to build a railroad that would run through the Las Vegas area. Finally, in 1902, she found a buyer for her holdings. She kept 160 acres and the family burial plot, and built new homes in Las Vegas and Los Angeles. She would help start—and

Helen Stewart, second from the left, displays some of her Indian baskets. Her second husband, Frank, who worked at the ranch, is on the far left. For keeping the ranch for nearly two decades after Archibald's death, helping to start the Mesquite Club, and aiding the local Paiutes, she is often called "the First Lady of Las Vegas." Special Collections, UNLV Libraries

name—the oldest women's civic organization in Las Vegas, the Mesquite Club. She collected Paiute baskets and, due to her interest in and sympathy for their makers, deeded ten acres of land for a Paiute colony, where a significant contingent of Paiutes still lives. When she died in 1926, she was remembered, as she is today, as the First Lady of Las Vegas. By then, a new man and his partners had completely changed the little desert rest stop of several ranches into a railroad town headed for much bigger things.

BIRTH OF A RAILROAD TOWN,
1902-1910

IN THE FIRST DECADE OF THE TWENTIETH CENTURY,
Nevada emerged from a twenty-year economic depression after the decline of the Comstock Lode, thanks to the discovery of gold and silver in
south-central Nevada and copper in eastern Nevada—and some hopeful
activities in such southern Nevada mining camps as Searchlight. Political
and economic power continued to reside with the mining industry in
Nevada's northern tier, but to the south a new railroad builder from outside the state promised change. Those changes eventually shook Nevada,
and many other places, to its foundation.

The first change involved ownership of southern Nevada. For most of
her two decades in Las Vegas, Helen Stewart had hoped to sell at least
some of her holdings for construction of a railroad. A couple of deals fell
through before her hopes turned into reality, courtesy of Montana copper
baron William Andrews Clark. In 1902, he bought most of her land for
fifty-five thousand dollars. Clark's advisers chose Las Vegas for several
reasons: first, it was on a more direct route to Salt Lake than the Pahrump
Valley or the rugged Colorado River Valley, and, second, it had plenty of
underground water—snowmelt from the Charleston range (Spring Mountains) to the west. The railroad also required a division point—a town—
with enough water for steam engines, repair shops, and residences for
workers. Helen Stewart's ranch met all these needs.

Clark knew how Stewart felt about overcoming difficulties and trying
to improve her life. Born in Pennsylvania, Clark later homesteaded in
Iowa with his parents. He worked in Colorado's mines before heading to
Montana, where he found the kind of prosperity that made him a classic
example of both Horatio Alger and the new rich of the late nineteenth
century who flaunted their wealth for all to see. His Anaconda claim pro-

duced the largest copper vein ever—fifty feet wide. It made him a multi-millionaire and led to the creation of the Anaconda Copper Company, which dominated both that industry and the state of Montana for decades. His original partner had been George Hearst, whose millions made from Virginia City and the Comstock Lode helped finance his son William Randolph Hearst's foray into journalism. And Clark imitated other western mining magnates by bribing enough legislators to win one of Montana's U.S. Senate seats in 1901. He also exemplified the scandalous acts associated with the Senate at the time: he built a mansion of more than one hundred rooms on Fifth Avenue in New York City and fathered two children with his mistress.

With all of that going on, the financial possibilities excited Clark's interest in railroad building in the West. As the twentieth century began, southern California was booming, but it had few railroad connections to the rest of the Southwest. Meanwhile, gold discoveries at Tonopah in 1900 and Goldfield in 1902 started a new mining boom in Nevada and opened the southern and central parts of the state to development. The combination was too much for Clark to pass up. In 1901, with his younger brother J. Ross, Clark began building the San Pedro, Los Angeles, & Salt Lake Railroad (SPLA&SL). But the Clarks faced competition. After going bankrupt, the Union Pacific (UP) rebuilt its reputation and profits under the guidance of financier Edward Henry Harriman, whose friends considered him shrewd and whose opponents deemed him ruthless. The Clarks won title to land the UP had acquired for a proposed railroad, then abandoned. But Harriman refused to concede defeat and sent in men, mules, and equipment. Both the Union Pacific and the Clark interests tried to lay track to the north in northeast Lincoln County through the Meadow Valley Wash, which was too narrow to accommodate more than one line.

Finally, in 1903, the two sides compromised. Senator Clark agreed to buy the Union Pacific's track. In turn, Harriman obtained half ownership of the San Pedro, Los Angeles, & Salt Lake line. Construction resumed, to be completed on the afternoon of January 30, 1905, when an engineer used his thumb to push a small gold spike into the last tie near Jean, about twenty miles south of Las Vegas. Passenger service began May 1. Now Clark needed a town where his trains could stop for repairs and their riders for refreshment—and to house those providing such services.

With the tracks being built through Las Vegas, a few people connected to the railroad began arriving. Halle Hewetson, the son of an Ohio doctor and a surgeon for the railroad who had taught at an Omaha medical school, became the area's first full-time doctor in 1904, using the first tent the railroad put up. That year, Walter Bracken came to Las Vegas and became the railroad's resident agent. Born in Ohio and trained as a civil engineer, Bracken first visited in 1901 as part of the group that recommended Las Vegas to Clark as the best route for the line. He served as postmaster, running the post office out of the tent in which he lived. He helped survey a proposed town site and set aside free land for any denomination that proposed to build a church.

But another surveyor had another town site in mind. Canadian-born John T. McWilliams had worked as a civil engineer in Las Vegas and Goodsprings in the 1890s. Working for the Union Pacific and Clark had familiarized him with their plans and practices. In 1904, he bought eighty acres from Helen Stewart and advertised the "Original Las Vegas Townsite"— now part of West Las Vegas, the area from A to H and Washington to Bonanza. "Get in line early, buy now, double your money in 60 days," said his advertisement. His plat became known as McWilliams Townsite or Ragtown for the tents housing most of its fifteen hundred residents and businesses ranging from stores and saloons to bakeries and three weekly newspapers.

Unfortunately for McWilliams, he picked a fight with an unbeatable foe. Obviously, the combination of Clark and the Union Pacific had access to far more capital than McWilliams could ever obtain. Even more significant for his town site's survival, Clark controlled the water rights to the Stewart Ranch. That forced McWilliams to depend on whatever wells he and the other residents could dig and made fire not merely a danger, but a likelihood. Besides, as historian Ralph Roske wrote, "The railroad would not let McWilliams reap what the Salt Lake route had sown." Given that they had worked together and known each other, the battle between Bracken and McWilliams became increasingly personal, and it continued long after a fire destroyed most of the McWilliams Townsite on September 5, 1905. The *Las Vegas Times* declared, "The old town is but a memory. . . . Bustle, hustle and jostle was its lot in its heyday. All is gone. Fire has consumed it."

By the time McWilliams Townsite had been all but destroyed, Clark's town site was off to a prosperous start. The senator and his top aides, his

The McWilliams Townsite, 1904–1905. Most of these businesses folded up and moved to Las Vegas after the Clark town-site auction. The wooden and tent buildings help explain why a fire destroyed many of the remaining structures in September 1905. Special Collections, UNLV Libraries

brother and executive C. O. Whittemore, formed a subsidiary, the Las Vegas Land & Water Company (LVL&W), to operate the town. From offices in a stucco building at the southwest corner of Main and Ogden, the LVL&W planned to sell lots between Stewart, Garces, Main, and Fifth Streets. Each of the forty blocks was three hundred feet by four hundred feet, separated by eighty-foot-wide streets with twenty-foot-wide alleys. The only two blocks on which businesses could obtain licenses to sell liquor were 16 and 17, at the north end of the town site. Set aside at Third and Carson for public uses, Block 20 became the site of the Clark County Courthouse.

Originally, railroad executives planned to sell lots to individual bidders. The terms were 25 percent down and the rest within two months, with corner lots going for up to $750 and interior lots for up to $500. But with so many bidders, Senator Clark's usually silent partners at the Union Pacific demanded action. All agreed, but not without controversy: J. Ross Clark unavailingly argued against it, and one would-be bidder called it "the simplest way of giving everybody a fair shake(down)."

The big day was May 15, 1905, a Monday. The railroad offered special round-trip prices of $16 from Los Angeles and $20 from Salt Lake City—and, as encouragement, a refund to anyone who bought a lot. It posted announcements at railroad offices all along the route. It put up an auction platform on the west side of Main Street between Fremont and Ogden. At 10 A.M., Whittemore announced that the LVL&W would guarantee to grade and oil all streets, build a depot and railroad shops to provide jobs, and make water available to all lots. Then Los Angeles auctioneer Ben Rhoades opened the bidding. The auction ended at 3 P.M. because the high temperature that day was 110 degrees, the first truly hot day of the year, and too much for the shade from the nearby mesquite trees to overcome. The carnations that California florists sent at a cost of a dollar a dozen soon wilted. The men, attired in three-piece and wool suits, removed their jackets—a major concession to the heat for those raised in the propriety of the Victorian era.

The LVL&W gave birth to a town—and a profitable birth it was. The auction sold the best 176 of the 1,200 lots for $79,566—many to southern California speculators rather than to Las Vegans. Land sales resumed at 8 A.M. the next day, but this time for fixed prices rather than through an auction. By the end of the day, about half of the lots in the Clark town site had sold for the grand total of $265,000—nearly five times what the copper baron had paid Helen Stewart, and with most of the acreage still available for sale. The railroad even made an extra $7 by selling the lumber from the auctioneer's stand. Almost at once, most residents of McWilliams's Ragtown literally folded their tents and moved east across the railroad tracks to be part of the main town site. And the railroad kept one of its promises: building a mission-style depot at Main and Fremont.

As successful as the auction was, not everything came out as railroad executives hoped. Economic problems and heat prompted the return of twenty-six business licenses during the summer of 1905. Plans to limit liquor sales to Blocks 16 and 17 fell by the wayside, thanks to a provision allowing hotels to sell alcohol. Naturally, hotels built along Fremont Street and elsewhere took advantage of the opportunity.

Also, Fremont Street failed to develop fully into the business district that LVL&W officials anticipated. Until the 1930s, the town's leading residential area would be on Fremont between Fourth and Fifth Streets. As if to prove it, from 1905 until 1942, Walter Bracken, the LVL&W agent and an investor in numerous important local businesses, lived with his wife, Anna, in a gray stone house at 410 Fremont Street that included a fashionable parlor and a collection of Paiute basketry. Charles P. "Pop" Squires, owner of a local newspaper and Bracken's fellow investor, lived nearby. At the northeast corner of Fourth and Fremont was the home of John S.

Walter Bracken became postmaster shortly after settling in Las Vegas in 1904. In 1908, he was still on the job. Although he left the postmaster's position soon after, he remained with the Las Vegas Land & Water Company until 1946. Special Collections, UNLV Libraries

Charles and Delphine Squires celebrated their sixtieth wedding anniversary, August 21, 1949, at the Flamingo, built on land he once owned. A 1905 arrival, he was active in numerous businesses, especially the *Las Vegas Age,* and she was involved in the women's club and suffrage movement. Special Collections, UNLV Libraries

Park, the cashier at the bank. At the southwest corner of Fifth and Fremont was the home of Dr. Roy W. Martin, long one of the town's two main doctors, both of whom worked for the Clark interests.

Yet the town's development and the role these men played in it signified from the outset that Las Vegas was a company town in the broadest sense. The traditional view of the company town was that one firm or businessman controlled literally everything and used scrip instead of money—much like the copper towns to the north in White Pine County or coal mining towns in West Virginia and Pennsylvania, all developing at about the same time as Las Vegas. That was hardly the case within Clark's town site, but no one could deny that the railroad was predominant. It was the major local employer and builder. It was also responsible for efforts to link Las Vegas to the rest of the state. Clark promised, "I will leave no stone unturned and spare myself no personal effort to do all that lies within my power to foster and encourage the growth and development of Las Vegas." The mixed results still affect the area's interplay with other parts of Nevada and reflected Clark's desire to expand his influence throughout the West.

Clark's first effort was to build a railroad to the boomtowns of Tonopah and Goldfield. Francis M. "Borax" Smith, a fellow millionaire known for his borax mines and twenty-mule team, already planned to build the Tonopah & Tidewater and thought that he had an agreement that would allow him to tie that line into Clark's road through Las Vegas. He was wrong. Clark incorporated and started construction on his own Las Vegas & Tonopah (LV&T) railroad, barred Smith's trains from using his tracks, and denied him discounts for hauling equipment. Smith finally conceded defeat, moving his line's terminus to California. For his part, Clark put his brother in charge and completed construction to Beatty, Rhyolite, and Goldfield, never reaching Tonopah. Worse, Las Vegas remained so small during the peak of construction in the fall of 1905 that it lacked facilities for the hundred-member construction crew, who instead lived in a nearby camp. But the LV&T connected Las Vegas with mining boomtowns in the hinterland, providing markets and additional employment for local businesses and residents.

Track repairs also affected Las Vegans. In 1906, a springtime storm washed out large sections of track in the Meadow Valley Wash near Caliente, stopping rail service for a month. Early the next year, another storm there wiped out the rails for two months. The biggest flood of all inaugurated 1910, destroying previous repairs and closing the line for nearly six months. Each time, Las Vegans wound up isolated from Salt Lake City, although not from southern California. Its economy suffered accordingly, with most of the employees needed to operate the railroad laid off, but the need for repair work also created a variety of jobs.

These track problems affected Las Vegas's growth and prompted the railroad to make sure that the rest of the line functioned properly. In 1909 the SPLA&SL expanded its local yards and built new repair shops at a cost of more than four hundred thousand dollars, increasing local railroad employment to four hundred and prompting a new round of home building. The SPLA&SL built about sixty-four houses on South Second, Third, and Fourth Streets, all with concrete blocks, wood frames, a rectangular layout, and a right entrance porch—all typical of the California bungalow architecture of the time. They cost about seventeen hundred dollars apiece to build and rented for up to twenty dollars a month for a four-bedroom house. Only a few remain standing, and several will be part of the Las Vegas Springs Preserve, while others have been combined or renovated as professional offices or larger buildings. The railroad subsidiary also built Hanson Hall, a two-story concrete building that doubled as a warehouse and meeting hall at the yards south of the town site, and a sixty-five-room apartment building for SPLA&SL workers.

Another railroad development crucial to the young town was the icehouse. Senator Clark personally chose the corner of Main and Bonanza on one of his rare trips through Las Vegas. Little did he know that the land belonged to someone else. Once construction was well under way, McWilliams proved that he owned the property—not the railroad, to which he offered to sell it. Instead, Clark's aides shifted construction to another site near the repair yards along South Main at Bonneville, where

Las Vegas, 1910. The rows of similar-looking houses are the railroad cottages, some of which still stand on South Second, Third, and Fourth Streets. South Main Street is in the foreground, with a two-story house built by Pacific Fruit Express for an official at the ice plant. Special Collections, UNLV Libraries

the ice plant burned down in July 1907—the worst time of year. The railroad replaced it with a 100-ton modern plant made of reinforced concrete, a 900-foot loading platform that could ice twenty refrigerated cars at a time, and a 175-foot-high smokestack, the town's tallest structure. It supplied all stations from San Bernardino to Salt Lake—and, to the pleasure of Las Vegans, local saloons and residences, which also benefited from the facility's power plant.

But while the railroad gave, it also took away. Its subsidiary, the Las Vegas Land & Water Company, operated under the thumb of executives at the corporate headquarters in Los Angeles. Until the 1930s, they allowed Bracken to play the role of heavy as resident agent in Las Vegas, but often without any real authority. Bracken refused to extend water lines beyond the original town site to allow for additional building—and since the railroad technically controlled local water rights instead of its subsidiary, options were limited anyway. The LVL&W failed to keep Whittemore's promise to pave all of the streets. Iron pipes would have been better, but water lines made out of redwood staves, held together with metal hoops, were cheaper and therefore the LVL&W's choice, prompting the *Las Vegas*

The original ice plant burned down, and this one was built to replace it in 1907. It burned in 1989, and served as a wake-up call to local officials who paid too little attention to historic preservation. Special Collections, UNLV Libraries

Age to warn in August 1905 that "all drinking water should be boiled." Consequently, would-be land magnates dug their own wells outside the town site. By 1910, more than one hundred uncapped artesian wells ran constantly within blocks of the depot at Main and Fremont—which helps explain the more than one-foot drop in the local water table in the course of a century.

One of Las Vegas's first and most important developers, future mayor Peter Buol, arrived just before the auction and understood the value of water. A Chicago native trained by his father, a master chef, Buol came west as a cook on Fred Harvey's dining cars on the Santa Fe Railroad. After eyeing Goldfield, Buol chose Las Vegas to live because he feared that his bankroll was too small for the mining boomtown. He probably was right: Goldfield became the basis for the empire of George Wingfield, who ended up controlling most of Nevada's major banks and many of its mines for the first third of the twentieth century.

Las Vegas was so small that it attracted little interest from Wingfield or anyone else in northern Nevada, but it offered ample opportunity for Buol's foresight and fortitude. He invested in insurance, mining, and real estate. The railroad's slothlike growth policies and the presence of artesian springs played into his hands. In 1905, he headed the Vegas Artesian Water Syndicate, which he formed with such local luminaries as Bracken (the same Bracken whom some residents blamed for the glacial-like pace at which his bosses extended the water lines), John S. Park, W. R. Thomas, and M. S. Beal. He began drilling wells and developing Buck's Addition, stretching from Bonanza to Fremont and Sixth to Ninth Streets. It joined the 400 block of Fremont as an upscale residential area.

Another developer involved in Las Vegas from its beginnings as a town was Captain James Ladd. He erected a tent hotel in preparation for the auction and displayed his own brand of ingenuity: to figure out whether travelers arriving from the desert heat were free of lice, he required them to sit by the stove and waited to see whether they scratched; if they lasted half an hour, they were acceptable. Ladd built a housing subdivision from Clark to Fremont and Twelfth to Fifteenth Streets, while other developers put up a tract from Ninth to Fourteenth and Mesquite to Fremont.

McWilliams continued to own and promote his land west of the tracks, but he had another development in mind. In the 1890s, while working as a surveyor and civil engineer, he claimed about thirteen hundred acres in the Spring Mountains. Unable to do anything with it just then, he learned in 1906 that the federal government had canceled his claims, prompting him to write to President Theodore Roosevelt, who was at the height of his trust busting. McWilliams blamed Clark, still a U.S. senator from Montana, for trying to punish him by depriving him of his land, and regained his acreage. In 1910, he and his wife set up a camp amid the pine trees and placed newspaper advertisements urging people to "bring your own grub and bedding." The area was Lee Canyon. When the Las Vegas town site began, the sawmill in Lee Canyon provided needed lumber, but McWilliams and other developers eventually added skiing, homes, and a park named for its owner.

While the willingness to seek water—and the LVL&W's unwillingness to provide it—contributed greatly to these developments, other residents looked beyond the original town sites for land and sought their own water to serve it. Ed Clark and C. C. Ronnow owned a ranch seven miles south of town, while Ed Von Tobel and Jake Beckley staked their claim southeast in Paradise Valley. They dug their own wells while relying on the local railroad subsidiary for water for their town-site investments. Other businessmen proved less tolerant of the LVL&W's faults: John F. Miller finally dug a well at the Hotel Nevada site at Main and Fremont because the water pressure was so low.

From the beginning, Las Vegans understood the need to take the initiative rather than waiting for others. One way in which they demonstrated this was by promoting their young community. They started forming a board of trade a few weeks after the auction and held meetings to discuss mutual concerns. Foreshadowing a longtime local interest in how the media portrayed Las Vegas, they passed resolutions condemning the *Los Angeles Times* for publishing an unfavorable description of local business conditions and lauding the *Los Angeles Examiner* for its full-page report describing Clark's town site in glowing terms. In 1908, they also set up the Las Vegas Promotion Society, a forerunner of the Chamber of Commerce.

One of the main goals of these organizations was to boost Las Vegas as a center for agriculture and mining. Given that Las Vegas was part of the Silver State and ranching ranked second only to digging for ore in its economy, that made sense. Reports predicted that Las Vegas would "one day be the center of an agricultural region of wondrous wealth." Urging readers to make agriculture an integral part of the city's future, the *Las Vegas Times* typically overexaggerated in describing "the finest vegetables grown in the country" and land "that properly cultivated and intelligently handled will prove a gold mine." Its editors also declared, "Vegas can be made the greatest mining metropolis of the greatest mining district in the world . . . more than a Denver of today." Las Vegas profited as the hub for a limited mineral hinterland that included Goodsprings, Searchlight, and Eldorado Canyon, but its mining success can be measured by the departure of the *Times*'s editors for a California mining camp by the fall of 1906.

The board of trade and the promotion society had their work cut out for them. While railroad officials hoped that Fremont Street would become a row of businesses, it boasted more vacant lots and dust in Las Vegas's early years. Block & Botkin's store between First and Second Streets was the first large men's shop in the summer of 1905. The two-story Palace Hotel sat on one side, with a nearby tent occupied by Dr. Roy Martin. The corner of First and Fremont boasted the Thomas department store, with the Ferron and Martin drugstore across the street. Benjamin Boggs also opened a store, with family members and investor Adolph Levy. Obviously, with numerous mercantiles and the railroad operating between major cities, Las Vegans rarely lacked for the basic necessities.

With the passenger depot on Main and the tracks parallel to it, the street proved to be a key business district. The town's first brick building housed the Las Vegas Drug Store and the mercantile of Crowell & Alcott. John F. Miller arrived from the mining boomtown of Beatty and built the concrete Hotel Nevada on the southeast corner of Main and Fremont. It opened in January 1906 and later became the Sal Sagev and, eventually, the Golden Gate. Across the street, John Wisner built the Overland Hotel, which later evolved into the Las Vegas Club. Down the block, the Lincoln Hotel opened in 1910.

But opening a store too far south on Main or First proved risky. Ed Von Tobel bought two lots at the May 15, 1905, auction, and opened a lumber-yard on the 500 block on South Main with his partner, Jake Beckley. He soon moved to South First Street near Fremont. As Ed Von Tobel Jr. later recalled, "Once the town was built, there wasn't enough business [for lumberyards]. My dad bought out two. It got to the point there wasn't enough business even to keep two families, so he bought out Jake, and Jake went to work for his brother Will, who had a men's clothing store," located for a while in the Hotel Nevada building.

These partnerships reflected a longtime trend that began in the town's early years: a few businesspeople involved in a variety of enterprises. The small population made this both inevitable and logical. But it also meant that Las Vegas quickly developed an elite whose members, elected or not, really ran the town—and, to an extent, that has remained true ever since.

Born in Minnesota, Charles P. Squires worked in title insurance and real estate in California before coming to Las Vegas. With J. Ross Clark and two partners, he borrowed $25,000 to create a bank, a tent hotel on Main Street between Stewart and Ogden, a lumberyard, and a real estate firm. The tent hotel included a dormitory, a dining room, and thirty rooms, each furnished with a bed, washbowl, pitcher, chair, and chamber pot. They set up First State Bank and imported Los Angeles banker John S. Park to run it. After opening in a store across from the depot and taking in $20,140.97 in deposits on the first day—a sign of success and prosperity if ever there was one—it eventually moved to a brick building at Second and Fremont that also housed the town's first post office boxes. Park's management proved so successful that during the panic of 1907, it was one of only two banks in the state that avoided paying customers in scrip instead of money. Squires, who also became secretary of the Consolidated Power and Telephone Company, incorporated in March 1906, bought several lots and built homes on them, and threw himself into the town's social and business activities. Besides serving as privy inspector and federal weather observer, he quickly became a leader of the local Republican Party. When he died in 1958, a revered local figure at age ninety-three, *Las Vegas Sun* reporter Bob Faiss wrote, "It seems strange that Las Vegas, a modern boomtown . . . established as one of the vacation centers of the world, should owe so much to the foresight of one man. But there is little we have today that wasn't given an initial shove by 'Pop' Squires."

Park, too, became a central figure in Las Vegas life. He not only ran the bank and invested in several other enterprises, but also bought the old Kiel Ranch north of town to serve as a showplace and summer home. He drilled for water there, built reservoirs that served as swimming pools, and planted various fruits and vegetables. His son, Dr. William S. Park, one of the first dentists in Las Vegas, also built a home at the ranch.

Squires's counterpart with the Democrats, Ed W. Clark, became perhaps the most important local figure in early Las Vegas. Born in California in 1871, Clark was the son of one of the first elected sheriffs in Storey

County, the heart of the Comstock Lode. Clark began herding cattle in northern Lincoln County while still a teenager and entered the freighting business, starting the Ed W. Clark Forwarding Company to serve southern Nevada miners and farmers across the Utah line with his partner, Charles C. Ronnow, a Mormon from Panaca. Clark also followed his father into Democratic politics and community service, winning election as treasurer of Lincoln County and an appointment as postmaster of Caliente.

But the railroad construction prompted Clark to move to the town site that his unrelated namesake from Montana was building. The forwarding company moved into a wood-frame building at Main and Clark (named, by the way for the western explorer, not for either local Clark) and became Clark County Wholesale. In addition to hauling freight from the new town to nearby mining camps, Clark and Ronnow adapted their freighting business to the boom-bust cycles of mining by providing food and other items in Las Vegas—everything from bridle bits and hay hooks to pocket combs and pocket knives, complete with pipes under glass to create solar-heated water. Clark also became a director of the First State Bank, an executive with the power and phone company, and a Democratic National Committeeman.

After coming to town to build the railroad's roundhouse, Canadian-born Edmund W. Griffith joined the others in pursuing a variety of investments. He opened a store in a tent on South First Street, then shifted to a block building on Fremont Street, where his goods ranged from oil to explosives. He rounded up burros that he kept north of town and sold to prospectors. This posed a problem when the prospectors left the burros behind and the animals wandered into town. Supporters of beautification built wooden coverings around small trees to protect them from the burros, who munched the plants and occasionally wandered into Block 16's saloons. For his part, Griffith supported rounding up the burros, and was popular enough with the townspeople to go on to represent Clark County in the state senate. As president of the Chamber of Commerce, he enthusiastically promoted his town, declaring, "Take care of five acres in Las Vegas and five acres will take care of you." Variations of that statement would be used to advertise Las Vegas for decades.

In 1906, the Wengert family migrated to Las Vegas. Frank Wengert became the first chief engineer of the Pacific Fruit Express Company, which ran the ice plant. His seventeen-year-old son, Cyril, drove the ice truck—a lucrative profession, given the local temperatures. Five years later, John S. Park noticed Cyril's excellent penmanship on a check and offered him a job as First State Bank bookkeeper, "plus the books for our electric light company here." He became the bank manager before rising to top executive positions with Consolidated Power and Telephone. Eventually, he built a large home at Sixth and Charleston that has become the home of the state bar association.

These leaders and the rest of the population enjoyed quality medical care—at least, as good as it could be in a dusty desert town where temperatures often topped one hundred degrees, without benefit of air-conditioning. Dr. Hewetson already was there when Dr. Roy Martin arrived and started practicing in a tent at Third and Stewart. While Hewetson served as SPLA&SL's chief surgeon, the Las Vegas & Tonopah awarded Martin the same title four months after his arrival as well as another tent hospital, complete with ten cots and what his daughter called "a makeshift operating room where only minor surgery was done, except in emergency cases." In 1906, he relocated his hospital to offices at First and Fremont that included a pharmacy, a private room, and twelve beds.

But Hewetson and Martin knew the limitations of their community and its medical equipment. Unless the case was an emergency, they tried to stabilize their patients and send them to Los Angeles for surgery. Otherwise, they preferred to operate when the temperature was at its lowest—at 4 A.M. They also resorted to old-fashioned ingenuity: Martin made a house call to a pregnant woman whose husband threatened to injure him unless he did something to ease his wife's pain. Martin explained later, "I knocked him out" and delivered their baby. And for those whose problems were beyond the abilities of Hewetson, Martin, and their colleagues in Los Angeles, the first mortician in town was William Roberts. As often happened, it was his sideline: Roberts also owned a dry-goods store. Eventually, his wife, Anna Roberts Parks, helped found the Clark County Museum in Henderson.

The founding of that county—how to divide existing Lincoln County and where the new county's seat would be located—proved to be the most important political issue of Las Vegas's early years. Pioche, long the Lincoln County seat, was more than 150 miles from Las Vegas and required a train ride to Caliente, followed by a stage trip. For residents of the mining camps south of Las Vegas—Searchlight, Jean, Goodsprings, Nelson, and

Eldorado Canyon—it was still farther, and it required a departure from the beaten path for the residents of the agricultural areas in the Moapa and Virgin Valleys. Obtaining a county business license or filing a mining claim proved far more elaborate and time consuming than most residents preferred.

Worse, Lincoln County faced the daunting prospect of paying off a huge debt. In 1872, county commissioners had approved construction of a new courthouse. Cost overruns, corrupt politicians and bidding, and accrued interest had driven the building's cost past the six hundred thousand–dollar mark by 1905. Whether in the newly created railroad town or in mining camps, residents of southern Lincoln County had no desire to pay the debt and questioned why they, as more recent arrivals, should have to pay it anyway. The *Las Vegas Age* declared, "Before the political financiers of Pioche saddle another courthouse debt on the county through the building of another courthouse, the south half should get out from under by division of the county," prompting the *Pioche Record* to dismiss the *Age*'s readership as "floaters, the shiftless and the reckless class." This was possibly because the *Record*'s editor believed it, he sensed the threat that Las Vegas posed, or the *Age* outbid the *Record* for the lucrative contract for county printing.

As the 1906 elections neared, residents of southern Lincoln County took action. Searchlight residents began calling for the county seat to be shifted to their mining town. About two dozen Las Vegas businessmen formed the Consolidated Political League of Lincoln County and teamed with counterparts in Searchlight, Overton, and other southern communities to back candidates who represented their interests. They succeeded: Ed W. Clark won the county treasurer's race. One of his first acts was to shift county deposits from Pioche to the First State Bank in Las Vegas. Granting that Clark owned a percentage of the bank, it was also the biggest, most respected bank in the southern portion of the county.

Understandably, Clark's move became a political issue throughout Lincoln County. From Pioche, Caliente, and the Moapa and Virgin Valleys came criticism of his actions, and Panaca businessman Henry Lee, a member of a pioneer Moapa Valley family, challenged Clark's bid for reelection in 1908. That year, Las Vegans countered by forming the Lincoln County Division Club. Its membership included every imaginable local leader: Bracken, Squires, Buol, Griffith, Miller, Clark, merchant W. E. Hawkins,

Helen Stewart's son William, and railroad employee Harley A. Harmon. The members raised more than sixteen hundred dollars to finance a campaign for their pet project and won endorsements from both local political parties. They met with railroad officials, and the *Age* proudly reported, "It is a most hopeful indication of the better understanding now prevailing between the people and the great railroad interests of the country that a committee of citizens may go before the high officials of a Railroad and receive the courteous treatment and fair consideration that was shown in this case." Yet, oddly, one of their failures helped breed success: Lee defeated Clark, but most candidates who backed division cruised to victory. The result symbolized the north-south split within the county and reinvigorated Las Vegans in their efforts.

The two Clarks played a role in the 1909 legislature's decision to create a new county. From his New York City home, the former senator from Montana—and, thanks to the railroad, Lincoln County's largest private landowner—made clear that he endorsed county division, and southern Nevadans welcomed the chance to name the new county for him. For his part, Ed Clark already wielded power among Nevada Democrats, who controlled the legislature and the governor's mansion. His lobbying apparently extended to a case of whiskey that helped convince the assembly and state senate of the justice of Las Vegas's cause. On July 1, 1909, Clark County was born to the sound of bells, cannons, and firecrackers in Las Vegas and a daylong celebration complete with a baseball game between Las Vegas and Goodsprings, burro and wheelbarrow races, a band concert, and a ball at the local opera house. Las Vegans were also pleased that one of their own, Hawkins, chaired the first three-man board of county commissioners, whose two other members came from the outlying areas of Logandale and Nelson.

Yet county division proved more difficult than it may have appeared. When the commissioners tried to regulate and change water rates, the LVL&W sued them and blocked the action, retaining power over local water for itself. Las Vegas also had to overcome claims by Searchlight, a mining camp farther south, to the much desired status of county seat, which meant the presence of county offices. A census taken in 1906 had found that the two towns were almost equal in population—around 320 — but the ephemeral nature of mining camps worked against the selection of Searchlight, which never mounted the systematic campaign that Las Vegans developed. Nor did it help Searchlight that the major railroad went through Las Vegas, which was Clark's creation. The birth of the new county also brought a steep price tag: Clark County agreed to accept more than four hundred thousand dollars of the courthouse debt.

In 1909, southern Nevadans had no opportunity to choose their county officials. Governor Denver Dickerson appointed the first slate. It was a Democratic group, given Dickerson's affiliation, but it also reflected that party's budding success in the Las Vegas area—and Las Vegas was well represented. Besides Hawkins as commission chair, Charles Corkhill served as the first sheriff, W. J. McBurney as assessor, Charles Ireland as public administrator, Ed Clark as treasurer, and Harley Harmon as clerk. Dickerson's choices made it clear that in the battle for county division, Las Vegas indeed had marshaled the largest battalions.

In 1910, Las Vegans immersed themselves in their first Clark County elections with mixed results. Pop Squires ran for the state senate, but lost to Democrat George Bergman. William J. Stewart, Helen's son and a Republican, lost his county commission bid to Democrat John Bunker, a member of one of the Mormon families farming in the Moapa and Virgin Valleys. Yet Hawkins failed to win a full term on the commission, losing to Republican T. A. Brown—and running behind another Republican, C. C. Ronnow. Harmon won a term of his own as county clerk, as did treasurer Ed Clark, who defeated fellow Las Vegan Ed Von Tobel. Republican Henry Lillis, one of the 1905 arrivals, won a term as justice of the peace.

Politics was a crucial part of the social life of any small town, but, typically, Las Vegans sought other outlets for building their community. With its population officially remaining below one thousand until about a decade after railroad construction began, Las Vegas fitted the typical image of a small town in many ways. Not only did businessmen invest together in a series of projects, but residents also took an interest in one another's lives and in building a sense of community. Creating a town also meant creating social necessities and social amenities.

One of the first was a volunteer fire company. The inspiration came in June 1905 when a gasoline stove burst in a restaurant, Chop House Bill's, on North First, rapidly razing three other buildings and causing thirty-six hundred dollars in damage. The Las Vegas Land & Water Company approved twenty-two fireplugs throughout the town site. Five local businessmen composed the Hook and Ladder Company of the Las Vegas fund-raising board, which sought money for a fire brigade and proper helmets, hoses, and hooks. Their work was cut out for them, but it helped that the Las Vegas Sanitary Committee promoted public awareness of cleanliness.

The sanitary committee did more than just push Las Vegas to avoid fires. Created by the Las Vegas Promotion Society, a precursor to the Chamber of Commerce, it lobbied the railroad to help remove waste that could cause not just fires, but even worse. Local leaders backed a forty thousand–dollar bond issue to build mains and ten septic tanks northeast of downtown by the old Stewart Ranch. Local newspapers agreed on the need for action, declaring that with "innumerable cesspools and toilet vaults, it is only good fortune that has prevented a serious epidemic." The bond issue passed.

The combination of lamps and fire had other long-lasting effects: the birth of an electric company. Local businessmen formed the Consolidated Power and Telephone Company, designed to provide the electricity that would make the dangerous lamps obsolete. Park, Squires, and their partners reached an agreement to use an extra generator at the Armour ice plant and redwood poles from a lumberyard. They added in several thousand feet of copper wire—yet another connection to northern Nevada and to the Montana magnate who created their town—and managed to provide coverage to most of the Clark town site. But growth and the limits of copper wire led to poor service, prompting the utility to buy "Old Betsy," a ninety-horsepower engine, and to replace the heavy copper lines with thinner, newer, better ones.

Another early project involved making education available, especially for families with children settling the town. The first school met in a tent under cottonwoods near Las Vegas Creek. Local residents paid to renovate the Salt Lake Hotel, a three-room wooden building at Second and Lewis Streets, for classes in the fall of 1905. Unfortunately, the school system ran out of money before the academic year ended, and in the next few years enrollment rose and fell with the economy, declining in the wake of the panic of 1907. Fire destroyed the school late in 1910, while the city was building a thirty thousand–dollar school between Lewis, Bridger, Fourth, and Fifth on land that the railroad had offered for a ten-dollar fee. For the next school year, students met in the First Methodist Church at Third and Bridger and in a building next door.

Las Vegans also sought to develop cultural and civic opportunities. They converged on the second floor (later called Beckley's Hall) of the First State Bank building at First and Fremont to go to the opera house, which rarely presented opera but provided space for lodges and public meetings. Las Vegas formed a baseball team that played teams from nearby towns, and welcomed occasional boxing matches and horse races. Las Vegans tried to obtain an endowment from Andrew Carnegie to build a library, but eventually had to develop one of their own. Lacking much in the way of theatrical companies, they mounted amateur performances. The volunteer fire company sponsored a Labor Day firemen's ball, including races. Harry Beale leased the old ranch from the Clark interests and turned it into a small resort that included a dance floor, with music provided by an orchestra from Salt Lake City. During the broiling summertime, Las Vegans welcomed the chance to frequent the ranch, with its creek, shady cottonwood trees, and bathing-suit rentals.

Social and fraternal organizations are important to many small towns, and Las Vegas proved no exception. The Eagles formed a lodge four months to the day after the town-site auction, bought a lot on Fremont near First Street at what is now the Golden Nugget, and constructed their own building. The Elks formed a lodge at the Hotel Nevada in the spring of 1906. In 1907, fifteen Masons who had moved from elsewhere formed a lodge—including Griffith, Bracken, businessman Frank Buol, Judge Henry Lillis, store owners William R. Thomas and Benjamin Boggs, and Park, who was the first worshipful master and held the meetings at the bank building until 1909, when they built a lodge on South Third Street. Women soon formed the Help One Another Club to help newcomers adjust to their surroundings. Businessmen formed the Rotary Club.

Religion also was a key part of building the small town. The first church to open was First Methodist at Third and Bridger. Christ Church Episcopal followed at the northeast corner of Second and Carson on land the railroad donated, and it remained there until moving onto donated county land at Maryland Parkway and St. Louis in the 1950s. In 1908, Catholics built a small chapel on South Second that evolved into St. Joan of Arc. In 1910 came the first Presbyterian pastor and the beginning of Baptist services. Local African Americans, discouraged from joining the local Methodist church, formed their own ecumenical church and conducted services in their homes. In 1905, the town's lone Presbyterian missionary sponsored a social that the *Las Vegas Times* promoted: "[I]n places where all are strangers to each other . . . something must be done to get to know one another."

As the only part of town where liquor could be sold, Block 16 certainly qualified as a place to get to know people. It could have developed in one of two ways: as an area where the elite gathered to imbibe in genteel surroundings or as a saloon district where rowdy gamblers and painted ladies moved across sawdust floors. But it turned out that Las Vegans could have it two ways. Both images fitted Block 16.

The "Queen of Block 16" was the Arizona Club, on the east side of the block at 219 North First Street between Ogden and Stewart. Three partners bought the lot at the 1905 auction, but J. O. "Jim" McIntosh bought out the other two and built what he hoped to be the most elite saloon and gambling hall in Las Vegas. For a time, it was. The front doors and fittings featured leaded beveled glass, and the fifty-by-seventy-five-foot bar and columns were made of mahogany. Gaslights lit up the bar, with electricity

The First Methodist Church opened at Third and Bridger soon after Las Vegas was founded. It was demolished in 1967. Special Collections, UNLV Libraries

This is the interior of the Arizona Club. On the right is the famous mahogany bar. When Block 16 shut down in 1942, it moved to the Gay 90s bar at the Hotel Last Frontier and disappeared during construction of the Hotel New Frontier in 1955. At the center of the photo, next to the banjo player, is longtime sheriff Sam Gay. Special Collections, UNLV Libraries

used only on special occasions. The Arizona Club included nickel slot machines, faro, roulette, blackjack, and fifteen-cent drinks—or twenty-five cents for two drinks.

The Arizona Club's neighbors were less elegant and respectable. The Gem, Red Onion, Turf, and Favorite apparently stuck with liquor and gambling; the Star Saloon, Double O, and Arcade reportedly included back rooms for prostitutes sometime in 1909. This disturbed some civic leaders, but others preferred to leave the area alone—so long as those on Block 16 never presumed to rise above their station. After McIntosh sold to another early Las Vegas arrival, Al James, the Arizona Club lost its more stately position by adding a second story with rooms and ladies. Thus, Block 16 became known throughout the West not merely as the place in Las Vegas to buy liquor, but also as a red-light district. Raised in Las Vegas, Ed Von Tobel remembered, "The girls were well regulated and they had to go to the city doctor once a week for examinations. . . . We lived on North 3rd Street and quite often in the night time we could hear rinkadink piano playing."

In the fall of 1905, Canadian-born Sam Gay went to work as a bouncer at the Arizona Club. He was built for the job: six feet tall, 260 pounds, and wearing a size 13 boot that he often deployed to the backside of difficult customers. Gay had enjoyed a checkered career as a streetcar conductor in San Diego, a miner in Alaska and Goldfield, and finally a bouncer at Goldfield's Northern Club, owned by Tex Rickard, who later promoted championship boxing matches in the area and eventually moved on to New York City and built Madison Square Garden. Gay's training and work at the Arizona Club prompted legendary Lincoln County sheriff Jake Johnson to make him the local night watchman. Gay won an election as town constable in 1906, and later became deputy sheriff for southern Lincoln County. His job could be difficult: he spoke for several other early residents when he recalled, "From 1905 to 1910, Las Vegas was a rough and tumble western town. Five men dead for breakfast one Sunday morning and ten men wounded."

When Clark County was born in 1909, the first sheriff was Charles C. "Corky" Corkhill, who kept Gay as his deputy. Their relationship would have a long-term effect on Las Vegas law enforcement. In the summer of 1910, Gay felt sorry for the prisoners in the Las Vegas jail at Third and Carson. Built of sheet metal and railroad ties, the small prison lacked windows and cool air, but not rats. Gay shackled the prisoners together, took them to Las Vegas Creek by the old ranch house, and tied them to cottonwoods so that they could be in the shade. The prisoners were cooler, but Corkhill was hot. He fired Gay, who ran against him for county sheriff as a Republican and defeated him in the November 1910 election. Except for an occasional controversy over his overimbibing on Block 16 and tendency to avoid enforcing laws he disliked, Gay remained sheriff for twenty years.

But Corkhill found plenty to occupy himself. The three weeklies publishing in Las Vegas at the time of the auction soon dwindled to one. The *Las Vegas Advance* disappeared within a few months. The *Las Vegas Times* belonged to a pair of veteran mining camp editors, James Brown and Frank Reber, part of a long tradition of newspapermen who moved from boom to boom, convinced on each occasion that prosperity merely awaited their arrival. Los Angeles–based C. W. Nicklin owned the *Las Vegas Age,* with Corkhill as editor, and they became a favorite target for Brown and Reber, who berated them as outsiders lacking in commitment to the community. Besides referring to the "Las Vegas Toilet Sheet," a "subsidized rag," and an "under-witted contemporary," the *Times*'s editors foretold the future better than they could have imagined when they attacked the *Age*'s out-of-town owner as the "Los Angeles dodger."

But Nicklin and the *Age* outlasted their critics. Brown and Reber left for another mining boom in 1906. In 1908, shortly after an economic depression struck the United States and hamstrung growth in Las Vegas, Nicklin decided to sell. He approached Squires, who had no journalism experience and replied, "What on earth would I do with a newspaper? I have troubles enough already." He meant it: Squires had invested in the local bank and power and telephone company, meaning that if the town was in decline, he would suffer, too. Finally, offered the weekly at what he called the "ridiculously low price" of twenty-three hundred dollars, Squires thought, "Now, just suppose I had a newspaper in Las Vegas; perhaps I could help revive the poor, sick little town." He took over the *Age* and its office at 411 East Fremont Street, across from the Bracken home and down the block from his own. He threw himself and his editorial support into the fight for county division and, in late 1910, helped draft the Las Vegas city charter. He kept publishing the *Age* into the 1940s.

While Squires supported virtually every opportunity to improve the town, he also belonged to the Republican Party. His hero was Theodore Roosevelt, the most popular politician of his time, but Las Vegas already boasted its share of Democrats. They wanted a voice and found it on September 18, 1909, with the debut of the *Clark County Review,* located at 113 South First Street and owned by Corkhill (who had left the *Age* when Squires purchased it), who declared that his newspaper would support the party, "provided that the Democrats behave themselves and 'come across' occasionally." By the time James Squires, the *Age* editor's son, conducted the 1910 census, Las Vegas's 937 residents had access to two weekly news-papers with divergent political viewpoints but similar goals: to boost their town, and thus themselves.

By 1910, Las Vegas boasted six hotels and several lodging houses, two churches, ten miles of graded and curbed streets, five general merchandise stores, four clothing stores, a hardware store, a women's clothing store, three barbershops, a bakery, six restaurants, a plumber, a blacksmith, five attorneys, two doctors, two dentists, "and best of all," as the Las Vegas Promotion Society boasted, "200,000 acres of fertile land with an inex-haustible supply of artesian water to irrigate it, waiting to produce every variety of fruits and vegetables, alfalfa, grain, or anything a successful farmer would desire, with a splendid local market at top prices for the products."

Las Vegas was typical of western towns that depended on industries other than mining. About half of the population descended from at least one foreign-born parent, who tended to come from the United King-dom or somewhere else in Europe. They included Germans like clothing merchant Will Beckley and his lumberman brother Jake; Buol and Von Tobel, the sons of Swiss parents; and Clark, Hawkins, and Lillis, born to Irish mothers. Canadians enjoyed prominent local representation with McWilliams, Griffith, Gay, and Western Union manager William B. Mundy. Most of the residents settled in Las Vegas from outside the state; few migrated from within the state, given that most towns with a mobile population relied on mining.

Las Vegas proved to be prejudiced, albeit no more so than the rest of the West. African Americans were few—sixteen in the 1910 census—but sev-eral wound up in Block 17, thanks perhaps to Bracken's warning to his cor-porate superiors that "our colored population, Mexicans, etc. is growing very rapidly and unless we have some place for this class of people, they will be scattered all through town." Befitting the railroad's quest for cheap labor, most of the few Japanese living in Las Vegas resided in construction cars or in the repair yards. Early in 1905, the *Las Vegas Times* reported that "Constable A. L. Murphy arrested a Jap . . . for polluting the limpid waters of Las Vegas Creek. . . . He was brought before Judge Ralph, the just judge of Vegas, who meted out $100 worth of the article to the inconsiderate Jap, who would take the Vegas valley pride for a bathing resort." The *Las*

In the spring of 1948, Apache Club owner P. O. Silvagni bought a lot on North Second Street at an auction. The lot had been the site of the old fire station and jail. Joining him were some of those at the original town auction in May 1905. At either end are George Thompson, then chief of police, and Sheriff Glen Jones, who later lost his job in a bribery scandal involving illegal brothel operators. Between them, *left to right,* are Fred Pine, Charles Aplin, Charles Squires, Ed Von Tobel Sr., Silvagni, and Walter Bracken. Special Collections, UNLV Libraries

Vegas Age tended to be more tolerant, although a story about a fight involving railroad crews inspired a reference to the "swarthy sons of Japan."

The local press varied in its treatment of those from Europe and Latin America. The *Age* reported a trial over a fight involving three Italians and fifteen Greeks working for the railroad south of town. "Judge Brennan was engaged as legal sponsor for the Greeks and Dan V. Noland appeared for the banana sellers," the *Age* said, with all concerned fined ten dollars apiece. The *Age* proved kinder to Domenic Pecetto, who built a liquor store on First Street between Clark and Lewis—outside the railroad's restricted area, although no one seemed to mind. Because they were fewer in number, Latinos and Latinas received less attention, although a Mexican eatery, the Spanish restaurant, opened in 1909. Most accounts of their lives focused on crimes involving them.

Jewish residents generally were the object of respect, not anti-Semitism. One prominent early Las Vegas landowner, Adolph Levy, opened a store on Fremont Street in 1906 in partnership with Boggs. Levy announced, "I have great faith in the future of Las Vegas and have staked my all here, and expect to see a nice thriving city of 6000 to 8000 here in a few years." Toward that end, he also staked several mining claims in the Charleston range and looked for investments in nearby camps. When he sold the store to Boggs in 1910, he kept a warehouse and several products.

The Las Vegans on the census included a few dozen "boarders" who may have been tourists. They reflected the area's long reliance upon visitors to boost the economy by leaving the train and heading for the establishments near the depot. But those residents also belonged to what was technically a shrinking population: while a local census found 320 residents in 1906, the population may have actually reached 2,000 by the following year. The social class and ethnic origins of these residents varied greatly, but all had one thing in common: they had cast their lot, even if temporarily, with a young railroad town that they looked to make into a home and a success.

A NEW CITY TAKES SHAPE, 1911-1920

BETWEEN 1910 AND 1920, THE POPULATION of Las Vegas more than doubled, from 937 to 2,304. This began a trend felt even more profoundly since that decade: in every decennial census, the local populace has doubled or come close to doing so. Today, that means such problems as traffic jams, air pollution, and schools bursting at the seams. At the same time, though, the increase filled in open spaces inside and outside the original town site. Yet some of these issues proved timeless, especially the availability of water, the impact of national and international events, and the area's relationship to the rest of the state.

The 1910s marked the high tide of the Progressive Era, which began with Theodore Roosevelt's ascent to the presidency in 1901. Roosevelt (1901–1909) and his successors, William Howard Taft (1909–1913) and Woodrow Wilson (1913–1921), agreed that government should play a larger role in individual lives than their late-nineteenth-century predecessors, who believed that if government involved itself in the economy, it should be on behalf of business. The three presidents and their counterparts in the states backed legislation to improve protection of the environment, expand and support democracy, make government and business more professional, ease poverty, enhance workplace safety, and promote WASP society. Wilson's efforts culminated in World War I, fought, as he said, to "make the world safe for democracy."

Nevada's leaders generally proved far less progressive than these national figures—or governors such as Robert LaFollette of Wisconsin and Hiram Johnson of California. During this decade, George Wingfield consolidated his power as the state's dominant political figure. He owned many of Nevada's productive mines, the major bank in several towns, and substantial properties in Reno, where he lived. When his old business partner, George Nixon, died in 1912, Wingfield turned down the governor's offer to appoint him to succeed Nixon in the U.S. Senate—because he felt that he could accomplish more by remaining in Nevada. What he hoped to accomplish included making sure that the state did as little as possible to interfere with the profits of businessmen like himself.

Still, Nevadans displayed progressivism, within limits. Francis Newlands, a longtime representative and U.S. senator from the state, played a large role in winning approval for a reclamation act designed to build irrigation systems throughout the West; northern Nevadans benefited from one such project, and Bureau of Reclamation officials began pondering a massive dam and irrigation system on the Colorado River. Newlands and other Nevadans also reflected the progressive belief in a white, Anglo-Saxon, Protestant society: Newlands supported repealing the Fifteenth Amendment, which gave African Americans the right to vote, and the state legislature passed a law requiring English to be spoken in the mines. Nevadans approved the initiative, referendum, recall, direct election of U.S. senators, and woman suffrage to expand the power of voters. They created state commissions to keep a closer eye on banks, mines, railroads, and utilities. In keeping with the progressive belief in moral reform, they tried to legislate the elimination of legal gambling and an increase in the residency requirement for divorce, but both efforts ultimately failed when the state's economy, especially around Reno, suffered due to the lack of visitors who wanted to take advantage of Nevada's libertarian approach. Nevadans also backed Prohibition but ignored the law with impunity. They also fell into line in backing World War I against Germany and Austria-Hungary, with Minden's Lutheran church patriotically declaring that it would offer services in English and Ely's Serbian Benevolent Association writing to Wilson to assure him that its members supported the war effort.

The summer of 1919 was one of the hottest on record across the nation, in more ways than one. Not only was the climate unpleasant and the effects of a recent influenza epidemic still being felt, but the recent Bolshevik revolution had also resulted in a communist dictatorship in Russia, whose leaders were trying to hold onto power during a civil war. While communism maintained at best a tenuous hold there, it gained strength in several European countries in which World War I devastated the economy. Americans feared the same or worse. The result, the Great Red Scare, led to the passage of legislation against socialism and communism, depor-tation of those suspected of advocating them, and confrontations be-tween radical unions like the Industrial Workers of the World and the civic authorities. In Las Vegas, the main heat remained related to the weather: the Chamber of Commerce, its business members, and local home owners complained that the heat and lack of rain meant the water pressure in city pipes and fire hydrants was too low. But Las Vegas had felt and contributed to the effects of the Progressive Era, and it would face its own debate over unions and radicalism soon enough.

The decade began auspiciously for the railroad town. On January 11, the San Pedro, Los Angeles, & Salt Lake completed an extensive renova-tion of its yards and began work on a branch line into the Moapa Valley, providing quicker access to an important farming hinterland with which Las Vegans could buy and sell. That March 17, Governor Tasker Oddie, a one-time miner from nearby Nye County, signed a bill incorporating Las Vegas as a city, including the Clark and McWilliams town sites. A mayor and board of four commissioners would govern it, making it the first Nevada town to adopt the commission form of government, which began in Galveston, Texas, and spread to more than one hundred cities as part of the progressive quest for more honest, efficient government.

Despite the early creation of a volunteer fire department, fires re-mained a problem for the still predominantly wooden town site. The opera house burned, but other meeting places quickly replaced it. More important and timely, the original Overland Hotel burned only a week before the referendum on incorporation. Such fires served to help pro-mote the fight to incorporate Las Vegas as a city. The Overland fire prompted Pop Squires to point out in the *Las Vegas Age* that with a city government, services would improve—which they did in 1917, when the town finally bought its first fire truck.

On June 1, Las Vegans approved the city charter in a special election. They chose their first mayor, developer Peter Buol, beginning a long tradi-tion of putting veteran businesspeople in charge of the government. Join-ing him as commissioners were William J. Stewart (Helen's son), Ed Von Tobel, J. J. Coughlin, and C. M. McGovern. The first city clerk, former railroad engineer Harley A. Harmon, doubled as city clerk and welcomed the additional twenty-five dollars a month in salary for the additional duties. Las Vegas's new governing body soon demonstrated its commit-

The Overland Hotel, built on the northeast corner of Main and Fremont, burned in 1911. Some of Las Vegas's population of about one thousand gathered to survey the damage. The Overland was rebuilt and now is the site of the Las Vegas Club. Special Collections, UNLV Libraries

ment to civic improvement by introducing a badly needed forty thousand–dollar sewer bond issue, exploiting the new power to borrow that municipal incorporation gave Las Vegas.

That fall, 111 elementary school students (through eighth grade) and 17 high school students began attending a new facility on Las Vegas Boulevard, just south of Bridger. The two-story, fourteen-classroom mission-style building cost eighty thousand dollars to build and included a heating plant and an electric fan for ventilation. The Las Vegas Post Office moved into a new business building that E. W. Griffith constructed at Second and Fremont Streets, which soon became the site of the Majestic Theatre. The Las Vegas Land & Water Company prepared to move to its building at Lewis and South Second that included offices on the first floor and rooms for railroad crews on the second.

In 1911, the members of the Las Vegas Promotion Society, and other recent arrivals, turned their attention to forming a chamber of commerce. About sixty businessmen gathered at the opera house on July 18, 1911, to elect officers and adopt bylaws. The chamber soon began promoting the city more systematically, although not always with great foresight: one of its early efforts was an attempt to convince outsiders that Las Vegas soon would be an agricultural paradise of fruit, vegetables, and grains. But the chamber kept growing and spearheaded numerous efforts to promote the city. Its first major project was to support incorporation, including a charter that called for commission government. Local leaders, seeking both respect and investment from businessmen outside the town, saw commission government as proof that their town was progressive in every sense of the word.

But the chamber did far more, providing harbingers of the boosterism that so greatly affected Las Vegas's development in the last half of the twentieth century. In 1913, in conjunction with the Automobile Club of Southern California, it placed an advertisement in *Sunset Magazine,* owned by the Union Pacific, to try to attract drivers from southern California. In 1915, it printed a postcard of one of the largest artesian wells in the world— located in Las Vegas, of course—and provided them to all the trains and cars coming through en route to the Panama-California Exposition in San Diego.

As they did at the beginning, local officials remained convinced in the 1910s that Las Vegas offered agricultural opportunities, and the chamber joined the effort to pursue them. In 1911, the railroad leased one thousand square feet of space at the Land and Products Exposition at the Los Angeles Exhibit Building, and Clark urged the newly created Chamber of Commerce to send as many exhibits as it could—at railroad expense—to show off for about forty thousand potential investors "seeking new investments or locations brought into southern California by the railroad." Building upon their other business successes, Ed Clark and C. C. Ronnow sold thirty-five acres of alfalfa that they had planted for four thousand dollars in 1912, and other ranches planted forty bushels per acre of wheat and forty-five bushels per acre of corn. In 1914, Buol's Southern Nevada Land and Development Company planted forty acres of cantaloupes on land that the town's first mayor, by then a legislator, had leased. The *Clark County Review* hoped that this would "induce the ranch owners of the valley to plant at least a portion of their acreage to cantaloupes" that they could ship "in carload lots." While Clark, Ronnow, and Buol fared well enough, agriculture never became the cash cow for which early Las Vegans hoped because the local soil was so high in alkalinity.

For all its success, 1911 also included a portent of troubles that would change the little town its residents were trying so hard to build. For the first time, but not the last, Las Vegas faced labor problems. That September, railroad shop employees went on strike, seeking acknowledgment of their union. They declared, "There is only one question at issue between the men and the railroads. This is recognition of the Federation." Once the railroad accorded that recognition, the workers returned to their jobs.

The railroad provided not only jobs, but also a block of the town site for a county building. However, it took nearly a decade after the 1905 auction for the block to be used for that purpose. On Block 20, at Third and Carson Streets, a small block building housed the first county offices in July 1909. But Clark County officials immediately began planning some-

The Murray and Buol Well prompted a postcard promoting Las Vegas's ample water supply, but leaving the wells uncapped like this was wasteful. The man sitting beside the well appears to be Las Vegas's first mayor, Peter Buol. Special Collections, UNLV Libraries

thing bigger. It cost fifty thousand dollars to construct a more elaborate two-story building, dedicated on December 7, 1914, with marble halls and granite steps. Designed by noted Nevada architect Frederick J. DeLongchamps, whose work still dots the state's landscape, it was designed in Spanish colonial revival style. They held public meetings on the steps, while a grassy area with numerous trees kept the audience in the shade. The offices were on the first floor, while district court convened upstairs, but not daily: Clark and Lincoln Counties composed a judicial district, the judge held court in both county seats, and the elections of Judges Charles Lee Horsey and William Orr demonstrated that candidates with long connections to Lincoln County were likely to fare better than those wholly associated with Las Vegas.

The completion of the new county building prompted the inevitable question of what to do with the old one nearby. The City of Las Vegas took half of it and used it as a city hall into the 1940s. The Mesquite Club petitioned city commissioners to fund a library in the other part of the building. They went along but provided no funds, prompting the club to hold a fund-raising drive to buy books. Clark County commissioners enhanced the area still more by beginning a beautification project to improve the lawn and trees around it, making it an even more appealing public place.

These improvements required cooperation from the railroad and its subsidiary, the Las Vegas Land & Water Company. Walter Bracken kept busy tending to numerous problems for the LVL&W. For one, the pipes kept breaking, leaving the entire town without water for a day at one point and prompting experiments to find pipes that would survive the alkali in the soil. Clark County commissioners objected to LVL&W plans to work in Block 20, the courthouse area that the railroad had ceded to their control, prompting negotiations involving county officials and railroad lawyers. And Bracken had a new building, complete with occasional boarders, to oversee.

In 1912, J. T. McWilliams found another opportunity to hound Bracken—and a just cause. Bracken and C. O. Whittemore had strained every nerve to keep the local water supply clean—and, of course, to make sure that everyone knew it. But McWilliams knew better. One day in May 1912, he found railroad shop workers emptying the cesspool from the yards into the Las Vegas Creek. He wrote to Bracken, "Near the slaughter house on the famous Las Vegas Ranch is a fine lot of hogs that wallow in the water

The Clark County Courthouse was built in 1914 on Block 20 at Third and Carson. It served as a municipal park and meeting place—and in 1931, when this photo was taken, the jobless gathered in the shade, hoping for work on Hoover Dam. Special Collections, UNLV Libraries

from the Creek. The only supply of meat in Las Vegas is butchered in the slaughter house, and the meat must be washed with sewerage water." McWilliams was also kind enough to take the time and trouble to notify Helen Stewart, whose dairy herd used the creek water, as well as a butcher shop owner, the ranch's lessee, and local doctor W. L. Fuller, who promptly notified the local health officer, Dr. Roy Martin.

Bracken deemed the matter unimportant. He described the controversy as "absolute rot, but the non-thinking employee's mind is being filled daily with such stuff as this." He dismissed McWilliams as a "crank," but that crank made his life difficult. Complaints from McWilliams prompted county and city officials to meet with Bracken and inspect the local septic tank, which turned out to have been emptied into the creek only once—

but once was enough. Acting as local health officer and registrar of vital statistics, Martin investigated and assured the state board of health that he knew of "no good reason for complaint on the part of any citizen of this community. . . . Las Vegas has never had a single case of sickness due to unsanitary culinary water. . . . If there was any excuse for criticism prior to two weeks ago, there is not now, as all defects have been remedied." But as Florence Lee Jones and John Cahlan wrote in their history of water in Las Vegas,

> Although he had been rebuffed, McWilliams had succeeded in arousing the town to the danger of the cesspool overflow into the Las Vegas Creek, in having a water line from the Ranch spring installed to supply the dairy and slaughter house, in assurance that the odious practice of dumping sewerage into the Las Vegas Creek would be abandoned, and in stirring the interest of health officials in Las Vegas, Clark County and the State of Nevada.

That interest paid dividends later. In 1916, city attorney Henry Lillis notified Bracken that the water supply again was unsanitary. Bracken and the railroad officials solved the problem with a new set of screens that did a better job of filtering the flow into the reservoir. City officials also proved willing to help when their West Las Vegas constituents demanded water lines: Mayor W. E. Hawkins and two of the four commissioners tried to remove the old town site from the city limits. "If water was carried over to the Old Town, it would be but a short time until Buck's Addition, Ladd's Addition, Pioneer Heights, and all other outlying farms would demand us to carry water out to them," Bracken warned. "I do not believe that we have any more water than is required for Clark's Las Vegas Townsite and the cultivation of our Las Vegas Ranch which we must maintain for the benefit of a dairy and butcher business absolutely required by employees who are living here." But the old town site remained part of the newer one, and soon it too had water lines.

As the debate over these issues showed, Las Vegans understood the benefits that the San Pedro, Los Angeles, & Salt Lake brought to their town, but they also grasped the problems. One was its handling of water and development. Another was the limits of local economic diversity—Las Vegas depended too heavily upon the railroad, and many of them knew it. Other problems manifested themselves. One was that passenger and freight rates were higher than local residents, hoping to import and export goods and services, thought wise or helpful. Although they often pushed for better rates, the railroad's executives turned deaf ears toward them.

Another problem was that the railroad left Las Vegas disconnected from the rest of the state. In 1917, arguing in the *Las Vegas Age* for better train service to northern Nevada, Pop Squires pointed out that reaching Reno was easier by way of Barstow and Sacramento or Salt Lake than it was through Tonopah. He encouraged better service that would promote commerce, with northern Nevada's livestock, lumber, flour, and sugar moving south. That meant, he said, "The promotion of intra-state business would increase our wealth by keeping our money within the state"— a complaint that tied Las Vegas even more closely to northern towns, given the frequency with which wealthy mine owners on the Comstock Lode had headed for California with the wealth that they had earned in Nevada. Instead, those mining camps to the north that the railroad did serve waxed and waned. The Bullfrog district petered out after 1912, eliminating the need for that train service. When Tonopah and Goldfield declined in the final months of World War I, the iron horse suffered, too. The Las Vegas & Tonopah reduced service to triweekly in 1917, and shut down on October 31, 1918—the fifty-fourth anniversary of statehood—a holiday that excited little attention in Las Vegas then and now, and less than two weeks before the end of the war and the demand it created for ore.

By the 1910s, railroads were beginning to give way to cars as a major mode of transportation. Las Vegas may have been a railroad town, but it wanted to be modern. With the Chamber of Commerce strongly advocating action, a highway was built to Goodsprings, enabling Las Vegas to take advantage of the zinc and lead camp's need for services and the desire of Goodsprings residents to spend their money in the railroad town. In 1914, local promoters began efforts to build a federal highway that would connect southern California with Salt Lake City and thus other points east. C. C. Ronnow's presence on the county commission also proved beneficial: he pushed for a route that included Las Vegas and went through his native Moapa Valley. A Las Vegas delegation represented the city in talks with Arizona and Utah, helping to induce Arizona officials to improve the portion of interstate highway through their state. The Southern Nevada Automobile Club organized in 1916 to promote highway building and interest in the horseless carriage.

World War I soldiers marched east on Fremont Street in 1917, and Las Vegans turned out with patriotic fervor. The post office sign at Second and Fremont is visible, and the flagpole beside it partly obscures the First State Bank building at First and Fremont. Special Collections, UNLV Libraries

Clearly, Las Vegans were taking steps to bring a major highway to their town, and E. W. Griffith proved to be the key figure in southern Nevada road building. He was a leader of the delegations that met with California and Utah officials about the highway. He opened a resort at Kiel Canyon in the summer of 1915, prompting road improvements. He and Ed W. Clark drove to St. George, Utah, to promote highway construction to that area. And in 1919, as Clark County's representative in the state senate, he pushed through two bills, with Chamber of Commerce support, that Governor Emmet Boyle signed into law. One measure provided for building a road from Mesquite, just inside the line from Arizona, to Las Vegas and on to Jean. The other authorized a road starting at Goldfield, heading southeast to Beatty, and then following the old LV&T roadbed to Las Vegas. For the first time, Las Vegas would be linked directly to the Reno–Carson City area.

Another link between Las Vegas and Nevada's dominant urban area was that they catered to visitors. But as part of the moral reform of the Progressive Era, Nevada legislators outlawed casino gambling in the state, to take effect on October 1, 1910. The ban proved short-lived, mainly because Reno's economy relied so heavily upon appealing to travelers along the old Central Pacific Railroad—and those travelers welcomed the easy access to gambling. By 1915, lawmakers had restored several forms of gambling.

In Las Vegas, not only had gambling continued in back rooms, but Sheriff Sam Gay also considered the laws silly and unenforceable anyway. Beyond that, his own staff often visited those back rooms. For this, Gay feuded with a fellow Republican, Clark County district attorney Albert S. "Bert" Henderson. At one point, Henderson filed charges against Gay's deputy Joe Keate for gambling. Gay responded by firing Keate—for a day. Keate then returned to work and finally went on to succeed Gay when he retired.

If that suggests law enforcement in Las Vegas could be quirky, the suggestion is accurate. Gay feuded with Henderson, who prosecuted him for gross intoxication when the sheriff shot out the lights on Fremont Street one night. Already in trouble once for overimbibing, returning to the office he shared with the more prim and proper town librarian, and singing bawdy songs, Gay responded by promising, "So long as I am sheriff of Clark County, I will not take a drink of intoxicating liquor. If I do, I will hand in my resignation." Meanwhile, Keate once tried to fight a duel with Justice of the Peace William Harkins over a fine of five dollars for contempt of court for failing to produce a prisoner with a one-hour deadline. Henderson demanded that he arrest Keate, but Gay merely calmed everyone down. The district attorney urged the county commission to fire Gay. When it did so, the ousted sheriff took his case to the Nevada Supreme Court, which ruled in the commission's favor. Gay responded by running again for sheriff—and winning.

Meanwhile, Gay and his deputies ignored the laws against alcohol. In 1920, Mayme Stocker became the licensee for the Northern Club on Fremont Street. It supposedly sold only soft drinks, since Prohibition had taken effect. But it sold stronger stuff, and as journalist A. D. Hopkins wrote in a profile of Stocker, "its real mission was betrayed by its name." Virtually every town born during Nevada's twentieth-century mining booms had a "Northern Saloon," and the same was true of boomtowns outside of Nevada. Also, as Stocker's son Harold explained, he, his brothers, and his father worked for the railroad or hoped to, and "railroad men weren't supposed to have anything to do with things like that."

While Las Vegans ignored the Volstead Act, which enforced Prohibition, the law's mere existence—indeed, opposition to progressive ideals generally—fostered development north of town. In 1917, Thomas Williams arrived in Las Vegas from his native Eureka, Utah, and deemed the town too lawless for him. But he proved lawless in his own right. Intrigued with agricultural possibilities, he brought his wife and sons to the area and paid eight dollars an acre for 160 acres a mile north of town. He subdivided acreage, dug wells, graded roads, built irrigation ditches, ran power lines, and sold lots for ten dollars down. As Bracken had done in Las Vegas a decade and a half before, he offered free land to churches, which he expected to keep the peace because he preferred to include as little government as possible. That aided his efforts: of the first eighty lots he sold, thirty-one went to moonshiners who ignored Prohibition as openly as possible. This marked the beginnings of what became the city of North Las Vegas.

Prohibition flowed in part from World War I. Not only was it a classic case of progressive moral reform, but it also afforded an opportunity to take action against German brewers, Irish distillers, and other recent immigrants involved in the making of alcohol. But war affected Las Vegas in other ways. In 1913, Buol visited Scotland. When he returned, he announced that Scottish investors wanted to help develop Las Vegas, with himself as vice president of their one hundred thousand–dollar company. They deposited twenty thousand dollars in earnest money in the First State Bank. Buol contributed land near one of the outlying ranches, owned by the Laubenheimers, and his water rights for his stock. They proposed to build the Scotch Eighties, a housing tract southwest of the Clark town site in an area now bounded by Oakey, Waldman, Rancho, and Highland. The death of company president Sir John Murray, a noted naturalist and oceanographer, and the outbreak of World War I in Europe scotched their plans for a while, but today it is one of the more elite residential developments within range of the original town.

The war also stopped a couple of other projects—but, like the Scotch Eighties, only for the moment. Two men obtained a federal permit to build a power plant on the Colorado River and formed the Colorado River Hydro-Electric Company. Then the John B. Stetson Company followed suit and sent engineers, led by Fred Hesse, a future mayor of Las Vegas, to examine the feasibility of building a dam on the Colorado. World War I postponed their plans, which reached fruition through different means. These would come in the 1920s, a decade that served as a harbinger of things to come.

World War I also affected Las Vegas society—which, in turn, promoted community togetherness. Boosted by several Las Vegas women, including Frances McNamee, the wife of railroad attorney Leo McNamee, the Clark County chapter of the American Red Cross obtained a charter within two months of the declaration of war on April 6, 1917, and set up headquarters in the county commission chambers. They gathered hundreds of sweaters, shirts, and coats, either donated or made by chapter volunteers, for soldiers and refugees. A June 1917 war bond drive prompted the purchase of more than eighty-seven thousand dollars in bonds, including twenty-five hundred dollars in just one week by employees of the railroad repair shops. The 1918 Liberty Loan Drive was equally successful. Las Vegans also joined the nation in holding meatless and wheatless days. They worked with the Clark County Defense Council, formed in March 1918, and even agreed to its plea to close down gambling that August until the war ended. When peace came that November, so did the return of the games of chance—and the return of servicemen, who almost immediately joined the national effort to form the American Legion. Within three years, twenty-eight women had created its women's auxiliary.

The need for mineral resources boosted production at mining towns throughout the state. Goodsprings became a major zinc supplier, while Blue Diamond provided gypsum and plasterboard, giving Las Vegas even more of a hinterland to supply. When the Las Vegas & Tonopah line closed, Las Vegas managed to receive long-term benefits. Work soon started on turning the roadbed into part of the state highway system, meaning that the city remained tied to outlying areas.

Amid these changes, certain aspects of Las Vegas life remained the same: a small group continued to dominate local business and society, but newcomers during this decade either joined the group or began their ascent to leadership. For example, in 1911, Ernest W. Cragin arrived in Las Vegas as a sixteen year old. His father was a storekeeper with the railroad. Cragin's first job was as a railroad stenographer, and he picked up part-time work at the Majestic Theatre. By 1915, he had started running the Airdome at Third and Fremont Streets, an open-air theater that allowed residents to avoid payment by watching films from the surrounding trees, and bought out former mayor Peter Buol's insurance agency. The next year, Cragin added partner William Pike, and their business remains in operation today. Cragin also went on to play a prominent role in state and local politics as mayor in the 1930s and 1940s.

The nonwhite residents of Las Vegas began establishing themselves more prominently in the community. One of the first permanent Asian American arrivals was Yonema "Bill" Tomiyasu, a native of Japan who arrived in 1914 and established a ranch and farm southeast of town near today's intersection of Pecos and Warm Springs. He received encouragement from First State Bank, which loaned him twelve hundred dollars to lease his original 160 acres, befitting Park's involvement in the Chamber of Commerce and the belief of local leaders that agriculture might prove to be crucial to the local economy. Tomiyasu grew alfalfa, melons, and a variety of vegetables, which he sold to Las Vegans and their restaurants, as well as outlying areas like Beatty, Jean, Goodsprings, and Sloan, and, after 1930, to Six Companies at Boulder City. "Socially, we weren't integrated," said his son. "But as far as gaining respect of the community for what he did, my father got that."

Several important figures joined the Italian community—whether or not they were actually Italian. Although his name prompted most to consider him Italian, David Lorenzi immigrated from France and lived in several places across the country before settling in Las Vegas in 1911. He and his wife opened the Palms, a downtown store that sold candy, ice cream, and fresh fruit, and became highly successful in business, eventually expanding into groceries, a coal and wood yard, and finally a gold mine. He also bought 80 acres two miles northwest of the Clark town site. He started drilling and digging for wells, generating his own water supply, for grape yards where he cultivated wine. Italian immigrant Al Corradetti enjoyed similar success. He arrived in 1916 to work at the Troy Steam Laundry and Cleaning Works, located on North Main between Fremont and Ogden. He eventually went into business for himself, became an American citizen, and served several terms on the Las Vegas City Commission. Domenic Pecetto, another immigrant who really did come from Italy, expanded upon his liquor store to build the twenty-five-room Union Hotel near the depot, and his brother-in-law Joe Graglia joined him to run it.

The small but growing African American community expanded and suffered at the same time. Thanks to restrictive deed covenants that kept them from moving into the more elite residential areas, blacks were largely consigned to the outskirts of the town site. But African Americans also saw opportunity in the growing railroad town. One of them, A. B. "Pop" Mitchell, a native of Texas, arrived in town in 1913. He apparently worked as a machinist and contractor while trying to develop farmland and resorts, and his wife worked as a nurse. In 1919, their daughter Natalie became the first African American child known to have been born in Las Vegas. The Reverend J. L. Collins arrived from Goldfield and, in 1917, began the Zion Methodist Church with fourteen members meeting at a home on Thursday evenings and holding Bible study on Sunday afternoons. As another early black settler, Clarence Ray, put it, "Most of our people worked in the railroad shops and the railroad company owned a lot of land. They would encourage the employees to buy, so almost everyone had their own properties." Since they often lacked the freedom to buy, live, or work wherever they wanted, Mitchell and other residents took action. They founded the Colored Progressive Club and the Colored Democratic Club, chaired by Eli Nickerson, which met at First and Ogden Streets at his restaurant, Nick's, which specialized in southern cooking. They also began forming a chapter of the NAACP in 1918 to help the forty or so African Americans then living in Las Vegas.

As minority communities grew, so did a sense of community, within them and in Las Vegas in general. Las Vegas was a small town, and its social activities involved much of the local population. In common with gender roles across the nation, women often were at the center of the planning and the activity. The Methodist Ladies Club, among other organizations, held ice cream socials on the second floor of the First State Bank building—and since they often were held in the summer, they provided a cool respite from the heat for the attendees. The Mesquite Club, formed by the town's elite women and named by Helen J. Stewart, debuted in 1911 and held numerous meetings dedicated to education and civic issues. The next year, their Arbor Day campaign to "plant a tree and bless the earth" led to two thousand new trees to provide much needed shade and spruce up the appearance of the dusty town. In 1915, they lobbied county and school board officials into creating a kindergarten. They organized a fundraiser for a local library, which opened in April 1917 with five hundred books the club donated. And another women's club formed to concentrate more heavily on women's issues rather than just community service.

In unusual ways, the Las Vegas Land & Water Company played a key role in local social life. Bracken was active in numerous clubs and hosted gatherings at his house, and Anna Bracken, the resident agent's wife, involved herself in a variety of civic causes. More than that, rather than sending out bills, the water company simply expected customers to visit the building at Second and Lewis to settle their accounts. If they failed to do so for three months, the LVL&W would send out a letter warning that "the water would be shut off unless payment was made." But Las Vegans obtained their mail by visiting the post office at Second and Fremont, so they often paid in advance to avoid the inconvenience. In another civic contribution, the LVL&W heeded a group of Las Vegas women who prevailed upon the company in 1914 to donate ten acres of the old Stewart land to the city for a municipal cemetery to be located next to a private operation. Yet this created another problem for Bracken's office: supplying the area, nearly a mile north of the town site, with water. The company provided the line, and later the city signed a contract to obtain the water from a nearby well that Lorenzi owned.

Attempts to enhance the community combined with the need and desire for social activities to create an awareness of and involvement in a variety of civic events. When Las Vegas officially became a city in 1911, Mayme Stocker would recall, residents had access to three forms of entertainment: Ben Emrick's four-piece German band, which played on street corners on Saturday nights; the Princess Theatre, which charged five cents for admission; and Captain James Ladd's swimming pool and resort by his housing tract on east Fremont near Twelfth Street. Another form of entertainment that year was the Colossal Circus, whose human and animal acts marched up Fremont Street. Already partnered with Buol in a Fremont Street lumberyard, Adolph Levy built Economy Hall, with a store on the first floor and a meeting hall, which hosted a variety of events, on the second.

Nor did Las Vegans neglect their religious needs. While the already established churches continued to grow, in 1913 Newell Leavitt, an employee of Clark and C. C. Ronnow, the former Mormon bishop of Panaca, began holding Sunday school classes for Mormons at his home at Bridger and Sixth Streets. The owner of a prominent Mormon name himself, Leavitt was also related through marriage to the Earls and Bunkers, pioneer Moapa Valley families. And spiritual matters were indeed a cause for concern. The town was too small to insulate even the elite from what went on in nearby neighborhoods. When his family entertained after church on Sunday afternoons, Ed Von Tobel Sr. sent his eldest son, Jake, who was nine, to buy the requisite bucket of beer. The nearest bar doubled as a brothel, and he shopped there.

Las Vegans also sought to improve municipal services. The new school that opened in 1911 offered vastly better educational opportunities than its predecessors, and these improved further when a new $42,500 high school opened in 1918 at Fourth and Clark, adjacent to the elementary school, with seventeen classrooms, a gymnasium, and an auditorium. Power service improved in 1912, when the Consolidated Power and Telephone Company bought a second generator that nearly doubled electrical capacity. Yet power remained available only at night for lighting and cooking, with gas powering the town by day. Three years later, local residents took a giant leap forward with the advent of twenty-four-hour electricity when the company signed a contract with the railroad to expand service.

Health care also benefited from the combination of the town's growth and the entrepreneurial instincts of Dr. Roy Martin. With fellow doctors Forrest Mildren and F. W. Ferguson, Martin built a modern hospital. They bought the Palace Hotel and a pair of Second Street cottages next to it for about $10,000. Martin renovated the second floor to provide patients with their own balcony, with beds and offices, while a pharmacy operated on the first floor. Nor did Martin neglect the hinterland: he also built a hospital in the booming mining town of Goodsprings.

As its business and social communities matured, local politics also began to reveal long-term trends. At the municipal level, Buol's election as first mayor began a long line of businesspeople dominating local government. The ever active Griffith served as a city commissioner before moving on to the legislature, to be followed in office by such local businessmen as William Elwell and James Ullom. One of the first county commissioners, merchant W. E. Hawkins, won three two-year terms as mayor, and his successor, William E. Ferron, owned his own store. Otherwise, though, most of the city commissioners served only a term or two and then disappeared from the elective scene.

In the 1910s, Democrats increasingly demonstrated their political importance in Las Vegas. Their party carried Clark County in most federal and state races. But Republicans continued to win in several key local races, especially with candidates who had been pioneer arrivals to Las Vegas and thus enjoyed name recognition for their involvement in less partisan political and business affairs. Republican Peter Buol managed to win the 1912 assembly race with 398 votes, only six more than Frank Williams, a miner from the Goodsprings area and former assemblyman who was less well known in Las Vegas than the town's first mayor. Buol then copped a state senate seat in 1914, defeating county commissioner John Bunker from the outlying area, while E. W. Griffith went on to win Buol's old assembly seat in 1916 against Williams, then followed Buol into the upper house. C. C. Ronnow won a county commission seat, defeating Hotel Nevada owner John Miller. Henderson won the district attorney's office unopposed in 1914, beginning a long political career that would include three terms in the assembly, two terms in the state senate, and fourteen years as a district court judge—and a significant contribution to local architecture when, in the 1920s, he built one of the most prominent homes in town, a $10,000 two-story mission-style building on South Ninth that now houses law offices. Republican Henry Lillis moved up from justice of the peace to district court judge at a time when judicial races were partisan. To demonstrate the small-town nature of Clark County politics, Ed Clark easily won several terms as county treasurer, in one election defeating Republican Frank Doherty—whose father-in-law was Clark's business partner, Pop Squires.

Las Vegas and Clark County also got caught up in one of the leading political issues in the state: woman suffrage, which Nevada voters approved in 1914. Anne Martin, the leading Nevada advocate of votes for women, worked closely with several local leaders. Nationally renowned suffragist Charlotte Perkins Gilman spoke there—but caused a fight with the local leadership when she insisted on "speaking from her own platform or not at all," and refused to speak on the same platform as two Democrats, a party that she disdained. Not that Gilman was aware of it, but the first woman elected to office in Clark County also was a registered Republican: Helen J. Stewart, already the first woman to serve on a Clark County jury, who in 1916 defeated a woman opponent by almost a two-to-one majority to win a seat on the state board of education. Stewart well understood the educational issues facing the young town. She understood

Taken in about 1920, this photo shows the Las Vegas Creek in a diagonal line across the top. On the left are the railroad shops. The depot is right of center. In the lower left is the Clark County Courthouse lawn at Second and Bridger. The small building there was the city library. Across the street was Christ Church Episcopal. Special Collections, UNLV Libraries

even more, having written after Senator Clark bought her land, "Following the trail of the trapper and of the trail blazer, and the pioneer, came the iron horse, that great annihilator of time and distance, bringing all the modern ideas of advanced civilization in our midst. . . . The hardships were no more." But for Las Vegas, as the decade of the 1910s came to an end, hardships were about to return.

SETTING THE TONE, 1920s

NATIONALLY, THE ROARING TWENTIES WERE known for the bathtub gin and speakeasies that resulted in the prohibition of alcohol production, young women becoming increasingly aware of their own freedom and sexuality, the Ku Klux Klan's revival, reactions against nonwhites and non-Protestants, a rise of fundamentalism, a tenuous prosperity that benefited fewer than the number thought at the time, and a conservative reaction to the reforms of the progressive movement that put Republicans in control of the White House and Congress throughout the decade. As Las Vegas grew from 2,304 residents in 1920 to 5,165 in 1930, it faced many of the same problems and successes as the rest of the country. It also began changing its economy, out of necessity, from relying on the railroad to attracting tourists.

Early in 1926, the *Las Vegas Review* described a small town on the rise. "Las Vegas has five churches, two large banks, two newspapers, electric lighting and telephone systems, a good public library, and all the improvements of a modern community," it proudly reported. "Las Vegas is the center of millions of acres of undeveloped lands and the hub of a rich mineral territory. It is likely to become one of the great cities of the west. Irrigation now is carried on from many artesian wells. It is near the proposed Boulder Dam project to be constructed to block the Colorado River water for use in power and irrigation." Analyzing Las Vegas in its first quarter of a century as a town, historian Gary Elliott wrote, "By contemporary standards, the economic growth of Las Vegas from 1905 to 1930 seems modest. But in the context of the semi-arid West, with limited natural resources and a small population base, it was enough to inspire a political change that would lay the foundation for Southern Nevada's dominance in the late 20th century." If the foundation was about to be laid, the

1920s was the decade in which Las Vegas mixed the cement for that foundation.

As early as 1905, the federal government and residents of the Southwest had discussed the possibility of damming the Colorado River, the nation's wildest. In that year, the Colorado flooded the Imperial Valley of California, creating the Salton Sea. While Nevada prompted less interest in the Colorado's possibilities than the water and power needs of the burgeoning populace of southern California, state officials looked forward to taking advantage of whatever opportunities might be available.

That also required them to give Las Vegas and its leaders a new degree of attention. When Governor Emmet Boyle appointed the first members of the Colorado River Commission, they included longtime political and business leader Ed W. Clark and attorney Harley A. Harmon, both of whom shared Boyle's Democratic leanings, and Republican publisher and businessman Charles P. Squires. They increased their and Las Vegas's profile in ways that might prove beneficial later: one of the other commissioners was the state engineer and Boyle's political protégé, James G. Scrugham. As Boyle's successor as governor, he promoted a spate of highway building and the creation of state parks. Later, as a congressman, he helped shepherd bills through the House of Representatives that brought federal projects and funding to Las Vegas.

As preparations began for the process that would lead to the building of the dam, hyperbole ruled the day. A Union Pacific executive declared, "When the gigantic Boulder Dam project is started, Las Vegas will become the central distribution point. The Colorado River project is not an ordinary million dollar proposition; it may well go beyond the billion dollar point." While the dam cost less than that to build, it certainly paid dividends above and beyond that level. Bureau of Reclamation commissioner Elwood Mead visited the area in 1926 and told the Las Vegas Rotary Club that Las Vegas would eventually be "the center of a giant electro-chemical industry"—which almost proved true, but in a different way than Mead projected.

Meanwhile, the Bureau of Reclamation began studying the river, seeking the best location for the dam. Although geologists and hydrographers agreed that the ideal site would be Black Canyon, the name "Boulder" stuck—even after the dam was built and, in 1947, renamed for Herbert Hoover. As secretary of commerce in the 1920s, Hoover played a key role in bringing together representatives of the seven western states through which the river flowed and inducing them to agree on how to divide its waters. Without him, they might never have signed the Colorado River Compact, which stipulated the number of acre-feet of water (the amount required to cover an acre of land with a foot of water) that each state would receive—in Nevada's case, 300,000 of 7.5 million available.

Las Vegans hoped to receive something else: the dam workers. Hoping that their presence would lead to the building of perhaps thousands of houses, city fathers anticipated an economic boom. The problem was that Las Vegas lacked the infrastructure—everything from sewers to schools— to serve them. Nor did it help that Las Vegas already had a reputation for flouting the laws against liquor sales during Prohibition.

While Las Vegans undoubtedly would have wanted the financial bene- fits of the dam under any circumstances, another motivation was econom- ic necessity: the town needed help. The problem originated with a chang- ing of the guard as the 1920s began. On May 28, 1921, the aging William Andrews Clark announced the sale of his investment to his partner, the Union Pacific, which took control of the railroad, the land and water com- pany, and their holdings. J. Ross Clark, the senator's younger brother, remained active (at least on the board of the First State Bank), and Walter Bracken eventually gained the power over Las Vegas affairs that local resi- dents long believed him to have. Even then, though, Bracken answered to his superiors in one key way: while he could make decisions, he still lacked power over policy. If Clark and his minions had been at least mildly pater- nal, the corporate headquarters at Union Pacific adopted what historian Ralph Roske called "apathetic neglect."

The apathy created new problems and made long-term problems worse. When the Las Vegas City Commission filed a complaint with the Public Service Commission over the lack of water pressure, the LVL&W wound up having to repair the leaky mains and submit plans to replace hundreds of feet of pipes. Attorney Clarence D. Breeze started organizing a group to try to buy the water company and submitted a proposal to Bracken, declaring, "The present supply is inadequate. . . . We understand that your company will not extend its service to any of the additions and subdivisions outside of Clark's Las Vegas Townsite." Union Pacific officials responded by asking Bracken to justify the UP's continued ownership of the water system. Only after Bracken persuaded his superiors that the return on their investment was about 25 percent did they decide to keep ownership of the company.

But the Union Pacific also confronted more important issues that profoundly affected Las Vegas. An action by 400,000 national shop workers fighting a wage cut spread into the railroad town. After the Union Pacific fired 60 local shop workers, the union called a strike on November 25, 1921, but when the railroad agreed to negotiate, workers agreed to remain on the job. As part of a national action, Las Vegas workers finally walked out on July 21, 1922—all 63 car men, 54 boilermakers, 27 blacksmiths, 22 sheet-metal workers, 17 electricians, and 122 of the 123 machinists.

The workers had cause for hope. They had already formed a political action group that involved itself in campaigns and helped Caliente shop workers do the same. Some of the other railroad workers refused to step in and replace their striking cohorts in Las Vegas. Mexican and Japanese workers walked out with them, although the strikers believed that they obtained their jobs by agreeing to work through any strike and treated them accordingly. Sheriff Sam Gay appointed several strikers as special deputies—ostensibly to keep the peace, but also to demonstrate his feelings. City officials were strongly committed to the strikers, who, with their families, made up a substantial portion of the voting public. Local support was so great that Leo McNamee, whose family law firm represented the Union Pacific in Las Vegas for half a century, warned that if the railroad hoped for government help, it would have to be at the federal level. Accordingly, railroad lawyers began cataloging examples of threats and intimidation with the hope that a federal judge would limit picketing and other expressions of union solidarity.

Besides shutting down the railroad west of Salt Lake City, the strike proved ugly. The Union Pacific employed about 15 percent of the local population in its shops and affected the rest. Consolidated Power and Telephone, which relied upon the Union Pacific, cut off electricity to Las Vegas. The Union Pacific imported strikebreakers who were the targets of union gunfire, and several fights broke out. State and local law enforcement authorities arrested 18 strikers in the yards for trying to stop scabs from doing their jobs, and the Federated Shop Craft Union bailed them out. The local economy suffered without goods and customers coming in and out of town. Ultimately, the railroad broke the strike with help from federal injunctions, and the workers returned that September.

Union Pacific officials had understood the need to win over public opinion. Meeting with railroad executives and attorneys, Governor Emmet Boyle reported that while visiting Las Vegas, he found many residents concerned that the Union Pacific might move its repair shops out of town. He advised them to issue a public statement denying that they planned such a step. When they did so, it helped deflect some of the criticism of the railroad and enabled UP representatives to persuade some of the strikers to return. Bracken reported that "the Japs all returned to work and Mr. Comstock [a top Union Pacific executive] and I are working on the colored shop men today." The railroad also aided its cause by raising wages—proving right the workers who had claimed to be underpaid, but also enticing some of them to abandon the strike and return to work.

Las Vegas had been one of the strongest prounion cities on the Union Pacific line, and the railroad made the city pay. Claiming that its plans had been in the works all along, the Union Pacific announced after the strike was over that it was moving its repair shops up the line to Caliente. Las Vegans suspected that the UP had decided to punish them for their sympathetic response to the strike. For its part, the railroad tried to win its way back into their good graces by expanding its stockyards and building both an employee clubhouse and tennis courts. It also ran special trains to Overton in 1925 for a pageant on early Native Americans and life in the Moapa Valley.

The strike affected the community in other ways. The railroad imported several Japanese strikebreakers, but 40 Japanese mechanics joined the walkout, although some of them may have broken ranks. That may have contributed to the *Clark County Review*'s suggestion that "sons of Mikado" should be excluded not just from landownership, as they had been in California, but from entering the United States at all. Indeed, the strike may have had a long-term impact on the newspapers covering it. Squires and the *Las Vegas Age* favored the railroad, and suffered accordingly with those who sympathized with the strikers. While the *Review* faced financial problems in the immediate aftermath of the strike, it proclaimed itself "a friend of labor" and, under different leadership, went on to eclipse the *Age*.

The loss of the shops and their workers prompted greater efforts among Las Vegas leaders to diversify the economy. The results were mixed. In 1922, Corky Corkhill's *Review* welcomed the arrival of developer W. F. Holt, who had been instrumental in the growth of the Imperial Valley in California. Corkhill declared that Las Vegas had been a "parasite" living off the railroad and was "sick and tired of being treated like a child." He predicted banks, irrigation systems, and "cities and empires." Corkhill hardly realized that the flooding of the banks of the Colorado would lead to an irrigation system that promoted cities and empires in southern Nevada. It just would take longer than he hoped at the time.

Even if its leadership became less paternal, as Corkhill suggested, the railroad's subsidiary Las Vegas Land & Water Company remained the dominant force in the local infrastructure. In the 1920s, it began replacing the old redwood lines and purchasing some of the water companies that enterprising businessmen had created on the outskirts of the original town site. But its actions reeked of self-interest. It bought out the Hawkins Land and Water Company, which former mayor W. E. Hawkins set up to develop two tracts: from Bridger to Stewart and Fifth to Eighth Streets, and from Charleston to Garces and Main to Fifth. The company's interest may have been due to Hawkins's support for the railroad during his tenure as mayor (1913–1919) and the secretary of Hawkins's company, Leo McNamee, also serving as the Union Pacific's attorney. The other water company it bought belonged to S. W. Craner, who supplied the water in Peter Buol's old Buck's Subdivision and the Fairview Addition, from Mesquite to Fremont and Ninth to Fourteenth—and Craner also happened to work for the railroad.

As much as it pained Bracken and other executives to assist anything with which McWilliams had been associated, the LVL&W finally built water lines to his old town site. About one hundred residents petitioned the Public Service Commission, demanding the building of water lines. When McWilliams requested action from the land and water company, Bracken replied, "You are to organize a Public Service Corporation which will contract with the Las Vegas Land and Water Company for the furnishing of water and your company is to act as distributors. Your company will have to tap our mains at Stewart Street in Clark's Las Vegas Townsite," at the rate of one dollar per user per month, the same rate that it charged other suburban developments.

But that was more than the residents of McWilliams Townsite could afford, prompting protests and a combination of public-private action. The Las Vegas City Commission named a committee of merchant O. K.

Adcock, a partner of Clark and Ronnow, and lawyers A. A. Hinman and Clarence Breeze to investigate the local water supply. The Chamber of Commerce appointed engineer C. D. Baker and businessmen J. T. Watters and Robert B. Griffith to do the same. Their joint report concluded that in West Las Vegas, "The concessions have been very bad from the standpoint of adequate supply for irrigation, domestic use, sanitation, health, and fire protection," and merely bad in other parts of the city. In response, the city commission passed an ordinance allowing the LVL&W to build a system only for West Las Vegas. Local citizens noticed that no agenda item had appeared, and neither Bracken nor any of his aides showed up at the meeting. To compound the oddity, the company hired McWilliams to do the surveying. By April 1929, the work was done, and, thanks to a plea from Las Vegas School Board president Adcock and secretary E. H. Hunting, the water system even included the West Side Grammar School at Fourth and Washington, which had survived seven years without the water lines and was outside the residential area to be served.

That school was part of an expansion of local educational facilities—and an improvement in their leadership. In 1921, Maude Frazier arrived in Las Vegas. She was forty, a native of Wisconsin who came to Genoa, Nevada, in 1906 as a principal and teacher. She went on to teach at Lovelock, Beatty, Goldfield, and Sparks before moving to town in conjunction with her duties as deputy state superintendent of education for Clark, Lincoln, Nye, and Esmeralda Counties. Traversing the desert in a used Dodge that she named Teddy in honor of Roosevelt because, she said, "he was such a rough rider," she tried to inculcate her belief: "A good school is a thing of the mind and spirit, and not a thing of gadgets."

Frazier wanted a chance to turn her theories into practice, and Las Vegas schools needed a leader to confront new challenges. In 1927, she left her state job to become superintendent of the Las Vegas Union School District, overseeing two grammar schools and serving as principal of the high school that shared the two-story building between Bridger and Lewis Streets. Convinced that the building was a firetrap, she made plans for a new high school that could house 500 students. Her bosses on the school board questioned her judgment; the year before her hiring, the local school contained only 772 students, 139 in high school. Worse, she chose a site on what they considered the outskirts of town: Seventh and Bridger. But she campaigned successfully for a $350,000 bond issue to pass, and in

Maude Frazier spent twenty years running Las Vegas's schools, then entered one of the more active retirements on record. In the 1950s, as an assemblywoman, she led the fight to start a university in southern Nevada, to create the Clark County School District, and to pass a civil rights bill. In 1962, Grant Sawyer appointed her Nevada's first woman lieutenant governor. Special Collections, UNLV Libraries

1929, Las Vegas High School opened, while the old complex became known as the Fifth Street Grammar School. Las Vegas had taken another step on the long road to becoming a larger city—and with the pending construction of Hoover Dam, her foresight would prove valuable.

Not that Frazier intended it, but she also contributed to establishing a beachhead for Las Vegas's future. In 1929, she hired a teacher, Eva Adams, a native of Wonder, a tiny mining camp in Churchill County. In Las Vegas, Adams met important political figures who later became close friends and allies of Pat McCarran, a Reno native and longtime Democratic Party gadfly elected to the U.S. Senate in 1932. Adams eventually took over as McCarran's administrative assistant, running his Senate office in Washington, D.C., where the senator became one of the nation's most powerful men. With Adams's help, that power did a lot to build the Nevada we know today, especially Las Vegas.

One of those closest to McCarran and Adams was Al Cahlan, who became a local and state political power. But, like Adams, his first taste of Las Vegas was as a teacher. Cahlan came to town as a math instructor and basketball coach at Las Vegas High School. After he left Las Vegas to edit the Elko newspaper, Cahlan's successor at the school was Charles Duncan "C. D." Baker, a native of Terre Haute, Indiana, a graduate of Ross Poly-technical Institute, and a civil engineer. By 1924, he had begun his own engineering firm, and he went on to a long career in Las Vegas politics and business, including a term as state senator, two terms as Las Vegas mayor, and chairman of the state Democratic Party.

Another 1922 arrival was Reed Whipple, whose family had settled on several ranches in the Muddy and Virgin Valleys. He graduated from the high school, worked for the railroad, and started at First State Bank as a $145-per-month bookkeeper in 1926. By the time he retired in 1970 from First National Bank, which had bought out Las Vegas's oldest bank, Whipple was a vice president and had served several terms on the Las Vegas City Commission. Whipple also became influential in the local Mormon Church, which consisted of one ward when his family arrived—and it was part of the Moapa Stake.

This is an aerial view of Las Vegas High School not long after its construction in 1929 at Seventh and Bridger. It was then at the far end of town. Today, it is the Las Vegas Academy, a performing arts high school. Special Collections, UNLV Libraries

In 1923, James Cashman moved his automobile dealership and garage from Searchlight to Las Vegas. He already was familiar in and with the town; his first visit had been in 1904, when he worked as a waiter and dishwasher at the camp where the railroad track workers lived. His garage was attached to the Overland Hotel at Main and Fremont Streets, now the Las Vegas Club. He sold Cadillacs, LaSalles, Pontiacs, Buicks, Oldsmobiles, and GMC trucks. But his influence in Las Vegas extended well beyond his business. He was involved in winning support for the plan to build Hoover Dam. He became active in the local Elks Lodge, the Chamber of Commerce, and the Democratic Party. As a Republican, Ed Von Tobel Jr., put it, "It was hard to say no to Big Jim."

Another future political power arrived in 1923, the Bunker family. Brothers Berkeley, Wayne, and Wendell moved with their parents and siblings from St. Thomas, where the family owned a ranch. The brothers later operated a mortuary, and each of them went on to important offices in the Las Vegas area and beyond. After graduating with twenty-five others in the local high school class of 1926, Berkeley Bunker served two years on his church mission, and then came home and ran a gas station before beginning a political career that included terms in the assembly, the House of Representatives, and the Senate, while Wendell became a city commissioner.

As the town grew, so did its legal community. One attorney, A. J. Schur, signified the growth of the Jewish population; his relatives included the Gordons, Wieners, and Waldmans, local families that did a great deal to create Jewish organizations and institutions. In 1928, Roger T. Foley moved to Las Vegas with his wife and sons and won election later that year as a justice of the peace. Foley had come to Goldfield in 1910 and trained to be a lawyer by working in his father's law office. When the boom ended, the Foleys relocated to southern California before moving back to Nevada. His oldest son, Roger D., later said of the move, "My mother learned to love it, but she hated it then. It was dusty and dirty, and milk cost 25 cents a quart here when it cost 11 cents in southern California."

Arriving in 1929 amid the hope created by the proposed dam project, two Italian families went on to play a prominent role in the future development of Las Vegas. Attilio Ronzone and his wife, Bertha, left the declining mining town of Tonopah for Las Vegas and opened a downtown clothing store that remained in the family for decades; their son, Dick, later became president of the Chamber of Commerce and a member of the school board, the university board of regents, the assembly, and the county commission. Pietro Silvagni moved from Carbon County, Utah, and bought a lot that had belonged to Roy Martin at Second and Fremont Streets. In 1932, he opened the Apache Hotel, and it is now the site of Binion's Horseshoe—and his descendants remain among the owners of the lot.

When the Apache added air-conditioning, it became a particular favorite of Las Vegans during the summer, but they found other places to congregate for socializing. The combination of railroad passengers and local residents meant that Las Vegas always boasted several profitable local eateries. In the 1920s, the Oasis, on Fremont Street next to the Majestic Theatre, was considered the elite evening dining spot. One of the most popular gathering places in town was the Beanery, a restaurant at the western end of the railroad depot at Main and Fremont. Al Cahlan related a story that captured what it and the town were like. Newly arrived as a high school teacher in the early 1920s, he ate breakfast at the Beanery. As he did so for the third straight morning, Sheriff Gay sat down and asked Cahlan to explain his presence, given that the two were as yet unacquainted. Satisfied with the answer, Gay went on his way.

Las Vegas also enjoyed access to entertainment, whether from shows or of their own making. In 1924, J. R. Garehime opened a music and jewelry store on Fremont Street, offering everything from upright pianos to sheet music and wind-up gramophones. A violin and cornet player, Garehime came through Las Vegas en route to his intended new home in California. When he stopped in Las Vegas to visit his brother-in-law, banker John S. Park persuaded him to stay, and the Garehimes ended up building a home at Tenth and Stewart Streets. At the time, Las Vegas had no local radio stations, although residents could tune to fifty thousand–watt clear-channel stations from Los Angeles and Salt Lake City. They could listen to music from those stations or on the ten-inch records of such artists as Gene Austin and Vernon Dalhart.

The movie offerings also improved with the addition of the El Portal Theatre on Fremont between Third and Fourth Streets. It opened in 1928, just in time for the spread of the talkies that began replacing silent pictures, with a seating capacity of 713, a Spanish-style interior, and a lobby surrounded by colored tiles. Run by Ernie Cragin and William Pike, it included "a loge section, which meant it had big, comfortable leather chairs, and you paid extra to sit in there," recalled Harley E. Harmon, the son of the local district attorney, of the 84 cushioned, high-back chairs. Its management segregated black customers. And it opened with an unwitting link to Nevada's future. The first film it showed was a prerelease of *Ladies of the Mob,* starring one of the biggest movie stars of the 1920s, "It Girl" Clara Bow, who later married cowboy actor Rex Bell. They moved to Nevada and a ranch near Searchlight, and he became a leading Republican, serving two terms as lieutenant governor. Their son became a local lawyer who served two terms as district attorney.

Churches grew with the city. Baptists finally completed their own church at Fremont and Seventh Streets. In 1923, Las Vegas had expanded enough to warrant its first chapel and ward of the Mormon Church in a Carson Street chapel, although it remained part of the Moapa Stake until 1954. About 175 Mormons attended a wood-framed church at Sixth and Lewis under the leadership of Ira J. Earl, the son of Joseph Ira Earl, one of Bunkerville's founding fathers. Earl's successor as bishop in 1929 was Bryan Bunker, a member of a pioneer southern Nevada family.

Newspapers served not only a social purpose, but also as signs and reporters of growth. By the mid-1920s, when Las Vegas was struggling to build a new economic identity, neither weekly, the *Las Vegas Age* or the *Las Vegas Review,* could boast of great profits or success. Squires continued to publish the *Age,* while Corkhill lost ownership of the *Review* in 1922 to his wife, Mae, in a divorce settlement. She preferred to sell it, but proved unable to find a buyer until 1926, when she sold it to Frank Garside, who reported that the town had one weekly "three weeks behind, and the other two weeks late."

Garside knew how to rectify that. A veteran Nevada mining camp newspaperman, he came to the state from Kansas in 1910 and published several papers, most notably the *Tonopah Times-Bonanza.* Given his other holdings, Garside hoped to hire an editor for his new Las Vegas paper. He found his man in Al Cahlan, who was ready to leave Elko. Cahlan served as editor and business manager of the *Elko Free Press* for three years until he lost his job: Cahlan's criticism prompted a basketball referee to sue him for libel; while the jury awarded the victim only one dollar, the principle involved moved the publisher to fire him.

When Cahlan applied for the job as editor of the *Review,* Garside jumped at the chance to hire him. Cahlan arrived back in Las Vegas to find "a four-page weekly . . . of approximately 300 circulation, mostly unpaid—an old and broken-down press and an equally antique linotype machine, and not much else." He remembered "the sinking feeling I had as we stood there together. I almost wished I hadn't come. . . . A cheerful and smiling 'Doesn't look like much, does it?' represented the optimism of the new owner and at the same time presented a challenge to me."

Cahlan met the challenge. The paper started coming out twice a week by the end of 1926, then went triweekly, and daily in 1929. His younger brother John, whom he eventually appointed managing editor, said, "My brother took the attitude of 'Don't ever sell Las Vegas short,' and it was optimistic. The newspaper's attitude was optimistic all the way along. We didn't—in our news columns or our editorial columns . . . pick fights with anybody. We had the broad view that what was good for the community was good for the people." Whatever their philosophy, the *Review* had grown from a dying weekly into a prosperous daily. That spoke well not only for Cahlan's management, but also for the growth of Las Vegas.

Politically, though, the *Review* bucked a national tide. The 1920s began with a squeaker: Democrat E. E. Smith became the newest assemblyman by defeating Republican district attorney A. S. Henderson by two votes, 808 to 806. The closeness of the race was a bad omen for the Democrats, who were rising to power in Clark County. The 1920s were a decade of Republican ascendancy nationwide. Nevada elected a few exceptions—for example, Governor James Scrugham, a progressive Democrat, in 1922, and incumbent senator Key Pittman in 1922 and 1928. Pittman may have enjoyed the support of the bipartisan machine operated by George Wingfield, Nevada's political and economic boss. But Wingfield wielded little or no influence in southern Nevada, whose population remained so minuscule that it excited little interest among northerners, and Pittman cruised to victory anyway. And in 1926, Clark County demonstrated its distance from the rest of the state. Local voters supported Democratic candidates for statewide offices, yet strong majorities from the rest of the state enabled Fred Balzar to unseat Scrugham and Republicans to elect their candidates for the Senate, the House, and lieutenant governor.

In other ways, Las Vegas demonstrated that it remained too small to affect the statewide ballot. E. W. Griffith became the first Las Vegan to seek a major office in a general election. A Republican, he lost in 1922 to Democrat Maurice Sullivan, who won his third term as lieutenant governor and undoubtedly benefited from Pittman and Scrugham at the head of the ticket. Nor did it help Griffith to come from a part of Nevada with little statewide political influence, despite his six years in the legislature.

But while Las Vegans supported more Democrats than Republicans, long-term residents again proved the exception. Republican William Stewart won one of the two open county commission seats with almost the same number of votes as Cashman, the Democratic winner of the other seat. Republican Florence Doherty won the county clerk's office, but she may have benefited from the popularity of her father, Pop Squires. Henderson and Martin won assembly seats for the Republicans, as did McWilliams in the surveyor's office, and Henderson eventually moved up to the state senate. But several local Democrats gave signs of things to come. Ernie Cragin became involved in local government as deputy county recorder and then as court clerk. He and Al Cahlan won seats on the school board, and Roger Foley unseated Breeze to become justice of the peace.

While Las Vegas both reflected and departed from national political trends, it unfortunately became part of a national reaction against immigrants in the post–World War I era, becoming one of many towns across the nation and in Nevada with its own klavern of the Ku Klux Klan (KKK). Elected district attorney in 1921, two years after he passed the bar exam without ever attending law school, Harley A. Harmon eventually obtained the membership list and threatened to publicize it. That did a great deal to reduce the KKK's activities in southern Nevada. But Harley's son, Harley E., could still recall one of his first memories, seventy-five years later: a burned-out KKK cross on Fremont Street, the site of a KKK march in broad daylight in 1924. The next year, that march prompted newly elected mayor Fred Hesse to announce that he would tolerate no more KKK parades.

Hesse's stand also had something to do with local politics. Already active in forming klaverns around the state, the Klan opposed his election in 1925. One of the key issues was Prohibition, which Klan members supported and Hesse opposed. Indeed, Hesse demonstrated his opposition so openly that he, a police commissioner, and seventeen other local residents wound up under arrest in 1929 when federal agents caught them violating the anti-liquor laws; later that year, agents seized nine stills and four breweries, too. For its part, the Klan resorted to vigilante tactics, capturing not only bootleggers but also the bondsmen who posted their bail. Klan members would indict and try them in their own "kangaroo court," to use their own terminology. The Klan also demanded enforcement of all vice laws against liquor sales, prostitution, and gambling. The effort received some support outside the klavern from Las Vegans who feared that the government would deny their town the economic fruits of the dam project if they failed to conform with federal law. And they had cause for concern: the presidential administrations of Calvin Coolidge and Herbert Hoover were well known for their commitment to piety, and officials were unlikely to recommend housing dam workers in Las Vegas or even letting them near a place that so openly flouted the law. Although he was no fan of the Klan, District Attorney Harmon understood and shared local concerns to the extent that he ordered Sheriff Gay to shut down illegal blackjack games.

How committed the KKK's local members were to that organization's traditional beliefs seems debatable. The usual victims of KKK violence continued to suffer from the prejudices regrettably typical of the time—including an Elks Club minstrel show that included white performers wearing burned cork—but apparently the KKK never resorted to physical violence against those who lived in the Las Vegas area. By 1925, the estimated African American population in Las Vegas was about fifty, consisting mainly of railroad porters or track crew members and janitors or maids. Their votes were influential enough in a small town to attract numerous statewide candidates to a political barbecue held at Pop Mitchell's ranch in 1928. The Jewish community, another usual victim of the national KKK, kept growing in the 1920s. The Goldrings owned a store that reportedly sold kosher food, and Ira Goldring owned Desert Construction. In the late 1920s, Nate Mack moved to town and opened a haberdashery; by his death in 1965, he had invested in several important banks and hotels, and his son Jerome had followed suit. While the local KKK was atypical in that it appears to have allowed Jews to go about their daily lives, it may even have initiated some Catholics, a religion that it targeted in other states. Vestiges of the local KKK survived into the 1930s, although by then the town itself was changing—as were the conditions that promoted the group's revival.

Las Vegas also had more purely economic concerns and interests: attracting residents and visitors to their small town. The arrival of daily passenger air service on May 23, 1926, marked another significant moment in Las Vegas history—a moment several years in the making. In 1920, barnstorming flyer Randall Henderson visited Las Vegas with encouragement from Jake Beckley, whom he knew from business dealings in California. Henderson landed at a small airstrip built by a railroad employee, former World War I aviator Bob Hausler, and took several residents aloft in his Curtiss *Jenny* biplane. Henderson told the *Review* that "a mail route from Los Angeles east is likely to be established in the near future and that the course will run so as to make this point a landing station." For his part, in the *Las Vegas Age,* Squires declared, "Las Vegas has at last experienced the joy of flying, at least some of Las Vegas has. All the rest of us are taking treatment for dislocated necks and sun-burned tonsils."

Las Vegas immediately saw the opportunities. Hausler met with California officials eager to encourage flight and optimistic about Las Vegas as a landing spot for airmail service. In addition to calling for the creation of a local aviation club and starting passenger service throughout Nevada, the *Review* said:

> The value of the airmail to Las Vegas cannot be overestimated. Aside from the convenience of the service, the inauguration of this new route will bring a vast amount of publicity for this city which could not be purchased at any price. It is in the interest of every business man of this city that he avail himself of the new means of communication at every opportunity. . . . Las Vegas will be the only regular intermediate stop on the new commercial airway, which will place Las Vegas importantly and definitely on the air map of the country.

With other Nevada towns between Los Angeles and Salt Lake—especially Caliente and Pioche—seeking the airmail service, Hausler improved the airstrip and held air shows to promote it.

The Rockwell brothers had only recently bought Anderson Field. They saw an opportunity and leased the land to the Chamber of Commerce for free; in turn, Robert Griffith, son of pioneer merchant E. W. Griffith, served as go-between with Western Air Express (WAE). The company began airmail service between Los Angeles, Las Vegas, and Salt Lake City in April 1926, and saw that it could use its Douglas M-2 biplanes to transport passengers. Its first passenger rates were forty-five dollars one way from Las Vegas to Los Angeles and eighty dollars round-trip, including para-

A Western Douglas M-2 biplane landed at Rockwell Field in 1926. Maury Graham is believed to have been the pilot. Daily passenger air service began that May, adding to mail delivery by Western Air Express. Special Collections, UNLV Libraries

chutes for emergency use. The planes took off and landed at Rockwell Field, just outside the city limits at what is now the southeast corner of Sahara Avenue and Paradise Road, in the Sahara Hotel parking lot. And the traffic gradually increased: in 1928, Western Air Express began regular passenger-only service to Las Vegas from Los Angeles and San Francisco.

But in 1929, developer Leigh Hunt, planning to develop the airfield, bought the Rockwell family's 40 acres and canceled the Western Air Express lease. City officials would no longer have access to flights. Then P. A. "Pop" Simon bought 360 acres of land north of Las Vegas, signed a lease with the airline, and announced plans for triweekly service to Reno. That would be the municipal airport when federal officials worked out a deal for the Las Vegas Army Air Corps Gunnery School in 1941.

The 1920s brought another turning point: the completion of the federal highway connecting California with Salt Lake. Thanks to Senator

Tasker Oddie of Nevada, national highway legislation promoted road building throughout Nevada and aided states through a dollar-matching plan: the more federal land in the state—Nevada, for example—the more money the federal government would provide toward highway building. It was welcome news: as Florence Lee Jones and John Cahlan put it, "[A]nyone essaying a trip from Reno to Las Vegas had to prepare himself for a safari." Accordingly, the U.S. Bureau of Public Roads offered to pay more than four-fifths of the cost of paving Fremont, First, and Main Streets with durable concrete as part of the highway through town. That was only part of a statewide effort. Road construction became the most significant portion of the state budget in the 1920s. Nevada drivers could soon use Highway 6 to Reno and Highway 50 across the northern tier. For his support of these efforts and frequent visits to his constituents, Governor Scrugham became known as "Gasoline Jim."

To the south, Las Vegas leaders, with doctor and assemblyman Roy Martin at the forefront, persuaded state engineers to run Nevada's portion of Highway 91 through Las Vegas instead of Searchlight. And because it turned into Las Vegas Boulevard within the city limits, roadwork became more important to the city. Twenty years after the railroad promised to pave Fremont completely from Main to Fifth Streets, voters approved a fifty thousand–dollar bond issue to do the job. Clark County Commission chairman James Cashman declared that oiling and widening the road would create a "dustless and smooth highway all the way from the California to the Arizona state lines and will bring much more traffic into Las Vegas."

The Las Vegas City Commission contributed to the effort. In 1925, it voted to pave Fremont Street all the way from Main to Fifth and then provide an additional six thousand dollars to match federal funding to pave Fifth Street from Fremont for two miles south to the city limits at San Francisco Street, now Sahara Avenue. Highway construction had become a significant part of the state budget and prompted local communities to follow suit. Las Vegas proved no different from other towns around Nevada.

Improved transportation aided an initiative by civic leaders to promote Las Vegas as a tourist destination. Compared with later efforts, these would be embryonic at best. While not systematic, they certainly reflected an effort to build—and rebuild—the local economy. Nor were they original. C. O. Whittemore had proclaimed in July 1905 that the railroad was advertising Las Vegas "as a sanitarium—a haven for the winter tourist" and that in December, Las Vegas would have "an activity and liveliness to compare with beach resorts for its salutary winter climate." The Chamber of Commerce created the Hotels Committee, and Las Vegans looked for opportunities to convince passengers on the train and drivers on the highway that they could do more in the Las Vegas area than just stretch their legs.

One step involved the creation of resorts. In 1924, eastern investor Edward Taylor bought the Kiel Ranch from John S. Park. He announced plans to convert it into a dude ranch for tourists, drill wells, and plant fruit trees and grapevines. David Lorenzi dug two wells northwest of Las Vegas for a proposed "high-class resort," which he called Twin Lakes. It would include boating, fishing, an outdoor swimming pool, and a dance hall. Each lake included an island, one with a small building equipped with a trapdoor to hide the illegal whiskey and beer if the police showed up, the other with a band shell and a movie screen. His first Fourth of July celebration in 1926 attracted well over one thousand visitors. Expanding beyond the successful Overland and Hotel Nevada across from the depot, Joe Graglia built the Hotel National, while his son John became a pharmacist and co-owner of Boulder Drug Company. Another hotel, the Golden, also opened on Fremont.

Another step was building a local golf course not far from Rockwell Field, across the city limits on what are now the grounds of the Las Vegas Hilton and the Las Vegas Convention Center. Not that it necessarily resembled a modern golf course: the twenty-six prospective members invited to help build "one of the finest desert golf courses in the west" laid out gravel fairways and greens of sand. But as of 1927, the Las Vegas area at long last boasted one of the attractions that future leaders of the tourist industry would cite as crucial to their efforts.

The "New" Overland Hotel also symbolized a change yet to come. Rebuilt after a 1911 fire and still calling itself "new" two decades later, the Overland advertised the Boulder Dam Stage Office outside and offered a "Big Free Sample Room." That actually referred to a room in which salesmen could show off their products. Future Las Vegas hotel owners and politicians eventually built upon that idea to promote the convention business. And just outside the Overland and its neighbor across Fremont Street, the Hotel Nevada, stood the arch erected after passage of the

These were the buildings and pond at the Twin Lakes Resort, built by David Lorenzi in the 1920s for dining, dancing, flouting Prohibition, and escaping the blistering summer heat. Today it is part of Lorenzi Park. Special Collections, UNLV Libraries

Boulder Canyon Project Act: "Welcome to Las Vegas: Gateway to Boulder Dam."

The act became law on December 21, 1928. President Calvin Coolidge signed the bill introduced by Representative Phil Swing and Senator Hiram Johnson, both of California, formally putting the federal government behind the plans to build a dam on the Colorado River. Las Vegans celebrated what promised to be an economic boon. The railroad whistle blew continuously. Longtime local educator Elbert Edwards said, "The volunteer fire department turned out in full force, leading the parade. Bootleg liquor just flowed like water." Leon Rockwell, who teamed with his brother Earl to run the small airport just across the city line as well as an electric shop that provided sanitary and plumbing services, added, "There was people got lit that never had taken a drink before."

The celebrating also took more prosaic, economically minded forms. Downtown lots started selling for fifteen thousand to thirty thousand dollars. The Union Pacific announced plans to build a rail branch to the dam site and expand its downtown yards. The Bureau of Reclamation took over the Old Mormon Fort, erected a virtually new building, and used it as a laboratory for testing the chemicals to be used in building the dam.

For many Americans, the Wall Street crash of 1929 marked the beginning of the Great Depression. But in Las Vegas at the time, most of the signs pointed toward prosperity. The Consolidated Power and Telephone Company had been instituting large-scale improvements. In 1927, the firm replaced its entire electrical distribution system throughout the area. It

When the Union Pacific Railroad connected its Las Vegas tracks with Boulder City on September 17, 1930, it was cause for celebration. When Secretary of the Interior Ray Lyman Wilbur announced that the dam would be named for the unpopular president Herbert Hoover, the mood changed. Special Collections, UNLV Libraries

also discussed putting the system underground, but the Las Vegas City Commission backed off amid complaints from constituents that "the first time it rains, everybody will be electrocuted." The phone company expanded its building and started the first long-distance service. Then its parent company announced that it would divide into two entities: Southern Nevada Power Company and Southern Nevada Telephone Company. The town had grown too large for only one utility to provide such extensive service.

The other event that year was a telling change in local journalism. Scrugham, who started publishing the *Nevada State Journal* in Reno after losing his bid to remain governor, decided to start the weekly *Las Vegas Journal*. It proved unsuccessful: Scrugham was unfamiliar with the city, and Garside and Cahlan already provided a Democratic voice. They bought out Scrugham and turned the *Review* into a daily. The daily appearance of the *Las Vegas Evening Review-Journal* signified the city's growth —and the awareness of the potential for additional growth.

Another sign of impending change in 1930 was Sam Gay's retirement after five terms as sheriff. As early gaming operator Harold Stocker said of him, Gay "couldn't be bought away; he wouldn't take a nickel from Jesus Christ. Sam Gay was against everything but whiskey. . . . That was up to the federal government, and Sam left it to them." Gay had little use for anti-gambling laws, too, but the seventy-year-old explained, "I'm used to tough hombres who shot each other up once in a while. I'm used to gunfights. But I ain't much good at turning down racketeers." By 1930, Al Capone, the Chicago organized crime boss, had allegedly sent associates to Reno and Las Vegas to involve themselves in the gambling that was legal and to encourage the legalization of the rest of it. But Gay's departure also signified that newer, more modern police work would be needed in a newer, more modern town.

In 1930, advertisements began appearing in local newspapers at the expense of Thomas Carroll, a Las Vegas real estate developer. He suggested that a law making gambling legal would help Las Vegas become a tourist magnet. At a subsequent meeting at a back table of the Northern Club on Fremont Street, several casino owners, a city councilman, two legislators, and at least one state official reportedly agreed to support Carroll's efforts. That December, Congress approved legislation to put the Boulder Canyon project out for bidding, with construction to begin as soon as possible. As 1930 began, the *Review-Journal* announced, "We believe that Las Vegas today stands on the very threshold of that unparalleled development from which she is to emerge the metropolis of the state of Nevada and one of the great industrial centers of the west." At the end of the year, an Al Cahlan editorial declared, "No matter what is going on around the rest of the nation, there is no depression in Las Vegas." Indeed, Las Vegas was on the cusp of the changes that would affect not only its citizens, but also the world.

THE DAM ERA

Railroad Town into Tourist Town

AS THE 1930S DAWNED, LAS VEGAS BEGAN the long process of changing from a sleepy whistle-stop into a world-famous resort mecca. As Six Companies employees started work on Hoover Dam in 1931, the urban structure and physical appearance of Las Vegas resembled that of many American small towns that had undergone minor growth since their founding. In 1930, small neighborhoods or districts that evolved from the original town site housed the businesses and residents of this small town of fifty-one hundred.

Clark's town site, the 1905 nucleus from which the modern city grew, remained the main commercial and residential hub throughout the 1930s and 1940s. Fremont Street included casinos and hotels, and many of Las Vegas's large stores were located there into the 1960s. City government buildings dominated Stewart Street, and, to the south, residences flourished until rising land values in the 1960s and 1970s began to convert many of the old dwellings to law and business offices.

Twenty-five miles southeast of Las Vegas, work proceeded feverishly on the dam and its city. By 1931, Six Companies, Inc., the consortium of six construction companies chosen by the Bureau of Reclamation to build the dam, had already begun work on Boulder City, the federal reservation that would house the workforce and relieve the miserable living conditions of current workers and their families living in the river camps. In short order, Six Companies, largely following the blueprints of noted Denver city planner S. R. DeBoer, laid out a street system and utility networks. In addition, the company also built an administration building, a hospital, and a large department store. The latter was a Six Companies subsidiary that accepted the scrip with which dam workers were paid.

Eventually, complaints from Las Vegas merchants to Congress forced Six Companies to pay their workers in U.S. currency. For housing, the employers erected 250 one-room cottages, 260 two-room homes, and 123 three-room homes that married couples could rent, as well as 8 two-story dormitories for single men. A mess room fed the workforce, who used meal tickets, and a recreation room, complete with pool tables and gym, served as a leisure center. Completion of the Boulder Highway to Las Vegas via Fremont Street allowed residents to escape the humdrum life of a company town. Over the next few years, Boulder City increasingly took on the familiar appearance of an American small town by adding a school, police station, post office, railroad station, and cemetery.

Despite these amenities, Boulder City was still very much a company town in the early 1930s. It was not a rip-roaring mining camp or even a "last frontier" railroad town like Las Vegas. Under the watchful eye of its

On the shore of the Colorado River near Black Canyon, looking east, is Ragtown or Williamsville in 1931. Families pitched tents and hoped for work on the dam. Special Collections, UNLV Libraries

puritanical city manager, Sims Ely, Boulder City was strictly a company town created to build a dam and nothing more. As one veteran sourdough from the mines of Cripple Creek, Tombstone, and Pioche told a *New York Times* reporter, "A feller couldn't make a real old-time Western town out of Boulder City if he tried." He then added, "[I]f these fellers were after gold you might do something to stir up some life around the edges. But this crowd is only after jobs." By the late 1930s, however, many residents had decided to stay and make Boulder City a permanent place. Over the years, it has developed into a pleasant community and one of Las Vegas's most desirable suburbs.

The coming of the dam began to alter downtown Las Vegas's appearance. At Fremont and Main Streets, the old Hotel Nevada's owners added a third floor and fifty new rooms and renamed it the Sal Sagev. Even the tiny MacDonald Hotel nearby added sixteen rooms in anticipation of more business. These hotels had served railroad passengers on layovers for three decades. And while the Union Pacific would continue to deliver passengers for decades to come, their purpose in coming to Las Vegas shifted decidedly from business to pleasure. Hoover Dam and, to a lesser extent, the relegalization of gambling turned Fremont Street into a tourist center. These projects and the building of the Apache Hotel, which housed the city's first elevator, symbolized the beginning of Las Vegas's transformation into the throbbing resort city it is today.

And the changes extended beyond Fremont Street. To the north on Stewart, the 1933 federal building and post office was a major addition to downtown. It presaged the New Deal's construction of the American Legion War Memorial Building down the street in 1935–1936. These two facilities converted the area just north of the hotel-business district into the community's government center (city offices moved there in 1942) for the next three decades.

In the 1930s and early 1940s, a spate of residential construction helped the city shed its old railroad-town image. Housing became more diverse, and the architectural style reflected the prosperity the dam and war economies created. South and east of Clark's town site, between Sixth and Tenth, some of Las Vegas's leading families bought or built a series of impressive Tudor and Tudor-revival homes. Mission-revival architecture also enlivened the neighborhoods surrounding the downtown core. The Foremaster house (1927–1942) on South Seventh and other residences

Las Vegas Hospital, built in 1931 at Eighth and Ogden, where many a longtime Las Vegan first saw the light of day. Its prominent doctors included Roy W. Martin, one of its builders, and Clare W. Woodbury, a longtime school board member. Special Collections, UNLV Libraries

nearby were excellent examples of that style. This area south of Fremont housed some of the city's most prominent lawyers, political leaders, and businessmen. It also contained larger buildings such as Dr. Roy Martin's mission-revival Las Vegas Hospital (1931) at Eighth and Ogden, the new Las Vegas High (1930), the Mormon chapel at Carson and South Ninth (1932), the First Baptist Church (1940), the Huntridge Theater (1944), and other significant community centers that served local residents.

While population concentrated around downtown for many years, other neighborhoods developed farther out. Though platted shortly after the town's founding, these areas experienced little significant growth until the prosperous dam and wartime eras, which finally compensated for their distance from Fremont Street and relative lack of water. On the outskirts of town between Highway 91 and the railroad, south of Clark and down to the municipal limits at today's Sahara Avenue, the old Boulder, Southern, and Meadows Additions began attracting residents during and after World War I and many more in the 1920s and 1930s. The Meadows neighborhood exemplified the planning typical of the City Beautiful Movement in America's Progressive Era. Meadows Park at Fairfield Avenue and Boston Street was an attractive focus for a desert suburb on the city's sagebrush frontier.

World War II, with its visiting soldiers and California defense workers, further boosted the area by pouring more traffic past it along the Los Angeles Highway. By the 1940s, as motels, motor courts, and restaurants increasingly lined Highway 91 out to the newly emerging Strip, residents understood they would have to share some of their space with auto tourists unable to find accommodations downtown.

The Westside neighborhood had languished for decades. A mix of classes lived there, as the neighborhood's small cottages, frame homes, and occasional mission-style and period-revival homes would attest. The first (1921) and second (1942) Westside public schools as well as local churches helped anchor the early community, along with a smattering of stores and businesses. But the community suffered until the 1950s from a lack of pavement, sewers, streetlights, and other amenities.

While the Westside lagged, the rest of Las Vegas began to change dramatically under pressure from myriad forces. The relegalization of gambling and further liberalization of divorce (to a six-week waiting period) in 1931, the end of Prohibition in 1933, the emergence of the Strip, the birth of Henderson, the Basic Magnesium plant, the army gunnery school, and North Las Vegas's development all combined to propel and shape the urbanization of Las Vegas, creating a budding metropolitan area by 1950.

Other changes affected residents less than visitors. The New Deal funded the widening and improvement of Highway 91. The Union Pacific completed a modern new depot in 1941. Federal and local officials produced a new airport in 1948. All of these promoted easier access to Las Vegas for travelers—some of whom stayed. As a result, the city grew dramatically from approximately fifty-one hundred residents in 1930 to eighty-four hundred in 1940 and almost twenty thousand during the war.

Everyone knew that the Boulder Canyon Project Act of 1928 would finally rescue Las Vegas from the economic doldrums it endured in the six years following its bitter strike against the Union Pacific. Within weeks of its passage, signs of a boom began to appear. Investors announced plans to build the Egyptian Ambassador Hotel at Fremont and Ninth Streets, which proved to be, like many "paper hotel" announcements, a hollow promise. But there was no lack of real estate transactions. In 1929, John Mills of San Diego bought a corner lot on Fremont and Third for thirty thousand dollars—more than thirty times its 1905 value. He also purchased 130 acres next to the Fairview tract north of Fremont Street and announced plans to build two hundred houses. In July 1930, longtime banker and power company official Cyril Wengert sold his home at Fifth and Carson to the Virginia Hotel Corporation for thirty thousand dollars.

Clearly, the funding of dam construction in 1928 convinced many that southern Nevada would become not only a tourist site, but also a center for dam-related commerce. In January 1929, California officials budgeted almost eight hundred thousand dollars to pave Highway 91 (the Los Angeles Highway) from San Bernardino to the Nevada line, to improve access to Las Vegas. In addition, Arizona outlined a plan to pave its road between Utah and Nevada across the so-called Arizona Strip.

Eager to cash in on the stimulus that the dam project would give the local economy, local businessmen also invested in their city. In March 1929, Earl Rockwell opened a series of commercial buildings on Fremont and Second Streets that featured a coffee shop, cafeteria, and a Skaggs-Safeway grocery store. He also worked with other town leaders and school officials to realize local school superintendent Maude Frazier's dream of a new Las Vegas High School on Bridger (today's Las Vegas Academy) in anticipation of the dramatic increase in the city's resident population. The expectation that Las Vegas would house the dam's workforce sparked a rash of land deals and new subdivisions—for example, B. B. Tankell's purchase in 1929 of a 180-acre tract near Stewart and Fourteenth for a new subdivision.

Aside from this real estate growth, the dam would obviously require and foster improvements in transportation to make Las Vegas more accessible to travelers and tourists. Leigh Hunt's closing of Rockwell Field had left Las Vegas without an airport when the city's lease ran out in 1929. So Pop Simon's decision to build a new facility seven miles north of the city and begin triweekly service to Reno was a godsend. When Western Air Express regained its federal airmail subsidy in the mid-1930s, the airline leased the field, then purchased it from Simon, then refused to cooperate when Las Vegas sought New Deal money to buy the land and build a more modern facility to support the town's new tourist business. Only in 1941, under the pressure of war, did the airline yield. Thanks to intervention by Senator Pat McCarran, the city obtained federal funding to acquire the field from WAE and forced the airline to share its landing rights with other airlines as well as the army's new gunnery school.

A decent airport was only one of many improvements Las Vegas undertook in anticipation of dam-related growth. In July 1929, city commissioners awarded a $15,000 contract to build a garbage disposal plant. They also secured a quitclaim deed from the Las Vegas Land & Water Company for 32 acres to build a municipal park (near today's "spaghetti bowl" of freeways). In October, the city installed new ornamental streetlights and appropriated more than $100,000 to pave dirty streets near Fremont. At the same time, the gas company spent $175,000 for a new plant and pipe system, and Southern Nevada Telephone finally budgeted $400,000 to give impatient residents long-distance phone service. Clark County officials also responded to the expected boom by announcing plans for a new $100,000 hospital at roughly the site of today's University Medical Center, while federal officials promised to build a highway connecting the dam site with Las Vegas. The city was growing, and its services and infrastructure needed to keep up. Medical care was a case in point. In 1931, Boulder City Hospital, Dr. Roy Martin's Las Vegas Hospital, and the Clark County Hospital all began caring for patients.

These actions came just in time. As Six Companies began work on Hoover Dam, Boulder City, and the Boulder Highway, two related trends became obvious: Fremont Street would undergo a facelift, and the dam would draw more travelers than the railroad ever had. From the beginning, tourists descended upon southern Nevada to see the dam under construction, and Las Vegas immediately became the gateway to this spectacle. In 1933, 230,000 people visited Las Vegas, and the next year the figure jumped to 300,000.

Fremont Street gradually became more of a tourist center than a main street, as construction of the Las Vegas Club, the Apache Hotel, the Sal Sagev, and other properties indicated. But casinos exerted little influence upon this process during the early 1930s. Even before the relegalization of gambling in 1931, Bureau of Reclamation commissioner Elwood Mead had predicted that the dam would make Las Vegas "a mecca for hundreds of thousands of tourists during the construction." He urged locals to build "a

The dam helped advertise Las Vegas, which called itself the Gateway to Boulder Dam, then Hoover Dam. The Boulder Club's operators were happy to connect themselves to the eighth wonder of the world—and to Las Vegas's efforts to market itself in the 1930s and early 1940s as a western town—thus the other slogan, not in this postcard: The Old West in Modern Splendor. Special Collections, UNLV Libraries

modern tourist hotel" near the lake that would soon form and bear his name. He also boldly declared that "one of the greatest winter resorts in the country will grow upon the shore of Boulder lake." His prophesies came true, but Las Vegas, and especially its downtown area, not the lake, drew the hoteliers and tourists.

Of course, not all the action was downtown. A few clubs like the Pair-O-Dice appeared on the lonely highway approach to Las Vegas that would become the Strip in the 1940s. Gaming emporiums also appeared along the newly paved Boulder Highway, which was really an extension of Fremont Street to the dam site. In May 1931, California gambler Tony Cornero (Stralla) and his brothers unveiled the Meadows Club on Boulder Highway near Charleston and announced plans for a fifty-room hotel. That August, the Railroad Pass Casino opened just outside the Boulder City gate.

In the 1930s and later, new casinos proved to be powerful magnets, capable of spawning new subdivisions around them to serve workers and players alike. Though small, the Meadows was no exception. Expecting development along Fremont Street near this casino, subdividers planned

Joe Graglia, who owned the Union Club and Hotel National, and Frank Detra, who dealt at the Boulder Club, moved out to Highway 91 to open their Pair-O-Dice Club in December 1933 (near today's New Frontier Hotel). Eventually, Guy McAfee bought it and renamed it the 91 Club. Special Collections, UNLV Libraries

the Sunrise Park Division, with lots selling for $150–$250. Even before the arrival of the Basic Townsite and its giant magnesium factory in the 1940s, the Meadows Club, as well as Fremont Street's stores and casinos, lured dam workers eager to escape the tedium of a construction town whose puritanical manager, Sims Ely, regarded gambling as a sin and Prohibition as the law. While few major buildings appeared on the highway between Railroad Pass and the Meadows Club, the stream of tourist and Boulder City traffic demonstrated the symbiotic relationship between Las Vegas and the dam long before Basic Magnesium and its industrial landscape reinforced this line of development in the 1940s.

As the Las Vegas area's population more than doubled during the height of dam construction, thousands of new residents poured into the valley. This injection of new blood, new money, and new ideas was vital to progress. Entrepreneurs proposed schemes to build water systems, buildings, expanded streets, and other improvements that would modernize Las Vegas's appearance and boost its appeal. In 1930, "outside interests" even tried to cash in on the city's proximity to the latest "wonder of the world" under construction in Black Canyon by honoring the man who made it possible. A small group suggested renaming Las Vegas Hoover City, but residents opposed the idea, and just in time. Within a year, the shanties of jobless poor springing up in caves, under viaducts, and in trash heaps across the nation would be nicknamed "Hoovervilles" for the tradition-bound president whose policies did so little to help those made homeless by the Depression.

Geography, geology, politics, southern California's need for water, and a dozen other factors brought Hoover Dam to southern Nevada, created Las Vegas's prosperity, and spared the town from the destructive effects of

The Meadows attracted the Las Vegas elite. In the lower left, with open jacket and necktie, smiling, is owner Tony Cornero (Stralla). The second woman to his right is Alta Ham. Two women to her right is Patricia Hesse, the mayor's wife, and beside her is Harley A. Harmon. Attorney and businessman Art Ham Sr. is looking at the camera on the far right. In profile next to him, in bow tie, is Mayor Fred Hesse. Special Collections, UNLV Libraries

the Great Depression. However, still other factors at the time threatened Las Vegas's chances of getting the project or its workforce. Long before it became known as "Sin City" or the "Green Felt Jungle," Las Vegas suffered and sometimes benefited from a lawless image. The town's wide-open atmosphere of booze, gambling, and prostitution did little to help its cause with the straight-laced officials of the Coolidge and Hoover administrations. Although the State of Nevada had banned gambling in 1909 and permitted it to return on a limited basis in 1915, illegal games continued to prosper in various club and bar back rooms in Reno, Las Vegas, and elsewhere. In addition, liquor continued to flow throughout the 1920s in continuing violation of the Volstead Act. A statewide referendum in 1926, in which a majority of Nevada voters supported a petition to Congress urging repeal of Prohibition, merely testified to the law's unpopularity, especially in urban areas.

Even after Hoover's secretary of the interior, Ray Lyman Wilbur, decided to base the dam workforce in Boulder City, federal efforts to clean up Las Vegas continued. As one local observer reported, the Hoover administration was determined to enforce Prohibition in Las Vegas, because the government regarded illegal alcohol sales "as inimical to efficient and safe operation of laboring forces on the great Boulder Dam project." In February 1931, U.S. Justice Department officials dispatched a federal marshal to town to warn the Red Rooster Club on Highway 91 and its counterparts on Fremont Street to obey the Volstead Act or suffer the fate of the Arizona Club, which the government had closed for a year due to violations. A few months later, marshals backed up their words by arresting fifty-nine people in surprise raids. Embarrassed county commissioners responded by threatening to deny or revoke the gaming license of any establishment that ignored the Volstead Act. The campaign continued until December 1933 when Prohibition finally ended. But even then, Sims Ely refused to allow any bars or liquor stores within Boulder City.

Prohibition was unpopular with many Las Vegas residents. Indeed, the city had hosted a lively, if covert, bar business in the 1920s. Not only did these watering holes serve booze, but as late as 1929 one southern California editor reported well-policed gambling halls, featuring faro and roulette, in operation. While Las Vegas had its share of bootleggers, it was not a "wide open town." But support was building in 1929 to relegalize gambling. As the same California editor reported, "liberals" envisioned a "wide open boom—with the skies the limit," while "progressives" sought to combat the Depression by using Hoover Dam's expected power and water to entice manufacturing to the valley's cheap lands. Both groups proved to be right.

However, there was no stopping the roulette wheels and table games. Saddled with a low population, a stagnant mining industry, and myriad farms and ranches in tax delinquency, the state legislature relegalized full-fledged casino gambling in 1931 to encourage tourism and raise revenue. Ominously, just one year later, the Internal Revenue Service opened its first office in Las Vegas—no doubt drawn by the need to service dam workers. By the 1940s, however, agents shifted their attention to the casinos, where tax evasion became a common practice. Despite the concerns of Wilbur, Ely, and other moral conservatives, gambling, booze, and Las Vegas's overall party atmosphere only contributed to the dam boom and benefited from it.

From 1931 to 1935, dam construction brought unparalleled prosperity to Las Vegas. The city's stores and clubs did a brisk business with tourists, residents, and dam workers. As a result, while police, teachers, and other workers endured some wage cuts, the Las Vegas Valley largely escaped the Depression's effects, with none of the lengthy layoffs or mass firings that plagued other cities. Unlike in northern Nevada, where all twelve of George Wingfield's banks closed in a spectacular 1932 collapse, the First State Bank at First and Fremont Streets remained open.

The boom, however, did not last for all of the 1930s. Following President Roosevelt's visit to town in September 1935 to dedicate the dam, and the departure of many workers to Grand Coulee and other projects, Las Vegas suffered a slowdown. In the meantime, hotel and club owners, who had experienced five years of prosperity, were desperate to keep the boom going. To this end, business leaders sponsored several new events to promote and publicize the town as a tourist center. Beginning in 1935, they organized the Boulder Lake Regatta and other races on the newly formed lake. They started a golf tournament patterned after the Phoenix Open, which had been drawing visitors to the Valley of the Sun since 1932. But the most successful promotion for Las Vegas in the 1930s proved to be the Helldorado Rodeo and Parade, sponsored by the local Elks Club. The parade began in 1935, and the Elks added a rodeo several years later. Helldorado, a play on words for "El Dorado," celebrated the Wild West atmosphere of early mining camps. The Elks also exploited the recent popularity of William Breakenridge's novel *Helldorado* (1928), which had inspired Tombstone, Arizona, in 1929 to celebrate its fiftieth anniversary by staging what became the annual Helldorado Days event, featuring a reenactment of the infamous shootout at the O.K. Corral.

The first Las Vegas parade in 1935 drew an enthusiastic response from residents and media alike. This surprise, coming in the midst of the national depression, immediately made the parade a likely candidate to become an annual publicity event. As one local columnist declared, "Las Vegas is particularly well suited to popularize just this type of a Wild West celebration . . . [because it] is one of the leading tourist centers of the West, in the heart of the nation's most liberal state"—at least in the sense of gambling, twenty-four-hour liquor sales, and easy divorce and marriage. Indeed, as early as 1935, Las Vegans saw their newly adopted last-frontier theme as an appealing image for tourists. No longer just the "Gateway to Boulder Dam," Las Vegas advertised itself as "Still a Frontier Town" and "The Old West in Modern Splendor."

Even though it did not last for all of the 1930s, the Hoover Dam boom made certain important contributions. Aside from the prosperity it brought, the boom taught Las Vegas leaders not to tolerate economic downturns, but to take action to restore prosperity with events like the regatta and Helldorado. The dam boom not only reminded businessmen of the importance of maintaining prosperity, but along with the New Deal, also benefited labor by inducing workers to take forthright steps to protect their interests in an expanding economy.

Specifically, the dam's construction inaugurated a new round of union organization in Las Vegas. For years, the community had been a railroad town dominated by the brotherhoods, which played a major role in electing the sheriff, mayor, and county commissioners. The Boulder Canyon Project Act of 1928 made it clear that the expected urban expansion would bring many construction workers to town. Local and incoming carpenters, welders, and other building-trades workers responded by organizing for the building boom that Hoover Dam promised.

Unlike the rest of America, where the Red Scare and other events caused union membership to plummet in the 1920s, Las Vegas workers formed the Central Labor Council later in that decade. Hundreds of workers joined, and by 1930 council leaders could report that all skilled crafts had been unionized. They had no lack of projects to work on. Indeed, the benefits were immediate. In the midst of the Depression, these workers exploited Las Vegas's newfound prosperity. For a forty-four-hour week, electricians earned a daily wage of ten dollars, while carpenters and common laborers took home eight dollars and five dollars, respectively. In 1935, passage of the Wagner Act recognized labor's right to collective bargaining and created the National Labor Relations Board. Within three years, local hotel workers formed Local 226 of the Culinary Union, an organization that now represents thousands of resort workers in Las Vegas.

The private sector accounted for only part of the new construction that transformed the former whistle-stop into a thriving city. Franklin Roosevelt's New Deal continued the momentum. Mayor Ernie Cragin and his successors worked with Nevada's powerful Democratic senators, Key Pittman and Pat McCarran, to get the War Memorial Building at Stewart and Fifth Streets (later replaced on the same site by today's city hall), whose large auditorium served as Las Vegas's first convention center and a venue for concerts and prizefights into the 1950s. Roosevelt's public works programs paved the remaining dirt streets downtown and ran sewer lines to many of the lots in the town's newer neighborhoods. The New Deal not only finished the city park's athletic fields and other recreational facilities, but also built a new grammar school, a sixty thousand–dollar fish hatchery for Lake Mead, and a municipal golf course.

All of these projects greatly benefited the city during the national depression. As in other American towns, many of the street improvements and other public works projects had been on the drawing boards for years, awaiting the population growth that would provide the tax revenues to build them. But the Depression and Roosevelt's jobs programs changed everything. In Las Vegas, as elsewhere, the New Deal catalyzed the city's public works agenda.

Indeed, many projects the New Deal built in Las Vegas had long been planned. A modern and expanded sewer system had been a major priority for years. The city's original sanitary network, built in 1913, had become inadequate, threatening the health and ultimately the growth of the community. Residents well knew how infectious disease had deflected workers from many Ohio and Mississippi River towns as well as places in the Los Angeles Basin where malaria and other summer fevers prevailed. So urban health was a major issue, and residents saw a modern sewer system as the

panacea. As one local columnist reported in 1931, "[Y]ears of good fortune have lulled us into a sense of false security and we have come to believe that because serious epidemics and pestilence have not resulted from the present sewer condition, they never will."

The health issue was serious, because it threatened growth. As the *Las Vegas Age* warned, several large buildings being planned "may be delayed by the inadequacy of our sewerage system"—and since editor Pop Squires had once been a local privy inspector, he would know. However, the present crisis menaced not only commercial development, but residential growth as well. With the dam boom already filling Las Vegas with hundreds of new residents, the editor wondered: "[W]hat will the many who desire to build homes in the outlying portion of the city do?" Sewers were vital to Las Vegas's suburbanization, and in a city where revenues remained inadequate, the New Deal came to the rescue.

The underlying force guiding Las Vegas's prosperity and public works projects in the 1930s was strong political leadership. It came not only from influential senators like Pittman and McCarran, but also from local officials. Following almost a decade of political turbulence, punctuated by charges of corruption and voting fraud, Las Vegans recognized the need for a stable administration during the inevitable development sparked by the dam's construction. By 1931, Cragin, a respected theater owner and insurance broker, embodied the honesty and leadership that residents longed for.

In his campaign, Cragin promised an "efficient business administration" and reassured voters that no clique owned him, he owed no one a job, and his only concern was the public interest. This was just what the city needed. One supportive editor portrayed Cragin "as an investment insurance

---

(*Top*) In January 1935, New Deal funding allowed the American Legion to break ground on the War Memorial Building at Fifth and Stewart. It opened in June 1936 to house public events and small conventions. By 1942, the city moved most of its offices there until the building was razed in 1971 to make room for the present city hall. Special Collections, UNLV Libraries

(*Bottom*) In the 1930s, the old Las Vegas Grammar School, part of the high school, burned. This led to the building of the Fifth Street School, which still stands, a protected building now used as a downtown center by UNLV. Special Collections, UNLV Libraries

against graft, inefficiency, squandering of public funds, corrupt paving contracts, [and] collecting tribute from underworld machinations." Those who today associate political corruption in Las Vegas with the mob and the postwar casino industry might be surprised to find that the roots of Las Vegas's courtship with crime go far back in the city's history and were not always mob related. In a clear reference to events in the 1920s, the *Las Vegas Review-Journal*'s Al Cahlan assured voters that Cragin's election would protect them "against an actual sell-out of the community to those who have envisioned the opportunity for huge profit from an amalgamation of the liquor trade, narcotic industry, corrupt municipal contracts, and other enterprises which can be made to pay tribute."

At the same time, Cahlan saw Cragin's election as a potential turning point in the city's history, and the editor's vision of what Las Vegas could become was remarkably insightful. Indeed, Cahlan insisted that "if we are to become the city we hope to become—the city which will take its place along with Phoenix, Salt Lake, and Denver as great inland population and industrial centers," then honest businessmen like Cragin had to be given the reins of power. On the day after Cragin's election, Cahlan proclaimed that "for years our greatest curse has been that of dissension," but now with dam construction beginning, Las Vegas residents stood "on the threshold of our greatest period of development."

The new mayor would not disappoint his supporters. In a remarkable display of energy, Cragin, relying on the considerable power of McCarran and other influential Nevadans, secured federal funding for many public works projects that the city desperately needed. Cragin and his successor, Leonard Arnett, benefited from Roosevelt's policy of routing jobs programs through local politicians to share credit with them and earn their support for the president's agenda. In fact, Cragin was so close to New Deal programs and the bureaucrats who ran them that his opponents charged him with running a "political machine." On the national level, Republican leaders similarly complained about the Works Progress Administration and other alphabet agencies, which led to a 1938–1939 congressional investigation. Arnett, portraying himself as a reform candidate, defeated Cragin by three hundred votes in the 1935 election.

Once in office, Mayor Arnett also worked with the New Dealers to secure projects, including the highly controversial effort to build a municipal power plant and liberate Las Vegas from the price-gouging monopoly

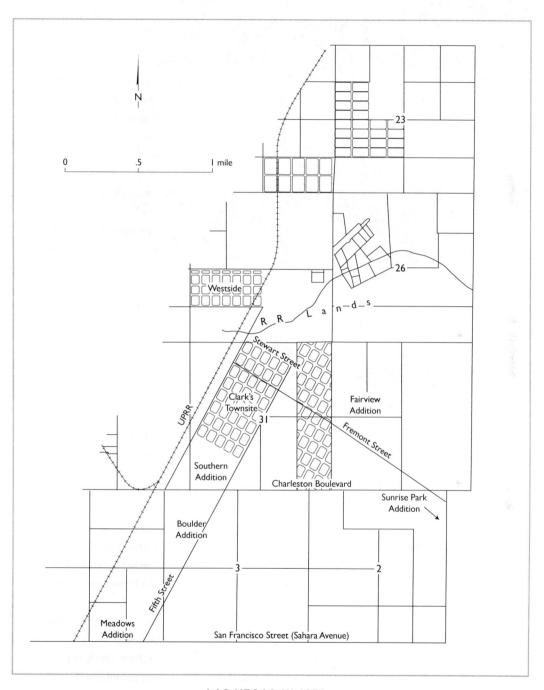

N

0   .5   1 mile

23

26

Westside

R R   L a n d s

Stewart Street

Fairview
Addition

Clark's
Townsite

UPRR

31

Fremont Street

Southern
Addition

Charleston Boulevard

Sunrise Park
Addition

Boulder
Addition

3   2

Fifth Street

Meadows
Addition

San Francisco Street (Sahara Avenue)

LAS VEGAS IN 1939

On September 30, 1935, President Franklin Roosevelt, in the white hat with black trim, visited southern Nevada to dedicate Boulder Dam. Standing in front of him on the left is Secretary of the Interior Harold Ickes. On the right is Senator Key Pittman. Special Collections, UNLV Libraries

of the Southern Nevada Power Company. This initiative dragged Arnett into a protracted conflict with the recalcitrant utility as well as fiscal conservatives such as John Russell and his followers in the Las Vegas Taxpayer's League, who objected to building an expensive electric power network (Southern Nevada Power had refused to sell the city its system) when the dam boom was over and a new 1937–1938 recession forced county commissioners to cut Las Vegas's share of property tax revenues.

In the end, city commissioners deserted Arnett on the issue, and in February 1938 he requested a sixty-day leave of absence for his health. Arnett moved to Petaluma, California, bought a chicken ranch, and never returned. The city commission declared the mayor's office vacant in early May, appointed city commissioner H. W. Marble interim mayor, and voted to delay construction of a municipal power system indefinitely. This represented a major victory for Southern Nevada Power, which, in revamped form, continued serving the valley into the next century. Marble remained mayor until 1939 when voters elected Las Vegas Taxpayer's League president John Russell mayor, an action they would eventually regret.

Despite the political turmoil at city hall, the 1930s marked an important watershed in local history. The dam boom changed Las Vegas forever. Not only did the project plant the seeds for the southeastern portion of today's metropolitan area by establishing another urban center more than twenty miles from Fremont Street, but it also created an umbilical cord between the two cities. Boulder Highway would serve as a major axis for suburban growth into the new millennium. The traffic between Boulder City and Las Vegas intensified during World War II, when the new chemical town of Henderson would generate even more traffic and development along the route.

Fremont Street was still residential on January 13, 1937, when an enterprising photographer took advantage of a Las Vegas rarity: a snowfall. Special Collections, UNLV Libraries

Looking west on Fremont in the 1930s, on the left are Beckley's, the Las Vegas Club, Las Vegas Hotel, Northern Club, and Sal Sagev. On the right is a mix of retail and tourist-oriented businesses, including the Las Vegas Pharmacy, a hotel, shoe shop, liquor store, delicatessen, cafe, J. C. Penney, and the Overland Hotel. The depot is in the center. Special Collections, UNLV Libraries

The 1930s also changed the Las Vegas cityscape with new buildings, streets, and industry. Tourism had always played a minor role in the city's economy. The railroad had delivered a few wealthy arthritics and consumptives to winter in town at places like David G. Lorenzi's resort (today's Lorenzi Park) and small ranches on the edge of town. But in the 1920s and earlier, Phoenix, Tucson, Albuquerque, Palm Springs, and other places with better highway connections, railroad service, and facilities claimed most of the winter business. While Las Vegas tried to compete from the outset, the real change came in the 1930s and 1940s. As it became Hoover Dam's gateway and a venue for legalized gambling, Las Vegas discovered its new appeal as a tourist center. Over the next decade, business leaders would build bigger and better hotel-casinos and develop the town's new tourist trade into a full-scale industry.

WORLD WAR AND ITS AFTERMATH

Gambling Becomes King

AS DEPRESSION GAVE WAY TO WAR IN THE 1940S,
America and Las Vegas began a new round of change and growth. World
War II transformed Las Vegas just as it did Phoenix, Tucson, Albuquerque, Los Angeles, and countless other towns across the West. With the fall
of France in spring 1940, and the Battle of Britain that summer and fall, it
became obvious the United States had to support its traditional allies in
the struggle against Germany. Key Pittman's death in November 1940
made Pat McCarran Nevada's senior senator, and he lost no time in securing military facilities for his state.

Even before the attack on Pearl Harbor in December 1941, McCarran
and others convinced Roosevelt's advisers that the giant magnesium plant
that America and its allies so desperately needed belonged in the Las
Vegas Valley. Since the German Luftwaffe's daily bombing of England
made it impossible to build a factory to make the "wonder metal" for
firebombs and airplanes in Britain, the United States, far beyond the range
of German bombers, became the best location. While Alcoa and other
large corporations could easily have handled production in California,
McCarran and officials at Basic Refractories of Cleveland (which held
many U.S. magnesium patents and owned magnesite mines near Gabbs,
Nevada) pushed for a site in southern Nevada. McCarran's argument was
convincing: Gabbs was only three hundred miles from Lake Mead, which
could provide the water to cool the magnesium ingots when they emerged
from the huge ovens that heated them with Hoover Dam's cheap power.

As early as 1935, a minerals executive from Salt Lake City came to Las
Vegas to look into constructing a magnesium factory near Hoover Dam, so
the idea preceded the war. The creation of Basic Magnesium, Inc. (BMI),

Las Vegas as the 1940s began. The railroad depot is at the center right, and to the left and at the top are the railroad yards. To the north and south, big changes loomed. Special Collections, UNLV Libraries

contributed substantially to Las Vegas and the eventual metropolitan area. It immediately added almost fifteen thousand to the local population, and provided a needed stimulus to Las Vegas's commercial sector and struggling casinos. BMI also diversified the valley's economy with a chemical and industrial sector that the railroad-tourist economy badly needed.

But BMI and the town of Henderson would make even more valuable contributions. As *Las Vegas Review-Journal* editor and Colorado River Commissioner Al Cahlan declared, BMI "solved two problems right quick

—[it] provided facilities by which Lake Mead water could be brought into the Las Vegas Valley and [BMI] brought about the installation of a generator to produce Nevada's power at Boulder Dam." In addition, the giant factory provided jobs and created a town, both crucial to the valley's development into a metropolitan area.

Senator McCarran's support for Las Vegas went well beyond Basic Magnesium. He played a pivotal role in convincing the army to base its gunnery school at Pop Simon's old airport northeast of Las Vegas. Although Western Air Express fended off city and New Deal efforts to buy its field and build a modern, municipally owned facility, there was no holding off McCarran or the army in the face of war. In 1940, WAE sold its airport to Las Vegas, which then gave the airline a thirty-year lease with

Basic Townsite in 1942–1943 boasted rows of demountable homes for white wartime workers. Basic Magnesium built Carver Park for African American employees, some of whom later moved to West Las Vegas. Special Collections, UNLV Libraries

landing privileges. Las Vegas officials then obtained federal funding to extend two runways and upgrade the facility for army training, which began in 1941. In an unusual deal designed to placate the city and WAE, the military agreed to share runways with tourists. Following Pearl Harbor, the gunnery school became a busy place, training more than fifty-five thousand gunners during the next four years.

Other federal operations changed the face of Las Vegas. Besides this facility, McCarran also encouraged the War Department to establish Camp Sibert, a small marine base near Boulder City, to guard Hoover Dam. Together, the camp, gunnery school, and magnesium factory brought thousands of soldiers and defense workers to Fremont Street's fledgling casinos. In addition, troops came from the Desert Warfare Center south of Searchlight. This temporary training facility prepared thousands of men for the rigors of desert combat in the upcoming invasion of North Africa and the Middle East. Moreover, marines from Twentynine Palms and soldiers from Camp Pendleton joined sailors from San Diego to contribute further to the tourist boom, which taught Las Vegans that gambling, not railroading, farming, or mining, would be the city's salvation.

These developments came with a price. In 1942, the army demanded that Las Vegas close down its red-light district on Block 16 (today a parking area for the California Hotel). City fathers balked at first, but later caved in under McCarran's prodding and the army's threat to issue an "off-limits" order for soldiers on Fremont Street. Later that year, city commissioners and casino operators agreed to ban prostitution and voluntarily close all bars, liquor stores, and casinos at midnight during the week and 2 A.M. on weekends.

The move was worth it. Not only did the town's venereal disease rate fall, but the money that soldiers and sailors dropped at the tables more

(*Top*) The two military men are unknown, but the white-haired man on the left is Senator Pat McCarran, standing by the airfield that would bear his name by the late 1940s. Special Collections, UNLV Libraries

(*Bottom*) Before Nellis Air Force Base, there was the legendary Las Vegas Army Air Corps Gunnery School. It closed at the end of the war but reopened and was named in 1950 for Searchlight native and Las Vegas High School graduate William Nellis, who flew sixty-nine missions over Europe before he was shot down in 1944. Special Collections, UNLV Libraries

than compensated for any loss of revenue from the girls. Moreover, the military saw Las Vegas was not just a wide-open party town, but a patriotic and cooperative community. This proved an important consideration during the search for fair-weather sites to base combat pilots during the cold war. Then in 1947, the newly established United States Air Force began to consider the old gunnery school range as a likely base for training jet pilots for the cold war—another world conflict that McCarran exploited to bring the military and its huge payrolls and supply orders back to Nevada. This time, McCarran pushed receptive city and county leaders to prepare for a more permanent federal presence by building a new commercial airport south of town to get the tourists off the military runways.

At the same time, McCarran brokered another agreement with the Truman administration to save Henderson and its chemical industry. In one of the more creative real estate deals of the time, the federal government agreed to sell BMI to the State of Nevada for a dollar down and twenty-four million dollars later, payable out of rental income. The state, of course, had no intention of owning the factory permanently. Following the suspension of magnesium production in late 1944, Pioche Manganese, Stauffer Chemical, and other chemical firms began renting parts of the factory. So the state, in effect, became the temporary landlord. Finally, in 1952, the tenants bought out the state and took over the plant. Through their creative efforts, McCarran and state, county, and city officials created two major centers that, for the rest of the century, not only helped expand the metropolitan area, but injected millions of dollars into the city of Las Vegas's economy as well.

With all of these events unfolding, along with the development of the infant "Strip" of hotels along the Los Angeles Highway south of town, Las Vegas obviously was on the brink of a new period of development that would eclipse the dam era. In April 1945, reporter Florence Lee Jones, in a column commemorating Las Vegas's fortieth birthday, remembered that in the 1930s, "Storefronts were more typical of the western frontier than of the modern resort familiar to residents today." The Meadows Club on Boulder Highway and the Pair-O-Dice on Highway 91 were "the acme of splendor in the night."

But the dam, the Depression, and the war changed everything for Las Vegas. Jones explained that Americans used their "pent up desires for travel and entertainment to erase the memories of the 'hard years.' During that time, they had been home-bound by lack of funds. . . . Americans had read almost constantly of the great Boulder Dam." During the late 1930s and even during the war, curious "visitors poured into the area by the thousands" to see this engineering wonder. With this tourist onslaught, "the need for hotel and auto court accommodations and recreation facilities was apparent," and new construction began.

Of course, the Mojave Desert's searing heat discouraged many, but technology came to the rescue. Air conditioners and swamp coolers spread throughout the Southwest, and especially Las Vegas—a major breakthrough in making the region and city comfortable. Jones noted that "while cooling systems were almost unknown in many parts of the nation, every hotel, auto court, restaurant business establishment, and home in Las Vegas now [in 1945] is cooled."

As a *Las Vegas Review-Journal* reporter from the time of her arrival in 1933, Jones witnessed the early stages of the process that turned the dam town into the world tourist mecca it has become. For soldiers and defense workers in the 1940s, the dam was less important. Jones attributed Las Vegas's popularity among gunnery school soldiers not only to the friendly women's USO that helped wives and sweethearts in California stay close to their men, but also to the club life and gambling hall atmosphere of the city itself. As she observed, Las Vegas differed from many other military towns: its "resort facilities and liberal laws provided a better background for the release of pent-up hysteria which characterized both military and civilian personnel."

Wartime Las Vegas was packed not only with tourists, but also with residents. "In rapid succession, three great additions were built where only sand and greasewood had been before." But even with the Huntridge, Mayfair, and Biltmore communities, the town still lacked enough housing for the added wartime population. As a result, "auto courts were jammed with residents who were forced to pay day-by-day rates which ate up almost their entire incomes." The boom put a tremendous strain on the city's infrastructure. Streets were improved in many new sections and in disrepair in older ones. The sewer system was inadequate, and the city badly needed parks, playgrounds, a public pool, and a larger jail. Public utilities struggled to keep pace. Because the power and telephone companies could not meet service demands due to wartime shortages, "transformers for extension of power lines were unavailable and telephones and wires were almost as scarce." Unsurprisingly, the area's water and power companies faced similar problems.

While defense spending altered the Las Vegas Valley's landscape with new bases, factories, and overcrowded housing, tourism also began to change the city's physical and cultural appearance. In the 1940s, tourist-related structures appeared on Fremont Street, Fifth Street, and other thoroughfares approaching the casino core. In the 1200 block of Fremont near Charleston Boulevard, the mission-revival Chief Hotel and the Regency Moderne Style Clark Inn Motel both appeared in 1940. Throughout the war and thereafter, motels, auto courts, and wedding chapels began appearing on what became Las Vegas Boulevard South and other arteries. Throughout the 1940s and 1950s, the city's growing resort sector started to commandeer one-time residential streets by pricing many homes out of existence.

Many of these displaced home owners moved out to the city's retreating periphery, especially on the southern and eastern sides of town. Between Charleston and San Francisco (now Sahara Avenue), Maryland Road (later Parkway) and its feeder streets became a popular new residential area during and after the war, as homes, stores, and churches began filling once empty lots. The First Good Shepherd Lutheran Church, an impressive mission-revival building, appeared on the thoroughfare in 1940. While bungalows had dotted the road just north of Fremont Street since the 1920s, the real thrust of development south on Maryland Parkway occurred in the 1940s, when federal funding built dozens of homes and apartments in the new Huntridge Addition for defense workers. The park itself, just south of Charleston, became a magnet for the instant wartime community and its residents. By the 1950s, the area would be home to a large group of middle- and upper-class residents, including doctors, lawyers, and some early University of Nevada, Las Vegas (UNLV), professors.

Just as it would late in the twentieth century, the city also pushed westward. During the 1930s and 1940s, municipal officials set the stage for the future growth of Las Vegas's western lands with expensive railroad underpasses at Bonanza west of Main (1935) and at West Charleston (1949). These two projects permitted traffic to move to the west, a vital prerequisite for developing lands along what would become Valley View, Decatur, and other western arteries in the 1960s.

But the most significant development of the 1940s occurred along the Los Angeles Highway, beyond Las Vegas's southern city limits. In 1940, James Cashman of the Las Vegas Chamber of Commerce and other members invited California hotelier Thomas Hull to Las Vegas to encourage him to build one of his El Rancho hotels in the city. A longtime local political and business leader, Cashman believed that Las Vegas could solidify its status as a resort city by attracting a hotel chain to town. Hull already owned El Rancho hotels in Fresno, Sacramento, and Indio. Cashman and his colleagues reasoned that an El Rancho Vegas, with a casino, would be the most profitable, and Hull could use his customer base from the other three properties to lure new visitors to Las Vegas. If the experiment worked, other larger hotel chains might be lured to the city.

To this end, Cashman and his associates showed Hull a number of potential sites for his resort on or just off Fremont Street. In the end, Hull shocked them all by purchasing a large tract of land off the Los Angeles Highway south of the city line (across from today's Sahara Hotel) in the county's desert flats. There he constructed the El Rancho Vegas, a sprawling, ranchlike building with attractive cottages and motel-like rooms. With this simple-looking resort, Hull launched the revolution that transformed the lonely stretch of highway into a world tourist destination and a dangerous threat to the city that inspired it.

For decades, gambling in America had been largely relegated to riverboats and tiny saloon clubs and hotel lobbies on narrow city lots near the docks or down the street from stage and railroad stations. In one stroke, Hull liberated the pastime from the cramped confines of ordinary hotels and put it where it belonged: in the leisurely atmosphere of a resort hotel.

But the real advantage of moving to the outer suburbs was space. On his desert acreage Hull had room to build a spacious casino, coffee shop, buffet, gourmet restaurant, pool, lush lawns and gardens, and, most important, parking for four hundred cars. While frustrated city leaders emphasized the advantages of being near the railroad and the city's water mains, Hull recognized that these traditional arguments were no longer valid. As a southern Californian, Hull understood that the growing dominance of cars, trucks, and buses made the highway more important than the railroad station for delivering supplies and guests.

While Cashman and others emphasized the advantages of municipal services, Hull knew that by locating beyond the city limits he would

The El Rancho Vegas was typical of the low-rise western architecture of the early Strip—and, indeed, other southwestern resorts. The view looks north, up Highway 91–Las Vegas Boulevard South. While the distance was only a couple of miles, the resort certainly looked far from the beaten path. Special Collections, UNLV Libraries

escape Las Vegas's slot machine and ad valorem taxes, which the county did not levy. Moreover, instead of paying a small fortune for Fremont Street lots, he bought the desert flats for pennies on the dollar. And he saw no need for city services. He could bore wells for water, dig cesspools for sewage, and hire hotel security to perform police and fire functions.

Finally, the major reason industry had located in America's downtowns for the past century was no longer valid. In the age of steam power, everyone needed city water mains to supply the boilers of steam engines. But electricity could be transmitted anywhere in the metropolitan zone, allowing people to work, live, and play in the suburbs. The car and electricity promoted the rise of suburbs in mid-twentieth-century America. No place epitomized this more than Hull's home base, the Los Angeles Basin. As early as 1930, Los Angeles had the largest percentage of single-family dwellings of any American city and one of the highest percentages of car ownership.

The El Rancho Vegas opened in 1941, and over the next seven years, it would be joined by the Last Frontier, Flamingo, and Thunderbird, creating an impressive line of resorts along the highway. Guy McAfee, who built the 91 Club near Hull's property and the Golden Nugget downtown, christened this new urban form the "Strip," because it reminded him of the Sunset Strip he had patrolled as a former Los Angeles police officer. The El Rancho and Last Frontier, like so many of the clubs downtown, were western in theme. But Billy Wilkerson's and Bugsy Siegel's Flamingo, with its classy Monte Carlo Florida-like appearance, set a new precedent, opening the way for the greater luxury and montage of themes that Strip resorts boast today.

As these resorts appeared, they, like their counterparts in the city, encouraged suburban development. In the 1940s, the first bubbles of suburbanization beyond the southern city limits appeared in small tracts of single-family homes and apartments built behind the El Rancho, Last Frontier, Flamingo, and other Strip hotels. As the Las Vegas area grew southward, surveyors abandoned the early grid pattern of Clark's Las Vegas town site, Park Place, and other early additions parallel to the railroad tracks. Later subdivisions ran at an oblique angle in the more familiar north-south direction so typical of American towns. These new blocks lacked the familiar alleys of Clark's town site downtown. The new blocks were also more rectangular than their earlier predecessors and oriented more to automobiles and trucks than to horses and wagons.

In the 1940s and later, as the casino core expanded along Fremont Street, wholesale and retail businesses moved to Main and Commerce Streets and farther east on Fremont. Roadside shopping centers began to develop even farther out on Charleston and even San Francisco (Sahara Avenue). The trend outward continued into the 1950s, as roadside casino resorts spawned new suburban developments on the lands between the railroad tracks and Boulder Highway—a process that continues today.

Both city and Strip flourished during the war, but their big profits came in the years thereafter. Following the war, Las Vegas braced for the inevitable wave of tourists. After all, the presence of BMI, the gunnery school, and Fremont Street's relative proximity to the giant bases and defense plants in southern California continued to award the town's casinos thousands of new players in the cold war era. As one local columnist rejoiced, "Now all travel bans have been lifted. . . . The tourist hordes are back on the highways and things are beginning to hum again."

Las Vegas business and political leaders looked with optimism at the postwar era. Now sure that gambling, not farming, ranching, or railroading, would be the valley's great industry, and with the Strip and Fremont Street hotels booming, they knew that more growth was in the cards. As

This chorus line appeared at the Hotel Last Frontier showroom in 1945. Most hotels employed attractive female dancers, from the Copa girls at the Sands at the height of the Rat Pack to those who now perform in such shows as Jubilee and the Folies Bergere. One chorine, Maxine Lewis, graduated from the production show to be the entertainment director at the El Rancho Vegas and thus the first woman executive at a Strip resort. Special Collections, UNLV Libraries

The Hotel Last Frontier boasted the Strip's first wedding chapel, the Little Church of the West, also referred to as the Hitching Post. Wedding chapels at local hotels and along the Las Vegas Strip remain an important attraction. Special Collections, UNLV Libraries

one columnist declared, "[W]e are standing on the brink of great expansion. Construction should bring us . . . numerous new business establishments with the foundation being laid for solid growth." Undoubtedly, downtown leaders saw the annexation of Highway 91's resorts as a foregone conclusion. They expected the city limits to march southward in the 1940s from their historic confines at San Francisco Street across the desert flats to tiny Alamo Field (part of today's McCarran Airport) and perhaps even farther.

It was little wonder that Las Vegans felt hopeful about their future. But there was widespread recognition, still present today, that postwar Las Vegas needed more than tourism to survive the one-industry fate that had relegated so many of Nevada's mining communities to oblivion. As one columnist explained, "[T]here may come a day when the great hordes will find a new playground and leave us. . . . If that day comes, . . . then the more industry we have in this area and the more diversified it is, we will not be too greatly affected by the fall-off in tourists." While the search for these new industries proceeded, Las Vegans could comfort themselves with a new chemical industry in Henderson and the hope of retaining the old army base north of town as a future site for defense spending.

In the meantime, business and political leaders worked to promote tourism, solve the ever worsening water problem, and build a new airport capable of accommodating the thousands of new visitors the city and its county suburbs hoped to attract. Securing a new home for commercial aviation was linked to Senator McCarran's effort to convert the old gunnery school into a major air force base. Help came from an unlikely quarter: Soviet leader Josef Stalin. His repression of democratic forces in Eastern Europe, combined with communist insurgency in Greece, Turkey, Indonesia, and elsewhere, forced President Harry Truman to increase America's military budget. By 1947, talks were already under way to convert the old gunnery school into an air force base. Indeed, the Pentagon was anxious to exploit southern Nevada's clear weather and endless tracts of federal land to train its pilots. As early as fall 1946, McCarran and city and county leaders discussed moving the commercial airlines to Alamo Field (south of today's Mandalay Bay) if the old gunnery school became a permanent military base. Two months later, in January 1947, county commissioners scheduled a May 6 bond election to buy Alamo Field and build a new county airport at the site.

Backed by the Lion's Club, the Elks, both major newspapers, and other social service and business organizations, the bond election garnered widespread voter support, as city and county residents eagerly made room for the new base. As one enthusiastic editorial predicted, once the commercial airlines left and the military training school opened, "there will be a large civilian payroll which will mean additional jobs for local people." As in World War II, the valley's growing economy would again benefit. Finally, after fifteen months of construction, the new county airport opened to the public on December 19, 1948. This facility, named for McCarran, served the city well over the next fifteen years until the jet age made it obsolete.

Building a new airport was just part of the effort to make Las Vegas a nationally recognized tourist center. As the airport commissioners demonstrated after 1945, boosting tourism increasingly became a joint venture between the casinos on Fremont Street and those on the newly emerging Strip. The same was true of publicity. In 1944, the Chamber of Commerce, recognizing the importance of propaganda in selling the war to Americans, decided to establish the Live Wire Fund. With Maxwell Kelch, owner of KENO, the area's first permanent radio station, taking the lead, chamber members pledged between 1 and 5 percent of their business's gross profits, while local resorts promised to match that figure up to fifty thousand dollars. In later years, the resorts contributed more as advertising costs grew. The Live Wire Fund was an immediate success, raising eighty-four thousand dollars in the first year. Local media applauded the chamber's program. The *Review-Journal,* for instance, noted that Las Vegas needed "better press. The town must convince tourists that there is something more here than gambling, divorces, marriages, and gangsters."

With this war chest, the chamber hired the nationally respected J. Walter Thompson Agency, which marketed Las Vegas as a new desert getaway for people eager to have fun and celebrate the permissive morality that became popular during the war. In 1947, the chamber switched to the West-Marquis firm, which invented the friendly Fremont Street cowboy "Vegas Vic" and his "Howdy Podner" greeting, as Las Vegas continued to play up its western heritage and "last-frontier" themes. A year later, the Live Wire Fund turned to the Steve Hannagan agency, whose most recent success was packaging Sun Valley as a skiers' paradise. By the late 1940s, the Live Wire Fund, like Helldorado, had become a mainstay in the valley's effort to attract visitors.

While Las Vegas leaders dreamed of creating a great resort center for tourists, they also realized that equipping the city and its suburbs with the infrastructure necessary to support this growth would cost millions. In the past fifteen years, they had seen how the dam and the war had changed the town, and how many new homes, schools, roads, and sewer lines had to be built just to accommodate that growth. They knew that continued urbanization in the desert required an expanded water supply. So far, local aquifers and wells had handled the increase in population from fifty-one hundred in 1930 to fifteen thousand or so during World War II, but well levels were running low even before V-J Day. Community leaders knew the valley's meager well supply and the Clark town site's old water system would never sustain the metropolis they hoped to create.

Discussions about creating a valleywide water district had begun in the early 1930s, so it was not a sudden crisis that began the process. Wartime tourism just accentuated the problem. With nine of ten Union Pacific wells experiencing a drop of 8 percent in annual output, the Las Vegas Land & Water Company called for a halt to more well drilling in 1944. Local newspapers demanded forming a "vigorous committee" to develop a plan for identifying future sources of water.

No one understood any better than Al Cahlan, editor of the city's largest newspaper and member of the state's Colorado River Commission. In a 1944 column he warned that "there must be fast action, not because of any critical shortage of water in the area at the present time, but as a protection for the future of the valley." Once again, city interests looked out for the interests of the entire valley, including what became the Strip. Las Vegas leaders were concerned about the current city. They also wanted to supply the center of the valley, especially the zone that would become the Strip—a tract the city expected to control someday. Clearly, if gaming on the Strip and Fremont Street expanded to any significant degree, the future of Las Vegas would be imperiled. Cahlan insisted that "we must solve the water supply problem . . . if Las Vegas is to grow. There is no other way to solve that problem except by bringing water in from Lake Mead."

The solution was to create a water district that would eventually encompass the whole valley. It would tap current and future generations for direct revenues and bonding approvals to buy the Las Vegas Land & Water Company's infrastructure, and expand it in all directions. The district would also have to build a vitally needed water line from Basic Magnesium to deliver Lake Mead water to the city and Strip.

Las Vegas's water problem menaced not only growth, but public health as well. However, city residents faced other threats to their welfare, including garbage and prostitution. With the wartime shortages of penicillin, the myriad diseases encountered on various world battlefronts, and the spread of polio, Las Vegas leaders were determined to improve the town's sanitary condition with a general cleanup in 1945. Shortly after v-j Day, Chamber of Commerce president Kelch, whose background in the sciences served him well, launched a vigorous offensive against garbage, flies, and polio. He marshaled support from the school board, the local military, and political leaders.

The media also helped. The *Las Vegas Review-Journal* complained that the city's sanitation ordinances had been ignored for years. It noted that "garbage cans, stacked full of stinking swill, are left for hours with the big green flies . . . buzzing hither and yon." The newspaper linked the growing number of polio cases and other diseases to the sanitary crisis. It also compared neighborhood conditions with "that of hillbillies back in the Missouri hills." Despite the appealing lights and false-fronted clubs and stores of Fremont Street, the city was a health menace. "We have pigsties for alleys, we have glorified cow trails for streets, and we have backyards which are a disgrace to a modern town." Las Vegans understood how tainted drinking water, sewage, and floods had damaged the early economies of other towns, and recognized the threat of infectious disease to an aspiring resort city. So the community responded positively to the postwar sanitary crusade.

Cleaning up Las Vegas's garbage proved a lot easier than stamping out prostitution. After the shutdown in 1942, the ladies continued to ply their trade in some of the clubs and hotels. But in 1946, with the gunnery school closing and Nellis Air Force Base still a dream, the question arose: Should legal prostitution be reinstated? Clark County faced the same problem, because the Formyle Club on Boulder Highway, the Kassabian Ranch, and other operations beyond the city line also encouraged the trade.

However, legal prostitution met strong opposition from the Chamber of Commerce and its influential president, Kelch, as well as Strip resort owners. As William J. Moore, executive director of the Hotel Last Frontier, reported in January 1946, "the gaming and liquor interests" had met several days earlier and agreed to "vigorously" oppose legalized prostitution in the metropolitan area. Dr. S. L. Hardy of the Las Vegas Hospital declared that the city's venereal disease rate had dropped significantly since Block 16's closure, and school superintendent Maude Frazier reported a similar trend among senior boys at Las Vegas High School.

Joining the chorus was Al Cahlan. Conceding that the trade had been a "necessary evil" in building the early railroad and resort economies of Las Vegas, Cahlan argued that doctrinaire morality and the image of the last frontier were no longer paramount. He asserted that since the war, "a metamorphosis in the thinking and the health angle has played a definite role in the change." He also saw economics entering the postwar equation. Cahlan noted that a recent meeting of fifty local businessmen raised almost eighty-five thousand dollars for a publicity and advertising campaign designed to attract tourists from across America. The businessmen felt, and the editor agreed, that "if the area went on record as favoring 'legalized' prostitution, . . . Las Vegas would be flying in the face of morals which decreed such practice to be taboo." The conclusion was obvious. Las Vegas, now seeking to appeal to a much broader customer base, had to rid itself of prostitution.

To that end, not only did city commissioners refuse to reopen Block 16 after the war, but county commissioners also agreed to close down the Formyle Club and deny liquor and gaming licenses to similar establishments. As Ira Earl, chair of the Clark County Board of Commissioners, declared in January 1946, "There will be no legalized prostitution in Clark County if I can prevent it." He and his successors would demand that both the district attorney and Sheriff Glen Jones take action against the Formyle and other brothels. However, despite the pressure of elected officials and businessmen, prostitution continued to flourish on the south edge of town in the county's jurisdiction.

Notwithstanding reassurances from the sheriff that the Formyle Club and the Kassabian Ranch had been under observation for weeks and stood to lose their liquor and gaming licenses, the illicit trade still thrived. Much of the problem lay in the failure of the sheriff's office to enforce the law. Finally in 1954, Hank Greenspun of the *Las Vegas Sun* set up a sting operation in which his operative taped incriminating conversations. The

Sun caught longtime sheriff Glen Jones and county commissioner Rodney Colton expressing their willingness to protect brothel operations in return for "gifts." Greenspun's success reminds one of Joe Yablonsky's "sting" operation in the 1970s when local FBI agents netted several elected officials taking bribes.

From a law enforcement perspective, prostitution was easier to root out (or at least minimize) than the gangsters whose expertise and capital became increasingly vital to the local gambling industry. The mob influence in Las Vegas's casino economy grew slowly but steadily. In the 1940s, the gangsters gained control of more than just the Flamingo, but nonmob operators continued to own most of the clubs and resorts in the area. And while city and county elected officials knew the managers of every club, these politicians were wary of licensing race books or taking public actions that would give the mob a stronger presence in town. Tough talk from sheriffs and district attorneys kept men like Flamingo operators Gus Greenbaum and Davey Berman discreet. Given their part in illegal activities like gambling and bootlegging, they knew that discretion was the better part of survival.

On the other hand, both mob and nonmob casino operators opposed what they considered strict regulations by state politicians. Witness their efforts in the 1950s to weaken the Nevada Tax Commission and oust its zealous leader, Robbins Cahill. But the connections between mob and nonmob operators ran deeper. Respected southern California contractor Marion Hicks, a main builder of the El Cortez downtown in 1941 and the Thunderbird Hotel on the Strip in 1948, was tied to underworld kingpin Meyer Lansky. Low on funds during the Desert Inn's construction in 1949–1950, Wilbur Clark joined forces with Detroit and Cleveland mob figure Moe Dalitz. Moreover, in the 1940s and later, some mob and nonmob interacted frequently, even working with each other. In April 1945, when J. Kell Houssels and an associate refurbished the Las Vegas Club, Phoenix bookmaker Gus Greenbaum and Moe Sedway, an old friend and ally of Lansky and Bugsy Siegel, became casino managers.

In the later 1940s and 1950s, some nonmob owners on the Strip and downtown sold their properties to mob-related buyers. While the nefarious effects of the mob's presence in Las Vegas have been accurately reported in any number of exposés, it is also fair to say that Las Vegas needed the mob. Until the 1970s, few reputable lending institutions provided

In the 1950s, the Thunderbird Hotel possessed a distinctive entry, a jewelry store that was an early example of the shopping to be found at Strip resorts, and featured Bert Lahr of *The Wizard of Oz* and Broadway fame in the hotel's showroom. Special Collections, UNLV Libraries

funding to build the great hotels on the Strip and in the city. From the 1940s into the 1970s, the mob not only provided valuable expertise in casino management, but also supplied vitally needed capital for resort development. The Dunes, Stardust, Flamingo, and many other Strip and downtown properties owed their early success to the mob. Not until Governor Paul Laxalt and state legislators liberalized the corporate gaming law in 1969 could giant companies like Hilton and MGM begin to replace the mob with the kind of money and expertise needed to build the megaresorts of today—and even then, the process took several years.

Prostitution, sanitation, lack of water, and the presence of mobsters were all problems that municipal leaders had to address in their effort to steer their city through the maze of problems caused by Las Vegas's tumultuous growth. Politically, however, one of the most troublesome issues was street improvements, because failure to widen, sewer, or light a street affected property values. Whether home owners obtained a public works job they wanted or were assessed for a job they did not want hit them in their pocketbooks. Making the wrong decision could cost an elected official votes. In a small city with so many elections decided by small margins, public works policy making was a risky business.

But in a city undergoing rapid economic and population growth, public works was a necessity. Even the relatively small resorts of the 1940s boosted the population and commercial economy enough to force expensive projects to handle the traffic and urban expansion. It was hard enough to enlarge the water supply or clean up the garbage. But city commissioners realized that accommodating the growth they expected would require a dramatic expansion and modernization of Las Vegas's road system. This process would include reflagging or building new sidewalks and repaving, newly paving, or widening many existing thoroughfares.

In the 1940s, Las Vegas remained unprepared for the growth it was experiencing. Part of the problem stemmed from restrictive policies. For example, in fall 1945 the city wanted to pave a section of Seventh and Eighth Streets south of Garces, but contractors estimated the cost at eleven thousand dollars. Under Nevada law, lot owners could be assessed only a small percentage of the assessed value of their property. In this case, the formula left benefiting residents three thousand dollars short of the money needed. In larger cities, government often expanded an assessment district, claiming that the improvements benefited all lot owners in the area, or officials simply paid the remaining cost out of its general revenues. But in Las Vegas, the city had to convince lot owners to pledge the extra money, almost like a donation, in prorated payments. Commissioners would have to discard this small-town approach in favor of more big-city, growth-oriented policies to finance improvements more easily. This was clear even to those who had built the original small town, like Pop Squires. As his *Las Vegas Age* noted in a 1941 editorial, "[P]ublic works must also be carried forward by the city to provide for the growth which already is beginning to spread the city into new areas."

Rapid urbanization from the existing city outward to the eastern and western desert lands would require widened roads, large-diameter sewer pipes, and constant public works projects. That meant a need for larger assessment districts and frequent bond issues. Las Vegans approached this process with mixed feelings. While they loved growth and its benefits, they bristled at the cost. Expanded tax bases, while desirable, did not immediately pay for the growth that spawned them. This was especially true for Las Vegas, which had to service an urban and suburban area growing toward a booming Strip zone that paid no taxes to the city.

Political leaders recognized that Las Vegas had to alter its government structure if it was to engage in the type of big-time city building that Phoenix, Tucson, Albuquerque, and many medium-size California cities were already undergoing. But they had many obstacles to overcome. One was that residential property valuations were inordinately low, because many homes and businesses had not been reassessed for years. In 1949, the city manager urged immediate updating of the valuation of properties that had not been reassessed. City commissioners did what they could, recognizing that many of their constituents wanted a modern-looking city and neighborhood, but cringed at the thought of higher taxes or onerous assessments. However, these fears did not escape the notice of a generation of county assessors who were cool to jeopardizing their chances for reelection.

As a compromise, the city sought other revenue sources. Recognizing that many white and black suburban neighborhoods still lacked sidewalks, Mayor Ernie Cragin insisted on using revenues from the gasoline tax to pay for them, because, according to him, "95 percent will be collected from our tourists." Unfortunately, the black Westside needed paved streets and gutters as well—a project too expensive for the gasoline tax to fund. Anxious to save money and possibly indulging his racism, Cragin refused to establish assessment districts for this work, insisting that Westside land values were too low to raise enough money. Overall, the improvements process was slow, even in white neighborhoods. The failure of municipal services to keep pace with growth plagued Las Vegas into the late 1940s.

In May 1949, work began on the Charleston Underpass to create another east-west traffic artery free from passing trains. This "improvement," however, soon became an impassable lake during heavy rains. Of course, the city also made progress. In 1949, crews completed a large storm drain down East Charleston to Tenth Street with laterals to the side streets. As one columnist cheerfully reported, "Mayfair and Vegas Verde streets now have less flood water, which is drained off to the flats north and east of town." While true, the statement demonstrated the short-sighted approach of leaders and residents who eagerly sought growth but were unprepared for its future consequences. By the mid-1950s, commercial and residential developments filled the so-called flats north and east of Charleston, and flooding would continue to plague East Charleston until the 1990s. For the next half century, the Charleston Underpass symbolized Las Vegas's inadequate response to flood control. The route would not be properly drained until century's end.

Postwar growth not only strained the city's street and sewer systems, but forced the construction of more schools as well. While the origins of the Las Vegas school crisis lie more in the 1950s and 1960s, when the resort industry's dramatic expansion raised population and triggered an acute classroom shortage, the immediate postwar tourist boom also created problems. Before the Clark County School District's creation in 1955, the city was its own school district. In 1946, sensing that growth would intensify, Las Vegas authorities began to consider building another high school and creating a junior high (today called a middle school) division. From 1945 to 1955, the city built additional classrooms and other facilities in response to the early baby boom. But not until the mid-1950s could the Clark County School District undertake the major construction program needed to accommodate the thousands of students the resort boom produced.

Politics necessarily colored these policy and public works decisions. While the leadership at city hall was generally good, political controversy continued to nag Las Vegas in the 1940s, as it had in the previous decade. Just as Las Vegas entered the momentous year of 1941, when construction began on the Basic Magnesium plant and officials negotiated with the army to convert the municipal airport into a gunnery school, the city became embroiled in perhaps the most contentious political crisis in its history. Contributing to the turmoil was the irascible mayor, John Russell, the conservative critic whose unrelenting attacks on public power had pressured Mayor Arnett into resigning in May 1938. In late 1940, Russell engaged in a series of major disputes with city commissioners over the city's tax rate and other issues. Shouting matches, lawsuits, recall efforts, and mass resignations virtually ground city government to a halt. In January 1941, disgusted city commissioners resigned en masse, prompting a delighted Russell to solicit nominations from community groups for an interim board he hoped to appoint. However, the duly elected city commissioners reconsidered, and city police (no doubt fearful that Russell's budget cutting would result in wage cuts for themselves and others) refused to allow the new board to be seated.

For the next few months, two boards of city commissioners met, and no one knew which was the legal one. Russell and his four appointees met at the old city hall on Bridger Avenue, while Commissioner Herb Krause, acting as mayor pro tem, presided over the old board's meetings at the other end of the room. Both mayors and both boards had to sign every document. Duplicates were made of every board action, including two lease agreements with the U.S. Army for the gunnery school. The chaos continued until district court judge Harry Watson of Ely ruled that the original board had not formally resigned and was therefore the legal city commission.

Residents watched this daily circus with amazement. A frustrated Pop Squires, editor of the *Las Vegas Age,* complained that "just now when Las Vegas is entering on her most important era of development, there should be no washing of our dirty linen in public." Indeed, he advised officials to keep the dirty linen hidden, "rather than tell the world that Las Vegas is a quarreling, quibbling, disgusting community from which it was better that investors stay away."

The impasse finally ended on May 10, 1941. The elected commissioners conducted a malfeasance hearing regarding Mayor Russell. They found him guilty on eight counts and removed him from office. The city commissioners then appointed one of their own, Herb Krause, interim mayor. Several weeks later, voters elected two new commissioners who, with two appointees, ran the government. Local mortician Howell Garrison agreed to serve as interim mayor until the next regular election in 1943.

Given the momentous events nationally, as well as locally at the gunnery school, at Basic Magnesium, and elsewhere in the valley, the Russell crisis could not have come at a worse time. Ernie Cragin's election in 1943 finally ended this turbulent period, and none too soon. In electing Cragin, voters sought a return to normalcy. As a prominent businessman who, as mayor, had supported Roosevelt's New Deal projects for the city, Cragin was seen as the man who could again work with Roosevelt, now in war, to obtain military bases like the gunnery school. Trying to steer voters to fellow McCarran Democrat Cragin, *Las Vegas Review-Journal* editor Al Cahlan also emphasized the need for stability, reminding readers that Mayor Russell's removal in 1941 occurred because "his further presence in the administration offered . . . a reason for the re-continuation of the battle that has raged for twenty-four long months." The editor warned that "Las Vegas cannot afford to embark on a new period of municipal strife, lest the door to this development be permanently slammed shut in our face."

Russell was hardly gone when a new controversy racked city hall even before Cragin's election. Adoption of the city manager plan in 1943 largely resulted from the Russell controversy. Las Vegas leaders were determined to put a modern face on city government to please potential out-of-state investors, the federal government, and crisis-weary residents. But the campaign to approve the reform prompted bitter exchanges. City attorney Harry Austin took out a full-page advertisement in local newspapers opposing the hiring of a city manager, charging that the latter could be co-opted or, with the support of just two commissioners, seize control of the city government. Obviously, the memories of Russell's abortive coup lingered in many minds. Supporters of the reform countered that "there is only one thing involved in this election—a certain group desires to control the city." The rhetoric only added to the confusion, leading to a narrow victory (982 votes to 827) for the city manager position—a reform that, over time, contributed much to effective government. But as one editorial asserted in 1945, "[T]he majority of the citizens of Las Vegas heartily will concur with the plan of the city commission to place the administration on a sound and business-like basis. Laxity has been tolerated in the past because it didn't make any particular difference in the life of the residents." Now it did. Voters eliminated the potential for more conflict by rejecting the reelection bids of M. C. Tench and Al Rubidoux, the two incumbent city commissioners who had opposed the city manager plan.

In the same 1943 contest, voters returned Cragin to the mayor's office. Cragin's support for the city manager position and forward-thinking approach to other problems led one writer to portray him as "an ideal choice to guide the city through the important period ahead." Clearly, residents were anxious to put bickering behind them. Of course, despite the increasing controversy surrounding them, recent administrations and commissioners made some positive contributions: finishing the War Memorial Building, laying the foundation for a new hospital, and constructing a new sewer system for downtown. But the city still lacked many urban amenities, including a new library, a comprehensive park system, and a modern and expanded street system.

Many in 1943 considered Cragin the one to implement this agenda. Certainly, he would preside over an era of rapid growth and the first great round of gaming expansion in the valley. Population growth and new construction marked the wartime and immediate postwar eras, but Cragin lacked the kind of federal assistance this time that he had enjoyed during the early New Deal. While the city's street system expanded, there would be no comprehensive system of parks. Most of the major accomplishments, such as the creation of a water district, construction of a new airport, and building of more schools, came with help from county officials, Basic Townsite leaders, and other groups in the suburban communities rapidly forming beyond Las Vegas's borders. This was also true of the emerging hotels and adjacent residential areas along the Los Angeles Highway, whose annexation became a Cragin obsession and, ultimately, a bitter defeat.

Las Vegas never got the Strip, but not for lack of effort. Although disappointed that Thomas Hull did not further strengthen Fremont Street's growing casino corridor by building the El Rancho there, Cragin, Cashman, and other leaders no doubt consoled themselves with the notion that someday the city would annex Hull's resort and any others that might spring up around it. During the 1940s, Las Vegans tended to see the El Rancho, Hotel Last Frontier, and other resorts along Highway 91 as their own, because there was no indication that these places would stay outside the city. The local newspapers reinforced this view. When Hull opened the El Rancho Vegas in 1941, the *Las Vegas Age* declared that "through the close cooperation of the Hull System with the great hotel systems of the East, an even more widely spreading field of favorable publicity is opened to us." The city saw Hull's sprawling resort not as a new urban form or revolution in casino operations, which it was, but as a profitable appendage that would contribute to the city's coffers.

As the *Age* editor recognized, "[F]or many years, Las Vegas has bemoaned the absence of high-type resort hotels and the wealthy class such would draw to us." No longer would Las Vegas casinos merely cater to train passengers, soldiers, defense workers, and dam tourists. Squires realized that the El Rancho "will be the example which the others will follow." But he never imagined what a spectacular direction the Strip's development would take and how frustrating it would be for the city. Fremont Street would benefit from the construction of some large new hotels, like the El Cortez in 1941, but these would be few and far between over the next six decades. Virtually all of the major action into the twenty-first century would be south of the city limits.

Just five years after the El Rancho's completion and before the Flamingo even opened, Mayor Cragin moved to annex the Strip. In April 1946, he justified this action as "purely and simply an effort to secure badly needed additional revenue to save our city, streets, sewer system, and other vital services." He was particularly eager to modernize and rebuild the sewers "in the older sections of the city" downtown. Cragin countered the determined opposition of Strip residents and resort owners by declaring that "the places on the 'strip' are actually part of Las Vegas. They derive their revenues as part of Las Vegas, and there is no reason why they should not help pay the costs of maintaining our municipal government." At the time, Cragin was right. In the mid-1940s, Fremont Street, with its neon lights and famous clubs, was the lure that brought most tourists to the area. Ten years later, it would be the Strip.

Despite their lack of population and political clout, Strip operators and residents fended off the initial annexation effort. This was crucial because the early Strip, with only a few hotels, was especially vulnerable. But Strip executives, including mob front men like the Flamingo's Gus Greenbaum, rallied residents (many of whom were hotel employees) against the higher taxes Las Vegas would impose. The second victory over the city, four years later, was easier. In 1950, when Cragin tried once more, the Strip again blocked him by using a new law pushed through the 1949 legislature by Lieutenant Governor (and Thunderbird part-owner) Cliff Jones that prevented any city from annexing an unincorporated township without the county commission's approval. According to former city attorney and mayoral candidate George Franklin, Strip owners in 1950 feared, among other things, that a strong-minded politician like Cragin's successor, Mayor C. D. Baker, would pressure them for campaign contributions. When Moe Sedway asked Franklin about the city taking the Strip, Franklin told him that the city could annex any contiguous area without the county commission's approval except for an unincorporated township. Paradise A came first in December 1950 and Paradise B in the next year. In 1953, they were renamed Paradise and Winchester, respectively. According to Franklin, the county commissioners created two townships "to keep [the] unincorporated towns coinciding with the several school districts in the valley."

Despite Cragin's efforts to annex the Strip and run the city efficiently, he again faced the kind of political criticism that defeated him in 1935. Years of New Deal spending programs and increased city expenditures to cope with growth had created a loose faction of concerned citizens who scrutinized every project for evidence of mismanagement or corruption. It was born in the 1930s when Mayor Arnett tried to take the city's electric utility away from Southern Nevada Power and the airport away from Western Air Express to make them public institutions. For conservatives, these actions were needlessly expensive, even socialistic. John Russell led this faction in the 1930s, and Charles Pipkin became its unofficial spokesman in the 1940s. In general, its members consisted of some businessmen and ordinary residents. While not opposed to growth, the faction was suspicious of club owners who were politically close to city hall. In general, the group functioned as a "good government" advocate, exposing political scandals, both real and imagined, and emphasizing the city's increasing devotion to spending.

In the late 1940s, Pipkin and his group grew increasingly vocal about Cragin's supposed favoritism toward certain casino interests. In particular, they criticized his close relationship with J. Kell Houssels and other Fremont Street club owners who supported Cragin with campaign contributions and received good treatment. Cragin, however, was not the only target: some city commissioners faced similar criticism.

The late 1940s became a period of intense political bickering and recrimination. Car dealer and beverage company owner Pat Clark and restaurant owner Bob Baskin, both respected members of the business community and city commissioners, faced an unrelenting attack by the newly named Las Vegas Taxpayer's Association and its president, Pipkin. Throughout the 1949 city election campaign, Pipkin blamed both men for

Las Vegas's $300,000 deficit and its $103,000 "emergency loan" request to the State of Nevada. He also hinted at corruption. Specifically, Pipkin called Baskin the key man in the "Houssels Machine" of downtown casino interests that ran city hall. Pipkin boldly asked the two commissioners: "Why do you frequently exclude representatives of the press from Star Chamber meetings of the City Commission?" And why was the vote on controversial issues almost always "3 to 2?"

Pipkin claimed that favoritism was blatant. Certain business interests used the municipal government to benefit their own properties. "Why," he asked, "are there paved streets in certain areas which have increased the value of property owned by various influential citizens?" Clearly, charges like these helped to erode the image of business-like government that Cragin and the commissioners wanted to project, and gave business interests on the Strip another reason to oppose annexation.

Of course, part of the reason for the city's debt was its effort to support rapid wartime urbanization with new public works and an expanded bureaucracy. Baskin, Cragin, and Clark may well have seen things Houssels's way, but downtown businessmen were committed to extending Las Vegas's growth, an expensive proposition that exposed officials to public criticism. Many leaders cracked under the pressure. Clark eventually left elected office, and many 1950s-era politicians met a similar fate. Franklin called Bill Peccole another good city commissioner who left office because "he couldn't take the pressure anymore."

Still, men like Pipkin were necessary in a town where some business leaders used elective office not only to guide the city, but also to benefit their own interests. Pipkin and his conservative allies were part of the informal checks-and-balances mechanism that kept city government responsive to the public—a mechanism still vital today when growth, taxation, and spending are more controversial than ever.

And not just higher taxes kept Thomas Hull, William J. Moore, and other Strip operators from joining the city; so did the power of city officials to favor Fremont Street over Strip interests. Strip executives who feared the misuse of municipal authority had to take Pipkin's charges seriously. In the days when mob associates operated in both casino centers, and downtown gaming moguls like Kell Houssels and Guy McAfee enjoyed much influence at city hall, Strip resort owners had to be wary of a political machine where the police could conveniently pull the business,

The "1905" on the Golden Nugget sign refers to the location of the original 1905 town site. The Eldorado Club was the casino below the Apache Hotel, later to be replaced by Binion's Horseshoe. Special Collections, UNLV Libraries

liquor, or gaming license of a casino outside the inner circle. Already, in their effort to herd black businesses out of downtown and into the Westside during the war, Cragin and the commissioners used license renewals as a tool for accomplishing this, and the Strip resort owners knew it.

Political controversies were certainly more the rule than the exception in the 1940s. But following the ouster of Mayor Russell in 1941, city hall leaders did their best to guide Las Vegas through the tumultuous growth in gaming, tourism, housing, and military spending that marked the era. The 1940s were significant, because in that decade Las Vegans recognized that gaming-tourism would be their main industry. Future operators like

Benny Binion, Sam Boyd, Jackie Gaughan, and others began their Las Vegas careers in this decade dominated by Hull, Houssels, McAfee, and a diverse assortment of talented, mob-related casino managers. Las Vegas had to wrestle with a variety of problems, including the presence of mobsters and nonmob gamblers whom other states considered outlaws. Through it all, however, Las Vegas continued to progress. Fremont Street's casino core expanded, and gambling made it to the suburbs. Unfortunately for the city, those suburbs would escape Las Vegas's grasp for the rest of the century, even as they did much to change the city, its appearance, and its image.

7

CITY AND STRIP

Laying a Metropolitan Foundation

AS THE 1950S BEGAN, IT WAS OBVIOUS that tourism and defense spending would be the two industries that would drive the growth of Las Vegas and its emerging metropolitan area. City, county, and state officials would spend much of the decade courting the Pentagon and the Atomic Energy Commission (AEC), using their congressional delegation to do it. But tourism would receive most of the attention. In a determined effort to improve Las Vegas's accessibility and allure, local politicians and businessmen worked to increase the number of resorts, build a spacious convention center, expand the airport into a jetport, and prepare for the arrival of Interstate 15. Their success stimulated new rounds of growth that enlarged the city and suburban populations as well as the government budgets needed to service them.

For proof that Las Vegas was spreading out in the postwar years, look no further than where its residents did their shopping. The retail chains, resorts, and other new businesses continued to locate not only downtown, but also in the newer suburbs. J. C. Penney opened a new store on Fremont and Fifth Streets, and Cornet and Woolworths enlarged their downtown emporiums. But in little more than a decade, Woolworths and J. C. Penney would open much larger stores on Maryland Parkway south of Desert Inn Road in the county suburbs. A major indication that retail was moving away from Fremont Street and out to the city's periphery occurred in 1950 when Safeway opened a large store on East Charleston near Maryland Parkway. Other stores headed out of the Fremont Street area, lining Commerce, Main, and other streets southward to Charleston Boulevard and beyond.

Increased banking facilities also reflected the growth of the city and the suburbs beyond. First State Bank, founded in 1905, responded to the suburban trend by selling its landmark building on the northeast corner of First and Fremont. New owners demolished the structure in 1958 to make way for the Birdcage Casino, which Del Webb later incorporated into the Mint. John S. Park's old bank became involved with suburban branch banking as it was absorbed into the large system that became First National, First Interstate in the 1970s, and Wells Fargo in the 1990s, with offices across the entire valley.

By 1950, Fremont Street near the depot had become mostly a gaming center, although a few stores can be seen mixed in. Note that the bus depot was nearby, and that a municipal park with grass and trees sat outside the depot where the Plaza Hotel is now. Special Collections, UNLV Libraries

During World War II, First National Bank was formed, and other small banks came in the 1950s to serve the valley's growing population. The most significant new financial institution of the decade was the Bank of Las Vegas, created in 1954 by a group of local businessmen (including Nate Mack and his son Jerry) and some out-of-state (primarily Utah) investors. This venture, soon headed by E. Parry Thomas, became the first bank to loan or negotiate major loans for casino-resort construction in southern Nevada. Thomas aggressively sought financing even from such notorious figures as Teamster Union president Jimmy Hoffa. The bank (later re-named Valley Bank, later absorbed by the Bank of America) was crucial to raising development and construction money for key city and especially Strip properties in the 1950s and 1960s. This was vitally important, because virtually no banks would loan casinos money until the late 1970s, when Atlantic City's success finally made it socially acceptable for eastern lending institutions to finance casino construction projects.

The gaming industry, however, was not the only stimulus for development. Government at all levels was another source of money for metropolitan expansion in the 1950s. In fact, new government buildings symbolized Las Vegas's growing importance and the expanding county, state, and federal presence in town. In 1958, the new Clark County Court-

Nate Mack was one of the most important leaders of Las Vegas from his arrival in the 1920s until his death in 1965. He invested in several Strip and downtown casinos and was a major investor in the Bank of Las Vegas, later Valley Bank. Special Collections, UNLV Libraries

house replaced the old 1914 structure at Third and Carson. Four years earlier, on Nevada Day 1954, officials dedicated the new Nevada State Office Building at Second and Bonanza. These structures reinforced the city's role as the government center for the metropolitan area and Clark County, and for the whole southern portion of the state. They also complemented a growing federal presence at the Test Site and Nellis Air Force Base, which reflected a trend common to Phoenix, Tucson, Albuquerque, and southern California cities. The Defense Department looked increasingly to the Sunbelt for sites to locate new military bases and research facilities, and Las Vegas was a leading beneficiary.

Defense spending not only provided a lot of business for chemical producers at Basic Magnesium and Henderson to the south, but also powered the development to the north. Along with other cold war threats in Europe, Asia, and the Middle East, the Korean War made the new air force base (at the site of the old city airport and army gunnery school) north of town a major source of federal dollars in the 1950s, greatly increasing the facility's workforce, payrolls, supply orders, and off-base housing—all of which aided the economies of Las Vegas and North Las Vegas. Nellis Air Force Base (named in 1950 for Lieutenant William Nellis of Searchlight, who was shot down over Belgium in 1944) would become a major tactical combat training center during the Vietnam War and a permanent part of the valley's landscape.

Obtaining the nation's nuclear test site awarded the Las Vegas area another major installation. In the late 1940s, as the cold war heated up and the Soviet Union detonated its first atomic bomb, the United States moved to expand its testing program. In the immediate postwar years, the Defense Department and Atomic Energy Commission had conducted nuclear tests in the Far Pacific at the Bikini Atoll. But this location had numerous disadvantages. With the fall of China to communism in 1949 and the start of the Korean War a year later, communist espionage seemed more threatening. At the same time, shipping supplies so far from the American mainland became costlier. Finally, radioactive leaks into the ocean were also posing growing environmental concerns.

Enter Senator Pat McCarran. His powerful positions on the Judiciary and Appropriations Committees made him a force to be reckoned with—and his state a recipient of federal money. Accordingly, President Truman and AEC officials chose a portion of the Nellis bombing range as the new location for nuclear testing. Work began on what became known as the Nevada Proving Grounds (or, more popularly, the Test Site), and the AEC detonated the first bomb in January 1951.

While delighted to secure additional federal payrolls and supply orders, Las Vegas officials worried about the health risk. The AEC, however, moved quickly to minimize the concern. In a series of meetings in January 1951, atomic scientists assured residents that nuclear tests at the Proving Grounds near Mercury posed no safety threat to the city. Once convinced, Chamber of Commerce president Vern Willis and Mayor C. D. Baker viewed the spectacular aboveground tests as another spur to development. Some resorts even used the giant mushroom clouds as a marketing ploy to attract tourists who could see the residual smoke from the blasts through their hotel windows. Only later in the decade did it become apparent that Las Vegas's only protection from radioactivity was the prevailing westerly winds that blew most of the dangerous radiation over eastern Nevada and Utah.

In the 1950s, this increased defense spending encouraged the first major construction of homes in the northern and western portions of the city. In 1950, Prudential Homes announced plans to erect 640 moderately priced homes in the west end of town on forty acres near Twin Lakes (today in Lorenzi Park) and the municipal golf course. The California developer credited the Korean War with making Las Vegas "one of the hubs of the present defense activities," and accurately predicted that the conflict would not trigger a national shortage of building materials, as World War II had.

However, much of the new commercial and residential development was not in the city, but in the emerging Strip suburbs. Throughout the decade, new resorts on Las Vegas Boulevard South (the old Los Angeles Highway) lured an increasing number of home builders, store owners, and other businesspeople south of the city limits into county lands east of the Strip and railroad. Urbanization fanned out into the mostly empty desert between Las Vegas Boulevard and Boulder Highway, with Desert Inn Road, then Flamingo, then Harmon Avenue, and finally Bond (today Tropicana) Avenue acting as the unofficial border. These lands filled with homes, apartment complexes, and large and small shopping centers, spreading inexorably southward and eastward into the 1960s.

The Strip's continued growth was the force driving development. By the mid-1950s, the El Rancho Vegas and its three neighbors on the Strip had been joined by the Desert Inn, Sands, Sahara, Dunes, and Riviera. When it opened in 1955, the valley's first high-rise, the Riviera, demonstrated the feasibility of building tall buildings in the Las Vegas area. Engineers had speculated that this might not be possible on a desert floor composed of unreliable caliche and other clays, as well as high water tables created by the valley's aquifers. Some of the problems encountered in the late 1990s during Mandalay Bay's construction vindicated their concern. But the girder, elevator, telephone, and electric lighting that made the great vertical cities of Manhattan and Chicago possible in the late nineteenth century worked their magic on the Strip in the years after 1955.

But the road to prosperity proved bumpy. Overbuilding in 1955 led to the closure of two of the weaker new properties, the Royal Nevada on the Strip and the Moulin Rouge in West Las Vegas, while others teetered on the brink. The Strip faced a drop in business during the "Eisenhower recession" of the late 1950s, forcing the Dunes's brief closure. But Major Riddle saved the resort with an ambitious building program that gave the Dunes a golf course, a gourmet restaurant, a high-rise, and the Strip's first topless revue, all of which revived the property.

Like the Dunes and Riviera, the Hacienda, Tropicana, and Stardust hotels also contributed to the early Strip's success. They continued the tourist momentum created by the 1940s resorts and the Desert Inn, Sands, and Sahara by offering a variety of features that attracted increasing numbers of visitors. For example, the Stardust boasted a golf course (still behind the Boulevard Mall), the largest pool and sign in the world, a grand prix racetrack where Spring Valley is today, and the technically complex stage show for the topless Lido de Paris production. The showroom's six hydraulic lifts moved props, musicians, and performers thirty feet below or ten feet above the stage, a precursor to the modern Siegfried and Roy extravaganzas of the 1990s.

The Hacienda and Tropicana also made valuable contributions to the emerging Strip. Ben Jaffe, a former part-owner of Miami Beach's Fountainbleu Hotel, came to Las Vegas in 1955, bought a forty-acre tract far south of the Dunes and Flamingo, built an elegant tropical resort that exuded the ambience of old Havana, and acted as an early magnet for drawing tourists to the largely empty south Strip. Today, the area possesses some of the most popular hotels in the world.

The Stardust opened in 1958 and, two years later, was highly successful with its Lido de Paris Revue of 1960, which ran for three decades in the resort's showroom. Tony Cornero, builder of the Meadows, began construction. When he died, Moe Dalitz's group from the Desert Inn finished the work. For years, charges of mob skimming plagued the hotel, which later became the subject for the 1995 film *Casino*. Special Collections, UNLV Libraries

While less physically stunning than Jaffe's Tropicana, the Hacienda Hotel benefited from the innovative marketing ploys of its owners—and other resorts benefited in the process. Warren and Judy Bayley, who had successfully operated a small chain of Hacienda Hotels in California, bought land south of the Tropicana and opened their Hacienda Hotel at the far end of the Strip (where Mandalay Bay is today) in 1956. It was in the 1950s at the Hacienda, and not at Circus Circus in the 1970s or in the family-friendly campaign of the 1990s, that Las Vegas first appealed to families. The resort's seventeen thousand–dollar quarter-midget racetrack for kids, its multiple swimming pools, and other attractions drew a large family following. On the other hand, the resort's ingenious Hacienda Holiday promotions in California (where customers paid sixteen dollars for food and lodging and got ten dollars back in casino chips upon check-in) appealed to gamblers. The resort also operated an airline that flew gamblers to the Las Vegas area from all over the West and Midwest.

In the 1950s, the city of Las Vegas was able to match some of these advances on the Strip. Certainly, the Mexican-theme El Cortez of 1941 was almost enough to offset Thomas Hull's El Rancho Vegas, but no other large hotels downtown challenged the Last Frontier, Flamingo, and Thunderbird. While Guy McAfee's 1946 Golden Nugget, with its blazing neon sign (added two years later), did a lot of business, the casino had no hotel until later years. When Texas gambler Benny Binion opened the Horseshoe Club in 1951 (where the Apache Hotel had stood for twenty years), it proved to be a lively addition to Fremont Street. But the only two large resort hotels that opened in Las Vegas during the 1950s were the Showboat (later the Castaways) in 1954 and the Fremont (1956).

The Showboat (originally the Desert Showboat Motor Inn) was relatively large, but its location on the Boulder Highway was problematic. Fremont Street and Las Vegas Boulevard were the main centers for gamblers and tourists. Even Tony Cornero, whose 1931 Meadows Club was the first gambling hall on the Boulder Highway, closed the place in 1935. And

The Hacienda opened at the south end of the Strip in 1956. At the time, it seemed far from the action. Mandalay Bay occupies the site today. The marquee suggests both the old and new Las Vegas: the rider astride his horse, typical of the town's Old West theme, and the advertisement for "Strictly Burlesque" and "Topless Models" along with Hank Henry, a fixture in Las Vegas lounges and revues. Special Collections, UNLV Libraries

In the 1950s, the El Cortez was in the downtown elite. Run by veteran gaming operators like J. Kell Houssels and later Jackie Gaughan, it opened in 1941. Special Collections, UNLV Libraries

when he finally did build his big resort, the Stardust, it was on the Strip. It would be decades before Sam's Town, the Nevada Palace, and Boulder Station would come to the rescue.

J. Kell Houssels of the Las Vegas Club and William J. Moore of the Last Frontier built the two-story one hundred–room inn, which the Desert Inn's staff managed. But the Showboat struggled for several years until Joe Kelley's arrival in the late 1950s. Kelley did for the Showboat what Major Riddle did for the Dunes. Kelley revived the Showboat with forty-nine-cent breakfast specials and other promotions designed to lure locals. But the real panacea was bowling, a popular television sport in 1950s America. He built the original twenty-four-lane bowling center and sponsored state and regional championships that attracted bowlers-gamblers from across the nation and received regular television network attention for decades.

In 1954, the Desert Showboat Motor Inn opened on Boulder Highway, just southeast of where it turned into Fremont Street. Its operators included longtime gaming executives J. Kell Houssels and Moe Dalitz. Special Collections, UNLV Libraries

The Fremont was a major addition to the downtown skyline. At fifteen floors, it was Glitter Gulch's first high-rise and the tallest building in the state, coming just a year after the Riviera. The Fremont was also the first place downtown to feature big-name stars in its Carnival Lounge: Pat Boone, Helen Reddy, and a very young Wayne Newton all performed there. A 1963 expansion added the fourteen-story Ogden Tower, one of the city's first vertical parking garages, and a swimming pool—the first on Fremont Street.

Despite these new facilities on Fremont Street and Boulder Highway, the Strip began to pass the city in customers and gaming revenues. The construction of the Desert Inn, the Sands, and neighboring resorts was part of a century-long building trend that eventually made the Strip and its suburbs larger and wealthier than Las Vegas and its suburbs. However, while some tourists and residents might regard today's city as a mere adjunct to the Strip, Las Vegas historically was more than a mere nucleus for the future metropolitan area. From the 1920s, the city's leaders aggressively pushed congressional delegations, state legislators, military commanders, federal bureaucrats, out-of-state businessmen, and locals to promote all kinds of projects (including Hull's El Rancho Vegas) that would create new nearby development that in later decades could grow toward each other and eventually stretch the metropolitan area across the entire valley.

The city played a dynamic role in this process, just as Phoenix, Tucson, and Albuquerque did in their valleys. As Al Cahlan put it in a 1957 editorial, "[D]uring the early days, . . . had the pioneers stopped to think about the problems which attended plans for expansion, the community still would have been a sleepy little village where visitors paused only long enough to get gas and a sandwich before going on their way." Despite its ultimately glittering success, at no time in the 1950s was Las Vegas's future ensured. As Cahlan shrewdly realized, "Las Vegas could have died after Boulder Dam was completed . . . [h]ad people like R. B. Griffith, Al Corradetti and C. V. T. Gilbert started to reckon the 'impossibility' of getting the Air Force Gunnery School here."

Las Vegas's road to glory proved most challenging in the 1950s because danger lurked at every turn. Many within and outside of Nevada bemoaned the conversion of Reno and Las Vegas into gambling meccas and tried to kill the vulnerable industry. In 1957, for example, the Nevada

The Fremont Hotel opened in 1956. Run by Ed Levinson, an investor at the Sands, it was downtown's first high-rise and an early home of Channel 13. Its lounge featured a teenage performer named Wayne Newton. Special Collections, UNLV Libraries

Council of Churches demanded that state legislators end twenty-four-hour gambling and drinking by closing bars and casinos from 2 A.M. to 8 A.M., reform the liberal marriage and divorce laws, and fund a study of the social and economic effects of gambling upon the people of Nevada. Needless to say, Las Vegas and Reno interests had little trouble fending off this challenge in Carson City.

Federal initiatives were more troubling. The threat from the nation's Bible Belt did not begin in the 1990s with Tom Grey and James Dobson. Nor were conservative Christians the only ones challenging Las Vegas and its gaming industry. In the most celebrated effort to stem the gambling tide, Tennessee Democrat Estes Kefauver led a whirlwind fact-finding tour with the Senate Select Committee to Investigate Organized Crime in America. In 1950, Kefauver and his associates held hearings in Las Vegas and assailed political and gaming leaders. Upon his return to Washington, Kefauver sponsored a bill that would have levied a 10 percent federal tax on all table-game and slot winnings. It took all of Pat McCarran's considerable influence to block the proposal in committee. Six years later, Nevada representatives again headed off another antigambling measure. In 1955, Senator Kenneth Keating (R-NY) led an effort by a small group of conservatives to increase federal taxes on casinos, but again Nevada's congressional delegation was able to block the bill. By then, McCarran was dead, but as his successors built their influence, they relied on his old allies: conservative southerners trying to block federal interference in their states for vastly different reasons. Ironically, though, Las Vegans engaged in similar bigotry toward their black population.

Despite these efforts to undermine its major industry, the Las Vegas area continued its vibrant expansion. New plans for great resorts and new roads appeared regularly for county commission approval, and projections for growth knew no bounds. No wonder that as the county's population continued to spiral, political leaders became more aggressive—not only with their northern Nevada counterparts over taxes and spending, but even with their western neighbors. Arguing that the new Pahrump Highway over the Charleston range made Pahrump Valley 110 miles closer to Las Vegas than to the Nye County seat at Tonopah, Assemblyman George Von Tobel and Clark County's state legislative delegation boldly tried in 1953 to annex Pahrump Valley over the objections of Nye County. The state legislature, dominated especially in the senate by Nevada's rural counties, said no.

Clark County hardly needed to take on the financial responsibility of governing a larger area, because the Strip's development saddled it with enough financial obligations, not the least of which was the need to build a new airport. While Senator Clark's railroad and later the Los Angeles Highway keyed the early rise of Las Vegas, airplanes gained importance after 1950. Not only the commercial airlines but also some of the hotels' airlines flew a growing number of regularly scheduled and chartered flights to Las Vegas. Both the Frontier and the Hacienda Hotels started airlines to fly guests to their properties. In fact, by 1959, Hacienda Airlines had more scheduled daily flights to Las Vegas than United, American, and TWA combined until the Federal Aviation Administration intervened.

All of this activity made the new 1948 McCarran Airport even more crucial. But new technological advances in aviation threatened to make the facility obsolete before its time. By the late 1950s, city and county leaders realized that commercial jetliner development threatened to make Las Vegas's cramped, little airport more of a liability than an asset. The county built the facility to accommodate propeller-driven aircraft, not jets.

Nevertheless, Las Vegas badly needed the jet plane for its tourist and convention business. Speed was the great advantage of this remarkable machine. Obviously, getting to Las Vegas would soon become easier. "Jet schedules made feasible by plane speeds of up to 575 miles per hour will allow more people to travel," one local column announced, and "the more airlines we get into Las Vegas the more tourists naturally will flow." In the 1930s and early 1940s, Western Air Express, with its control of the old airport north of town (today parts of Nellis Air Force Base) blocked competitors from delivering passengers from Los Angeles, St. Louis, and other cities. But the new public airport of 1948, while not particularly big, was a significant step forward in air travel for Las Vegas. It broke Western's monopoly and allowed TWA, United, and other airlines to enter the Las Vegas market. Local businessman Ed Converse started Bonanza Airlines to serve the state and region.

Of course, in this era before airline deregulation, Las Vegas had another potential obstacle to deal with: the Civil Aeronautics Board (CAB), the federal agency that decided which carriers flew where. For many years, McCarran's power in the Senate brought its bureaucrats to heel. The CAB, however, also counterbalanced firms like Western that sought to create monopolies. In this vein, the *Las Vegas Review-Journal* viewed the CAB as an ally in the fight to increase air travel to Las Vegas. In 1956, for instance, the newspaper was optimistic that the agency would approve Continental flights to Las Vegas from the upper Midwest and East. With air travel increasing and more airlines forming, local resort and government leaders recognized that more tourists would come to Las Vegas by air. But first the tiny 1948 airport would have to go. New transportation technologies were forcing not only Las Vegas but cities across the nation to undertake costly expansion projects.

In January 1958, the growing dominance of the car, bus, and airplane became even more apparent locally when the Union Pacific Railroad announced it was cutting service on the *City of Las Vegas* train to just three days per week. This was an ominous sign of things to come. By the end of the next decade, the old railroad town would raze its venerable station to make room for the Union Plaza Hotel.

The jet plane's anticipated arrival and the construction of a convention center went hand in hand. Hotels in New York, Philadelphia, Chicago, and other large cities had always dominated the convention business, because America's railroads converged at these points. But commercial jets could fly passengers anywhere, even to cities like Las Vegas served by only one railroad. So local businessmen in the 1950s knew that once Las Vegas built a jetport, building a large convention center would also make sense.

In the early 1950s, President Eisenhower and the Republicans led the way by amending the income tax code to allow generous deductions for travel to exhibit goods and for professional growth. Once this occurred, building a large convention center promised to deliver even more tourists to town. Casino operators like the Horseshoe's Joe W. Brown (Benny Binion, jailed for tax evasion, had lost his gaming license and sold the club) realized that conventioneers could be brought in to fill the hotels during the week when southern Californians were working.

To this end, Brown purchased the 480-acre site of Joe Smoot's failed racetrack behind the Riviera Hotel at a bankruptcy sale in 1955. Brown then offered part of the land to Las Vegas as a likely spot for its new convention center. The problem was that the parcel was south of the city line and therefore had to be annexed, but Clark County commissioners were hardly willing to award the city this valuable prize. In the end, city, county, and business leaders, recognizing the need for such a facility, formed a subcommittee composed of Brown, William J. Moore, and Ed Converse to select a site for the convention center. They discussed various locations, including some near the airport, but Las Vegas wanted the facility near the city limits. For that and other reasons, the committee chose a site on Brown's land behind the Riviera. Another committee decided in January 1957 to fund construction by levying a 5 percent hotel room tax and a 3 percent motel room tax.

The county scheduled a bond election to raise immediate funds until enough room tax could be collected to pay off the debt. Following a campaign in which both the *Las Vegas Sun*'s Hank Greenspun and the *Review-Journal*'s Al Cahlan vigorously supported the project, voters overwhelmingly approved the bonds. Construction began within weeks on a meeting hall and exhibit hall. In April 1959, the convention center opened to the World Congress of Flight meeting. This was appropriate: airplanes, not cars, would be the preferred mode of travel to Las Vegas for most conventioneers.

Las Vegas's growth depended upon attracting more tourists and making it easier for them to get there. Construction of a new airport in 1948 was a step in the right direction, but so was the building of Interstate 15. Shortly after President Eisenhower signed the Interstate Highway Act of 1956, engineers began drawing blueprints for a modern road to replace the old two-lane route between southern California and Salt Lake City. For Las Vegas the benefits were obvious. A modern four-lane freeway with a large center median and gentle banked turns would deliver tourists to Las Vegas at speeds of sixty miles per hour or more. This would cut the trip to four hours compared to the old tedious drive of seven or more hours on the Los Angeles Highway.

The problem was that it took more than a decade to get the road built, especially the last ten miles. Worse still, the route through the city itself had to rip through some neighborhoods due to the lack of open land all the way through Las Vegas, except its extreme eastern or western borders. No municipal officials wanted such a diversion, because the casinos and commercial businesses wanted an interchange that served downtown. Planning disputes over this and other issues continued into the 1960s and slowed the road's progress. Contributing to the impasse, Mayor C. D. Baker supported a route near Highland Avenue west of the tracks and opposed two alternate choices, one running east of the tracks and the other west of Highland, because they would "overload city streets which were built for residential thoroughfares." The mayor also rejected an east-side route that "would reverse the city planning and displace the present commercial and industrial area."

He neglected to mention that an east-side freeway would cut through the city's lily-white eastern and southern suburbs, causing a huge political fallout. Anything too far west would threaten new western white suburbs, where subdivisions like Rancho Circle and others on the drawing board would be endangered. The choice was obvious, just as it was in Chicago's south side, Nashville's north side, and so many other minority neighborhoods in urban America. The black Westside, with its depressed land values and rundown housing, was the route of choice. In later years, city leaders and freeway engineers bulldozed hundreds of dwellings there and split the community with a ribbon of concrete. The only concession would be an exit on D Street to give resident commuters who survived the wrecking ball a convenient route to downtown and the Strip.

The freeway, airport, and convention center all required the cooperation of city and county commissioners, who worked together uneasily. The need, for instance, to compromise over the convention center's location and funding pointed out the disadvantages of the city's earlier failure to annex the Strip. Despite the Strip's unwillingness to join the city, Las Vegas commissioners and the mayor continued to try to annex the increasingly valuable lands on its borders. These initiatives were not limited to Mayor Cragin. His successors also resented the loss of a resort sector the city helped spawn. Evidence of this frustration came in 1959 when Mayor Baker announced that city firemen would no longer help their county counterparts fight fires south of Sahara Avenue until the unincorporated towns there agreed to be annexed. This served only to antagonize an already deteriorating relationship and encourage insurance companies to raise fire rates on both sides of the municipal border. For their part, county commissioners responded by expanding the fire department they had created in 1953.

Turf battles also erupted on other fronts during the decade. Thwarted in 1946 and again in 1950–1951 in their efforts to annex the southern Strip suburbs, city leaders were in no mood to be blocked on their eastern boundary by the county or North Las Vegas. In 1957, the city commission moved to leave its growth path to the east open by threatening to annex four square miles on East Charleston to Nellis Boulevard to prevent residents of Meckle Manor from incorporating a town. A half-dozen other incidents also punctuated the decade before a major showdown in 1962, when Las Vegas and county commissioners worked together in a rare display of unanimity to prevent North Las Vegas from annexing lands bordering what later became Sunrise Manor. And while the larger city continued to battle with its northern neighbor over tracts north and east of Las Vegas, the major annexations came later in the century, mostly along the western and northwestern edge of town.

The conflict between Las Vegas and its southern suburbs went beyond the annexation question. Divisions also appeared within the resort industry. As the 1950s progressed, the interests of the Strip hotels and their downtown counterparts clearly diverged, even when it came to attracting tourists. In the 1950s, the *Las Vegas Review-Journal,* in particular, blamed these conflicts on a lack of community spirit. Editorials cautioned that the hotels needed to work together, as they had in the past, to boost the Las Vegas area's economy.

The publicity arm of the Chamber of Commerce became an early battleground. In 1956, one *Review-Journal* editorial bemoaned the failure of some Strip resorts to support the Live Wire Fund publicity war chest. In a clear reference to the newer Strip resorts south of the city that were beginning to fund their own publicity departments, the column complained that "the newer people in the [casino] industry . . . have developed a shortsighted policy of pulling out of civic enterprises." As a result, the Live Wire Fund was expected to have less than one hundred thousand dollars in contributions for the first time in several years. The column also charged that these "newer" interests "have failed to support community enterprises such as the Community Chest [and] Red Cross drives." Many "resorts" had chosen not to sponsor floats in the Tournament of Roses and Helldorado Parades. Clearly, as the Strip took on a life of its own, the community spirit so strong in the 1940s and early 1950s began to dissipate under the pressure of competing interests, although the Las Vegas Convention and Visitors Authority would later struggle to maintain some degree of unity. But even the authority, despite efforts to remain evenhanded, increasingly favored the Strip as its resorts grew in visitor popularity.

The Strip's growing indifference to the city's annual Helldorado Parade also angered local columnists like longtime resident and promoter Al Cahlan, who bemoaned the Strip's lack of commitment to traditional events that celebrated the city's heritage. "More and more," he complained in a 1957 column, "some of the establishments are taking the attitude that the residents of the local community do not mean anything to their economy, and they are dependent entirely on the tourists who come into the area because of the glamour provided by the Strip." In a scathing indictment of this new trend, Cahlan reminded Strip executives that "many of the later resorts were constructed on a foundation laid by Helldorado."

While resentment built within the community over the growing division between downtown and the Strip, Las Vegans displayed a surprising amount of tolerance for the continuing presence of mob-related figures in the casinos of both sections. Officially, state and local political and law enforcement leaders considered Las Vegas, like Reno and the rest of the state, off-limits to mobsters. Unofficially, they quietly accepted gang-related and former gang-related mob operators like Gus Greenbaum and Moe Dalitz. While out-of-state newspapers often echoed the views of critics like Senator Estes Kefauver that Las Vegas was mob-run, the local media, for the most part, tended to minimize the problem by ignoring or trivializing it.

In 1950, for instance, the *Oakland Tribune* charged that the "Capone-Siegel" mob was now in Las Vegas, using the city and the race wire that reported results from California and other tracks as a base for operations in the Golden State. Local newspapers carried the story, adding that Governor Vail Pittman doubted the charges. Surely, numerous associates of Siegel's old syndicate were in Las Vegas, downtown, and on the Strip, including the new Desert Inn. But no one locally, including the newspapers, acted as though this was true, although Greenspun's *Sun* often criticized them and questioned their associations. Clearly, people like Moe Dalitz, with their influence and access to capital, were vital to the city's casino development. As long as they kept a clean record, no one locally was inclined to investigate their activities.

Nevertheless, the mob's presence in Las Vegas and Reno convinced political leaders of the need for tighter state regulation of the gaming industry. In 1949, the legislature passed a law requiring potential casino operators to obtain a gaming license *before* they opened their doors for business. This gave the Nevada Tax Commission (which regulated gaming before the state gaming commission was created in 1959) time to investigate all applicants. While operators like Guy McAfee and Benny Binion had criminal records, Bugsy Siegel, Moe Sedway, and other figures with ties to organized crime were the real targets of early state regulators. The need to keep Nevada "clean" became paramount during the nationwide campaign against the mob in cities, in labor unions, and elsewhere. Such 1950s films as *On the Waterfront* (1954) and *Slaughter on Tenth Avenue* (1957) only reflected the sentiment that crusaders like Kefauver and other local reformers expressed.

Nevada's conservative Republican Party, and not the Democrats, supported the strict regulation of gambling in the early 1950s. Even after Siegel was gone, plenty of mob figures remained around town. The most obvious was Dalitz, a former leader of Cleveland's Mayfield Road Gang and an associate of Detroit's notorious Purple Gang. Dalitz and other mobsters used Wilbur Clark as a front man to mask their control of the Desert Inn. Even the Dunes's Major Riddle, who also owned the Silverbird (the old Thunderbird), the downtown Holiday Inn (today the Main Street Station), and the Silver Nugget in North Las Vegas, was an associate of Al Capone in the 1930s. Through their managers, mob leaders Jake and Meyer Lansky owned large shares of resorts like the Thunderbird until the crusading Republican editor Hank Greenspun revealed their role in the *Las Vegas Sun*. Several years later, former *Sun* reporter Ed Reid, along with Ovid Demaris, exposed even more Las Vegas connections in their 1963 best-seller, *The Green Felt Jungle.*

The mob trend continued into the 1960s and after at the Aladdin, Tropicana, Stardust, and other resorts. A series of U.S. attorneys general, from Robert Kennedy to Ramsey Clark to John Mitchell, used the FBI and IRS to investigate skimming and other illegal operations in casinos. The so-called Organized Crime Treaty of 1977, in which East Coast mobsters allegedly awarded Las Vegas to their midwestern counterparts in return for Atlantic City, did little to alter the FBI's conviction that the mob was alive and well in Las Vegas, both on the Strip and downtown. How much influence the mob, if such a coherent group exists, exerts in Las Vegas and on the Strip today is doubtful. Certainly, the invasion of the corporations after 1969, with their access to huge sums of capital, reduced the mob's presence significantly. The owners sold, but their loyal employees remained. The passage of time—death, retirement, and changes in management—eliminated any obvious influence mob figures still may have enjoyed.

Love or hate the mob, or even question its existence, the fact remains that it exerted major influence upon the development of Las Vegas's gaming industry in the mid-twentieth century. The presence of such financial figures as Dalitz and Jimmy Hoffa, and even more shadowy types like Sam Giancana, was an advantage to both the city and the Strip. In an era when almost all lending institutions refused to loan money for casino development, these supposed wise guys provided the cash or pension-fund loans to build the resorts and even some of the high-rises that downtown and the Strip needed to keep the boom going.

Local residents were committed to the growth of their valley. To this end, they courted the military, unofficially tolerated the mob, built airports and roads, and did whatever else they could to attract business. Support for a right-to-work law was unusual for a city and state where railroad craft and mining unions had always enjoyed some influence in the legislature. However, the ill-timed Culinary Union strike in Reno on the Fourth of July weekend in 1949 so antagonized even the average voter that employers across the state saw their chance to make the right-to-work law provision of the 1947 Taft-Hartley Act part of Nevada's constitution.

The bitter fight over the amendment initiative on two successive state ballots divided Las Vegans as few issues had before. Numerous antiunion groups supported the right-to-work amendment in the November 1952 election. In an effort to procure support from numerous job applicants in the casino industry, one Nevada Citizens' Committee advertisement declared that a yes vote would "eliminate labor boss monopoly controls of all jobs." In response, members of the culinary, bartender, and other unions, which composed much of the casino-resort workforce downtown and on the Strip, urged a no vote and spiced their advertisement with condemnations of auto dealer and former Chamber of Commerce president James Cashman, who led the right-to-work forces in southern Nevada. But union efforts were in vain. In 1952, 1954, and again in 1956, voters from all parts of Nevada supported the right-to-work provision as state law. In later years, the Venetian, Aladdin, MGM Grand, and many other businesses exploited this opportunity to operate in Las Vegas without having to negotiate with unions.

The right-to-work campaign reflected the rough-and-tumble nature of politics in the early 1950s. On the national level, the Republicans and Dwight Eisenhower ended two decades of Democratic Party rule in 1952.

At the state level, Republican governor Charles Russell battled former Democratic governor Vail Pittman and the casino lobby to maintain tough state regulation of the industry, while Pat McCarran's political dominance declined due to his own mortality and the growth of a population with no loyalty to him. In Las Vegas, McCarran supporter Ernie Cragin initially expected to survive the invective of his old nemeses, Charles Pipkin and the Las Vegas Taxpayer's Association.

In 1951, Cragin sought another term as mayor. Having been elected in 1931, 1943, and 1947, his selection once again seemed likely. In his campaign, he emphasized "the expansion of the downtown business district with the erection of many fine stores and office buildings, the opening of a great number of new subdivisions," and many newly paved, curbed, and lit streets. Cragin promised that, if reelected, he would enhance Las Vegas's appeal with the "installation of off-street parking to provide better downtown shopping facilities."

But this time the incumbent mayor faced renewed political opposition from foes like Pipkin who again blasted "the pseudo political organization on Fremont Street" and Cragin's cozy relations with J. Kell Houssels and other club owners. Pipkin criticized the city's "emergency loans" and failure to build enough parks and recreational facilities to curb the rising trend of juvenile delinquency. Pipkin and others dismissed the growth that Cragin took credit for as inevitable, given the defense boom and the rising popularity of gaming. All Cragin did, they argued, was respond to the growth, and not very well. According to his opponents, Cragin failed to provide Las Vegas with the quality services that other medium-size cities enjoyed. A particular target for the critics was the Southern Nevada Telephone Company, run by Cragin's old friend Samuel Lawson. The utility not only made new residents wait years to get a phone, but kept much of the city, including some of the Strip hotels, on four-party lines into the 1950s. Worse still was Lawson's unchallenged policy of making residents in new suburbs pay for poles and wires just to get service. As with McCarran, newcomers felt no loyalty to Cragin. They not only resented service problems, but also sensed that the establishment expected their deference.

Years of criticism, insinuation, and, ironically, growth took their toll on the mayor's reputation. In the 1951 municipal election, former city engineer C. D. Baker defeated Cragin and attorney George Franklin for mayor. Baker had served as a state senator and president of the Chamber of Com-

Mayor Ernie Cragin rides in the annual Helldorado Parade. Note the tags and slogans on the old-fashioned car. Special Collections, UNLV Libraries

merce, making him a safe choice for the business community. He based a lot of his campaign on the need for street improvements in all parts of town, including the Westside, and Baker's accomplishments as city engineer convinced voters that he was more up to the task than Cragin.

The city commission also gained a talented new member whose leadership contributed greatly to Las Vegas's development over the next decade. Reed Whipple, a prominent Mormon and manager of First National Bank on Fifth Street, defeated realtor William Peccole. The latter's opposition to rent control and public housing appealed to builders and businessmen, but won him few votes from renters and the impoverished.

The sometimes crusty and outspoken Baker and the quieter Whipple made an effective team. They and other city leaders wasted no time in addressing the problems created by the major force shaping city policy: growth. The dramatic expansion of the Las Vegas area's resort and defense industries in the 1950s was a mixed blessing. Everyone welcomed the construction boom and prosperity, but as growth continued unabated, so did the rising cost of paying for it. In 1955, Mayor Baker announced three bond issues for the May ballot: $2.5 million for a new city hall, then $600,000 for two fire stations and expanding the alarm system into new neighborhoods, and $500,000 for a railroad underpass at Owens to relieve crosstown bottlenecks in the rapidly expanding western suburbs.

C. D. Baker became mayor in 1951, but his career also included a state senate term, engineering, real estate, and service to the state Democratic Party. Special Collections, UNLV Libraries

Like Cragin in the 1930s and 1940s, Baker and his colleagues also sought federal assistance. Since the Korean War contributed significantly to local growth due to Nellis and the Test Site, the national government offered to help beleaguered local officials. In 1952, representatives from the U.S. Home and Housing Administration visited Las Vegas at the height of the war to gather information on what public works projects the city needed. Baker and other local officials met with John F. Lamb, the agency's regional engineer, and submitted a prioritized agenda. Topping the list was a $6 million water line from Basic Magnesium to Las Vegas. Baker and water district director Thomas Campbell told Lamb that, if built, the line would stand "as an integral part of the ultimately envisioned direct line from Lake Mead to Las Vegas"—later called the Southern Nevada Water Project.

Baker, like his predecessor, dreamed of Las Vegas someday becoming a major metropolitan area, but he recognized that natural gas as well as more water and power were vital to realizing that dream. As the city's former engineer, Baker also understood the importance of more localized improvements that would raise property values in all neighborhoods and serve as a base for extending the city's infrastructure outward. Therefore, in his meeting with Lamb, the mayor also requested $3.1 million for five miles of new 36-foot-wide streets equipped with sewer outfalls and mains, along with $50,000 for a new fire station and garbage processing facility.

Las Vegas's frantic growth also helped the effort to finally bring cheap natural gas to the valley. The private sector recognized an emerging market in southern Nevada. In 1950, El Paso Natural Gas announced plans to build a 433-mile line from its New Mexico fields through Topock, Arizona, to the Las Vegas Valley. At the time, the city relied on liquefied petroleum gas, which had to be delivered by truck. As one community spokesman said, this practice was "neither economical nor efficient. . . . [T]he availability of supply cannot always be assured." A natural gas line would provide a relatively cheap source for heating and fuel for the factories that Las Vegas promoters hoped to attract, but this industrialization never really happened. While a few small plants settled near Basic Magnesium and other pockets in the valley, Las Vegas never lured the industry that Phoenix, Tucson, Albuquerque, and other southwestern rivals did.

Part of the reason was a relative lack of electric power. Despite its proximity to Hoover Dam's generators, Las Vegas had to concede more than 60 percent of its power to California and share the rest with Arizona and other entities. By the early 1950s, Las Vegas's growth outpaced the available supply. Worse, Southern Nevada Power did not build enough new plants to supplement the dam. As early as 1951, the utility banned the use of space heaters, and the area's lack of electricity threatened to cut Federal Housing Administration loan guarantees for new homes, a move that could have threatened residential construction and ultimately growth itself. These concerns led Mayor Baker to seek help from California Edison and a share of electricity from Shasta Dam or a comparable facility.

The real solution was to pressure Southern Nevada Power into changing its management. This finally occurred when company directors replaced Samuel Lawson with a dynamic young executive, Reid Gardner, who immediately ordered construction of a new coal-fired generating plant in Moapa Valley and drafted plans for more. By 1956, the crisis had subsided. As the area's new steam-powered generating plant prepared to open in 1956, Gardner told grateful residents they could once again purchase space heaters and have load regulators removed from their homes.

Perhaps the worst growth-related problem was in education. At the time, Nevada possessed some of the nation's lowest-quality schools, but Las Vegas, in particular, faced an even greater crisis, worsened by the postwar baby boom and the city's rapid urbanization. The solution to the state's problem came when former Las Vegas school superintendent Maude Frazier, along with a coalition of concerned parents in Reno and Las Vegas, Mayor Baker, and other city and county leaders, pressured Governor Russell into funding a study by a blue-ribbon panel of experts from the prestigious Peabody Teacher's College in Tennessee. This group's findings gave Russell and other school advocates the ammunition they needed to convince voters and legislators to levy a 2 percent sales tax, increase property taxes, and use bonding power to raise teachers' salaries, improve libraries, upgrade the curriculum, and build more schools. A 1955 law replaced the state's two hundred or more school districts with just seventeen—one for each county. The Clark County School District, today the nation's sixth largest, was born.

Even earlier, the Korean War–induced growth of defense worker families in town prompted the federal government to help ease the pressure. It built a $650,000 elementary school. Built on vacant land near West

Charleston and Palomino, the facility helped relieve the classroom short-age for the mushrooming white suburbs south and west of Westside. This was crucial, because the city had to address the substantial development occurring in its southern suburbs approaching the Strip. In 1952, for example, southern California developer Philip Yousen announced plans to build eighty-eight duplexes and fifty-one single-family homes near Fifth and Oakey Streets. This new community, called Paradise Grove, arose near today's historic preservation district just east of the Stratosphere Hotel, an area of town where classrooms were at a premium.

Creation of the Clark County School District came just in time. By 1954, overcrowding plagued local schools. The forty-year-old Fifth Street School had become a firetrap, and many of the city's other facilities were no better. Due to budget shortfalls, school grounds maintenance had lost all priority. "Egg-sized" rocks sat in almost every playground, and broken fences exposed children to the danger of street traffic. In 1953, the Las Vegas Board of Education allocated only $15,000 for grounds. As newspa-per reporter Jeff McColl observed, the board's attitude was "let's get the children in classes first and worry about the recreation areas later." This was little consolation to parents worried about their children's safety. Years later, McColl would become head of the powerful Culinary Union Local 226, whose members, many of whom were parents, supported Maude Frazier's reform efforts in 1955. But even before her triumph, there was progress, as work continued on a new grammar school south of town along with the city's second high school.

Nevertheless, Las Vegas–area schools continued to face severe over-crowding, worsened by the city's spiraling population. In January 1955, the school board announced that half-day sessions would continue at Las Vegas High until Rancho opened later that spring. Rancho's completion would free up ten classrooms at Las Vegas High for grade school students. These buildings created only a brief respite until Las Vegas's next round of growth triggered more school construction. And this trend continued unabated into the twenty-first century.

The same growth that sparked the crisis in school construction drove population up to a point that justified building a college. Since 1887, when Morrill Hall opened, the University of Nevada in Reno had been the place where state residents went for higher education. Following the Com-stock's decline, Reno, with its national railroad connections, became the state's largest city. Even in 1950, Reno, with 32,497 residents, still comfortably led Las Vegas, with its 24,624, in the population sweepstakes. But that would end in the late 1950s.

The early pressure for building a new college in the valley came not only from high school seniors and graduates, who were unwilling or unable to attend classes at the Reno campus, but also from local teachers who resented having to leave their families each summer and go to Reno for graduate coursework. Additionally, Nellis airmen, promised a college education as part of their enlistment package, wanted to attend classes while they were stationed in the valley. The state board of regents, composed mainly of northern Nevadans, did little until the air force began negotiations with the University of Southern California to teach some extension courses on the base. At the same time, Brigham Young University officials also considered establishing an extension program in Las Vegas for local Mormons.

Apprehensive about losing potential enrollment and tuition for the state university and pressured by such state legislators as Clark County Assemblywoman and former school superintendent Frazier, regents established an extension program in Las Vegas in 1951. University officials tapped James Dickinson, a young faculty member from the school's English department, to run the night program in space donated by the school board at Las Vegas High. Even though residents and students wanted a college campus of their own, at a 1954 meeting regents opposed building a Las Vegas campus. Later, under intense pressure from southern Nevada residents, the board reversed itself and began seeking a location for a permanent campus.

After investigating several sites, including one in Boulder City, another in Henderson, and a third on West Charleston Boulevard where a campus of the Community College of Southern Nevada exists today, regents chose a parcel of land on Maryland Parkway owned by former Las Vegan Estelle Wilbourn. Wilbourn offered to donate sixty acres of land in memory of her mother, a pioneer Nevadan. However, to get the sixty acres for free, the university had to purchase an additional twenty acres for $35,000. In the 1955 legislative session, State Senator Mahlon Brown of Clark County sponsored legislation to provide $200,000 to construct the campus's first building, later named for Frazier. But the bill contained a provision that required Las Vegans to demonstrate their good faith to a skeptical north and raise the $35,000 necessary to buy the additional twenty acres, which the school needed if it was to have a campus large enough to accommodate future growth. The bill set a one-year deadline to raise the money or else the $200,000 would not be spent.

With help from Clark County school superintendent R. Guild Gray and others, Frazier moved into action, meeting with high school principals in Las Vegas, Henderson, and Boulder City to recruit seniors to solicit funds. In the so-called "Porchlight Campaign" in May 1955, local high school seniors visited the home of every valley resident asking for financial support to start what eventually became UNLV. Chamber of Commerce president Archie Grant lined up business support. The student effort and other donations eventually brought in over $50,000, more than enough to buy the land and provide some books, furniture, and other supplies for the Maryland Parkway campus's first building.

Classes began there in 1957 with William Carlson serving as the campus's first administrative head. Even though Carlson formed a small foundation to raise money to buy more land and construct more buildings, state funding was required, but it was meager and progress was slow. The struggling college did not graduate its first class (of only twenty-nine students) until 1964. Not until the 1960s did Nevada Southern University (renamed UNLV in 1969) begin to grow. Two events were crucial. First, the U.S. Supreme Court's "one man, one vote" decision in the early 1960s ended rural county control of both the state legislature and the board of regents, and gave populous Clark County more power to divert higher education funding to construct its school.

The next came in 1968. President Donald Moyer, working with Valley Bank owners E. Parry Thomas, Nate Mack, and his son Jerry, formed a new foundation that acquired all of the 335 acres of land needed to build UNLV. Irwin Molasky, developer of Sunrise Hospital, the Boulevard Mall, and virtually all of today's shopping centers on Maryland Parkway from Sahara Avenue up to the UNLV campus near Flamingo Road, also played a role in the process with his business partners, Moe Dalitz and Merv Adelson. Perhaps the college could have gotten off to a faster start in the 1950s with more local money. But the infant UNLV suffered from the same problem as the infant school district and many other public works priorities in the valley: too many growth-related needs and not enough money to fund them all.

In 1959, the Southern Regional Division of the University of Nevada consisted of Maude Frazier Hall on the left, Archie Grant Hall to the right of Frazier Hall, and, behind them, a gymnasium, now the Marjorie Barrick Museum of Natural History at what became UNLV. Special Collections, UNLV Libraries

Water supply was a case in point. The great Goliath threatening Las Vegas's future growth was not costly street improvements or even school construction, but lack of water. In 1947, the state legislature acceded to the requests of city and county leaders to authorize creation of the Las Vegas Valley Water District pending voter approval, which came on October 19, 1948. Although the district's first board of directors began work at that time, the district did not formally take over the Las Vegas Land & Water Company's system until summer 1954, when it issued bonds to finance the purchase.

The district's creation represented an important first step toward providing businesses and residents in this desert community with enough water to support a larger economy and population. But the district's task was daunting: obtain a supply for the entire valley, not just Las Vegas. In pursuing this goal, the board of directors tolerated no interference from city officials, including Mayor Baker. In 1953, when the Las Vegas Land & Water Company began negotiations to sell its plant and infrastructure (which were mostly located in the city), Baker was not even allowed to attend the meetings. Despite his insistence that city residents were not "outsiders" in the deal, district officials, asserting their authority, forced him to leave. The lesson was clear: the City of Las Vegas's power was limited not just by county commissioners and unincorporated townships, but by special service districts as well.

After purchasing Senator Clark's old water system, the water district next signed an agreement with Basic Management to build a pipeline from the factory to an expanding network of mains the district was busily laying in the city and Strip suburbs. This project, completed in December 1955, finally delivered the first Lake Mead water to Las Vegas, twenty years after the lake's formation. The added capacity immediately awarded the Strip and city the support they needed for additional resort and population growth.

In addition to all of these major concerns, the extension of municipal services was a continuing problem for Baker and city commissioners. This had been the case throughout U.S. history in all urban areas that underwent rapid growth. Even cities with vibrant tax bases like New York and Chicago lagged in delivering new police and fire stations to instant neighborhoods. In other cases, racial discrimination delayed the effort, diverting funds to new white areas. In the city of Las Vegas, the valley's original urban nucleus, West Las Vegas, platted a few months before Senator Clark's town site, had struggled for years with its rundown appearance and unpaved streets. The problem grew worse after 1939, as the city, especially under Cragin, pressured many black businesses into the area while refusing to support street improvements and other services.

Thousands of new African American residents recruited to southern Nevada by Basic Magnesium, whose Carver Park housing project could not accommodate them, ended up in Westside. The neighborhood's increasingly dense population and building pattern hardly contributed to the community's physical appearance or security. While the city police increased Westside patrols, there was no fire station until 1951, when Mayor Baker and city commissioners finally agreed to pay fifty-six hundred dollars for 2.5 acres at Bonanza near Tonopah Highway for a firehouse. Rapid urbanization of the black area as well as the construction of white-only housing on the periphery of this zone forced the city to act. Municipal officials knew that land developers would not build middle-income housing in the western suburbs unless an acceptable level of utility infrastructure and municipal services was already in place.

This is part of West Las Vegas, with Westside Elementary at the center right, in the 1950s. Special Collections, UNLV Libraries

Of course, the twenty-year struggle of Westside residents to obtain street improvements and services from the city was directly related to racism. And residents could do little until their numbers reached a critical mass to support an effective protest movement. This occurred by the mid-1950s, and civil rights soon became more of a burning issue. Although Basic Magnesium and World War II brought the first large influx of African Americans to Las Vegas, the postwar growth of downtown and especially the Strip created many low-skilled positions that paid better than similar jobs in the East and South. As a result, the city's African American population continued to soar, passing ten thousand by the late 1950s, much to the chagrin of many white residents. The community even formed it own Westside Chamber of Commerce in 1948.

The dawn of America's modern civil rights movement is often associated with the *Brown v. Board of Education* school decision of 1954 or Rosa Parks's courageous refusal a year later to take a backseat on a Montgomery bus. But local NAACP activists were pushing for change in the Las Vegas Valley long before these events occurred. Job discrimination was one source of trouble. In the 1930s, the local NAACP protested Six Companies's failure to hire any African American workers until July 1932. Blacks won a token victory that month when embarrassed company officials quickly hired ten men. But from 1930 to 1936, African Americans accounted for less than 1 percent of the total dam workforce. BMI had a better record, recruiting and employing hundreds of black men. However, except for a few black females working in the office, BMI hired no black women in the plant for most of World War II. Even though numerous white females and even some Latina employees worked in the factory, it took several years of pressure from Woodrow Wilson, a labor activist, and others before BMI gave in.

Job discrimination was not the only issue. Pressure for a local civil rights ordinance originated in the 1940s when Mayor Cragin's regime began enforcing residential segregation in public places such as downtown's retail, residential, and casino districts. By the mid-1940s, the Club Alabam was the only casino on Fremont Street that was integrated. Tensions rose during the war but, except for brief conflicts with police, never escalated beyond the control of local law enforcement. After the war and during the infamous McCarthy era, the fall of China, the Berlin crisis, the Korean conflict, and other cold war events discouraged dissent in the name of patriotism. But the 1953 Korean truce and President Eisenhower's election eased international tensions enough to allow civil rights advocates to speak once again.

The public debate over civil rights in Las Vegas, while never totally moribund, resumed in earnest in January 1954. San Francisco attorney Franklin Williams, representing the NAACP, prodded Las Vegas city commissioners to pass a civil rights ordinance. Williams insisted that all he wanted was the legal authority "to have a cup of coffee or throw a few nickels in the slot machine." To this end, he refuted a 1953 opinion by then city attorney and future U.S. senator Howard Cannon that the city charter did not expressly give Las Vegas the authority to pass a civil rights law. Cannon suggested that the power lay with the state legislature, which in 1953 had voted down a civil rights bill sponsored by local attorney and state assemblyman George Rudiak. Williams responded that Las Vegas was "a nonsouthern city with the pattern of the Deep South," and insisted that "there will always be discrimination and race trouble in Las Vegas if the ordinance is not put on the books." Commissioner Reed Whipple countered that if the city passed such an ordinance with so many southern businessmen now in town, "bloodshed and trouble" would ensue. Whipple's view prevailed, and the measure was defeated. But Las Vegas paid a high price in the long run. Racial violence, a dreaded curse for any resort city trying to lure tourists and vacationers, plagued Las Vegas until the late 1960s.

To a large extent, the Baker administration's solution to black demands to be admitted to casinos was to license the Moulin Rouge at the edge of Westside. Like the Showboat on the Boulder Highway, this was a rare suburban casino. In the first decade after the 1931 relegalization of full-fledged casino gambling, city commissioners limited the industry by ordinance to the areas along Fremont Street from First to Third, only later expanding to Fifth Street and beyond. A smattering of clubs also dotted the Boulder and Los Angeles Highways in the county's jurisdiction. For the most part, however, city officials were careful to keep large casinos out of the suburbs.

But the 1954 decision to approve a large new gaming property in the black Westside, though welcomed by many in that community, angered a small group of white residents on Bonanza Road who objected to any casino-hotel, much less an integrated one, in their neighborhood. They wanted such resorts confined to downtown or the Strip, but their protests were in vain. In a sense, the Moulin Rouge was the first large hotel-casino built in populated suburbs. This factor alone, aside from its integration policy, was enough to stir local controversy. The Moulin Rouge opened in May 1955, and catered to a mixed clientele. For six months the hotel was a popular late-night hangout not only for Westsiders, but also for Strip entertainers and some white tourists and residents. But the place lasted less than a year. Casino losses and poor management were the chief culprits. Local black residents sensed a conspiracy and even organized protests. Even today, some longtime residents blame Strip resorts, fearful of losing business to the upstart Moulin Rouge, for pressuring creditors to force the latter's demise.

The Moulin Rouge tower and hotel in 1956, a year after it opened. The building burned in 2003, but investors plan to rebuild and revitalize it. Special Collections, UNLV Libraries

But this was not the case. There was no nightly mass exodus from the Strip to Westside. The Moulin Rouge closed because Max Schwartz and his associates mismanaged money and most likely allowed profits to be skimmed or otherwise diverted, wittingly or unwittingly, out of the business. Whatever the cause, months after the Moulin Rouge's closure, Schwartz still owed money to the contractors who built the place, as numerous unresolved mechanics liens against the property show. In 1957, another white operator, Leo Fry and his LeRoy Corporation, reopened the Moulin Rouge, but Fry antagonized the community with discriminatory policies that eventually provoked a confrontation with the city in the early 1960s. There were other efforts to open black casinos in the area. In 1955, construction began on the Mardi Gras Casino on D and Owens, but it never opened. The city also granted a license to the smaller Town Tavern, which operated for many years.

Aside from civil rights controversies and growth-related problems, Mayor Baker also struggled with a series of weak city managers. Despite the mayor's undisputed honesty, his determination to be fully in charge created problems. Not the least of these was the embarrassing turnover rate in the city manager's office. In 1954, Baker defended the reform, but had to explain to the press why no one lasted long in the office. While he conceded that there had been four city managers in just the last year, he explained that "Chet Shelley and Raymond Carey could or would not carry out the policies of the board" of commissioners. Unlike Cragin, Baker promised that the city would begin to search for out-of-state talent as well.

While several capable men served in the position over the next decade, the municipality continued to hire managers who lacked the vision that a fast-growing city required. And despite Baker's reassurances, instability continued to plague the office. In 1965, respected newspaper reporter Jude Wanniski wrote a series of columns exposing the often fickle criteria mayors and city commissioners used to fill the office. Wanniski's series raised public concern about when Las Vegas leaders would finally choose a visionary like North Las Vegas's Clay Lynch or someone from a larger city.

Not only did mayors and the city commissioners have to deal with criticism from the *Las Vegas Review-Journal,* but the *Las Vegas Sun* also played a vigilant role. Herman "Hank" Greenspun, a New York attorney, came to Las Vegas in the mid-1940s. He worked in a variety of jobs, including a brief stint as Bugsy Siegel's publicity man. But Greenspun's decision to go into the newspaper business changed his life. Greenspun bought what became the *Las Vegas Sun* in 1950, and quickly transformed the typographer's union sheet into a worthy successor to Pop Squires's *Age* and a needed antidote to the *Review-Journal*'s pro-McCarran, Democratic Party bias. During his first few years as editor, Greenspun exposed a number of politically corrupt local officials. The editor also supported Russell and the state tax commission against a coalition of mob and nonmob gamers trying to weaken the state's regulatory powers and return Democrat Vail Pittman to the governor's mansion.

Greenspun, however, was at his best in challenging controversial Wisconsin senator Joe McCarthy in 1952. At the height of McCarthy's power, few in the national or local media had the courage to criticize "Tail Gunner Joe." But Greenspun was an exception. He believed that McCarthy was a fraud and that he and his ally, Pat McCarran, were both anti-Semites. Despite their local popularity, Greenspun took them on. In a series of daring columns about McCarthy, the editor questioned not only the senator's integrity, but his sexuality, too, calling him "the queer that made Milwaukee famous."

In October 1952, McCarthy made his only appearance in Las Vegas at a rally at the War Memorial Building to endorse Republican George "Molly" Malone for reelection to the U.S. Senate. Greenspun, who supported political newcomer Thomas Mechling, was in the audience when McCarthy characterized the editor as an "admitted communist" and "publisher of the 'Las Vegas Daily Worker.'" Greenspun immediately challenged McCarthy to a debate, but the latter abruptly headed out the door with Malone. The next day in his "Where I Stand" column, Greenspun charged that McCarthy was "afraid to debate openly." "He knows the truth will find him out," Greenspun thundered, "and show him to be the lying scoundrel history will prove him."

In the long run, history vindicated Greenspun's view, but, in the short run, a McCarran-inspired advertising boycott of the *Sun* by downtown and Strip casinos almost bankrupted the newspaper. Joining the fray was *Review-Journal* editor Al Cahlan (whose newspaper stood to gain from any hotel advertising boycott of the *Sun*), who launched a spirited attack against Greenspun. Cahlan not only raised questions about Greenspun's credibility, but also attributed the "notorious" editor's denial of admission to the New York Bar to "irregularities" on his bar exam. Cahlan also told readers of Greenspun's stint as Bugsy Siegel's publicity man, his violation of the Neutrality Act for running guns to Israel, and his registration with Las Vegas police as an ex-felon. Greenspun focused his efforts on attacking the boycott, firing back with lawsuits against a McCarran aide and all of the offending hotels. Several months later, the boycott dissipated due to a federal court settlement that proved Greenspun was here to stay. And so was the contentious relationship between the *Review-Journal* and the *Sun*.

Greenspun, however, did not just challenge state and federal leaders. Throughout his career, he kept a watchful eye on city hall. Two generations of city commissioners felt the sting of his invective when their actions struck the editor as incompetent or corrupt. City hall watched, for instance, when Greenspun leveled his guns at city commissioner William Peccole in 1953, accusing him of "trafficking in liquor and gambling licenses." Peccole, a respected businessman, angrily denied the charges. But Greenspun's pressure did little to help Peccole's political aspirations. Tired of the unproved accusations, Peccole eventually decided not to run for reelection.

While Greenspun, for the most part, supported C. D. Baker, the mayor recognized that as Las Vegas had grown, and as his office had become powerful, so too had the media scrutiny. It was not just the *Sun* but also the *Review-Journal* that weighed his every action. After all, Baker had defeated Cragin, Cahlan's friend and fellow McCarran supporter, and this did little to endear him to the longtime editor. Besides, for the past three decades, controversy had constantly surrounded the mayor's office, and antitax watchdogs and other members of the public were as vigilant as ever. It was no wonder then that Baker, exhausted from the pressure, decided in 1959 not to run for a third term.

In the wake of this decision, furniture and appliance dealer Oran Gragson, who had come to Las Vegas to work on the dam, challenged Wendell Bunker, a longtime local politician, for the mayoral post. In the heated campaign that followed, Bunker charged Gragson with being a casino-backed candidate covertly "seeking to introduce women dealers into the casinos along Fremont Street." Several club owners publicly denounced this charge and countered that Gragson was the best candidate for the city because he was a successful businessman who, unlike Bunker, was politically independent. In the end, Gragson prevailed, just as he would three times more. For the next sixteen years, Gragson would lead the city through some of its most tumultuous rounds of growth, including casino expansion, more civil rights controversies, and even greater urbanization.

Clearly, the political leadership at city hall improved markedly in the 1950s. Baker brought a degree of integrity and engineering expertise that his predecessors had lacked, and Gragson proved an able successor. The new jetport, freeway, and convention center contributed much to advance the Las Vegas area's accessibility and room occupancy. But, for the most part, these projects benefited the Strip more than the city as the century wore on. Baker, like Cragin, failed to annex the Strip. And while Baker immeasurably enhanced the city's infrastructure, property values, and building space with the public works he undertook, Las Vegas's inability to annex its growing southern suburbs proved troublesome.

Clark County commissioners, their position strengthened by the creation of Paradise and Winchester Townships, now sought to prevent Las Vegas, North Las Vegas, and the new 1953 city of Henderson from grabbing too much valuable land as the valley began growing into a true metropolis. Keeping the new jetport and convention center in the county proved to be lucrative victories. Once the lone city in the valley, Las Vegas by the 1950s began to suffer from the political fragmentation and suburban independence that plagued San Francisco, Los Angeles, St. Louis, and other great cities. Las Vegas was growing significantly—but so were its growing pains.

GROWTH AND COMMUNITY CONFLICT, 1960s

AFTER MANY DECADES OF MODERATE GROWTH interspersed with boom and bust, Nevada expanded rapidly in the years after 1940. The state's 71 percent population increase in the 1950s was followed by a 78 percent figure in the 1960s, and the Las Vegas area fueled much of that boom.

Tourism keyed the valley's urbanization in the 1960s, as it had earlier. In addition, defense spending grew even more than it had during the Korean War, once the U.S. commitment in Vietnam intensified after 1964. This partly resulted from the major role played by air force pilots in both conflicts. By 1967, Nellis Air Force Base had become only the third "tactical training center" in the world, boosting its force of fifty-two hundred to more than eight thousand during the decade. Estimates put the payroll at fifty-six million dollars, with the new F-III fighter jets injecting at least another twenty million dollars into the metropolitan economy. Moreover, Senator Howard Cannon (D-NV), of the Senate Armed Services Committee, announced plans to modernize old World War II housing and construct new dormitories at the base.

The expansion of Nellis promoted the urbanization of North Las Vegas. But Las Vegas also grew. This was especially true in its western suburbs, a response less to Nellis than to the increased activity at the Test Site and more directly to downtown's booming casinos. In 1961, the city experienced "exploding residential developments on the western side," as single-family homes and apartment complexes sprang up around Bonanza and Rancho, Vegas Drive, Decatur, and other locations.

But the real growth was southward, beyond Charleston and even Sahara into the emerging Strip suburbs. In the 1960s, Maryland Parkway slowly became a major commercial artery paralleling the Strip and catering to its employees. The suburbanization and decentralization of Las Vegas's retail sector threatened the traditional dominance of city stores. As one columnist noted, "[D]owntown . . . businesses are fighting to hold on in the face of a mushrooming of shopping complexes in outlying areas." Indeed, as construction began on Paradise Development's Boulevard Mall on Maryland Parkway (led by Moe Dalitz, Merv Adelson, and Irwin Molasky), the same writer reported that "competition, always keen, had become increasingly fierce." The center opened in 1967.

The success of Paradise Development, and especially Irwin Molasky, illustrates the tremendous business opportunities that Las Vegas offered in the 1950s and 1960s. The son of an Ohio businessman, Molasky came to Las Vegas in 1951 and quickly joined forces with Merv Adelson, who owned the twenty-four-hour Market Town grocery on Las Vegas Boulevard and Oakey. Together, they owned the Colonial House, a 1950s bistro on the Strip. They also formed the Paradise Development Company, which, over the course of the next four decades, developed the first major commercial artery in the Strip suburbs, Maryland Parkway. The construction of Sears and the Boulevard Mall was followed by a series of large and small shopping centers, including Sunrise City, Commercial Center, Mission Center, Best of the Boulevard, and other retail venues.

In the 1950s, Molasky teamed with other investors, including Adelson and his father, Nathan, Dalitz, and Allard Roen, to build Sunrise Hospital. This project demonstrates how nonmob businessmen and former mob associates could work together for the community's welfare. Dalitz, who had known Jimmy Hoffa since 1949, was able to convince the union leader to loan the developers one million dollars from the Teamsters' pension fund for the project. Sunrise Hospital, built with this money along with other financing, and the old Clark County Hospital (renamed Southern Nevada Memorial Hospital in 1951 and again renamed University Medical Center in 1986) have been the two largest medical centers serving the metropolitan area. With Merv Adelson as president, Sunrise Hospital opened in 1958 and, in its early years, catered heavily to Culinary Union and Teamster health plan members. Paradise Development also built the professional buildings that today surround the hospital and house many of its doctors' offices.

While Molasky, with the support of Merv Adelson and others, made millions in Las Vegas real estate, he contributed mightily to the community's health care services. Aside from Sunrise Hospital and his numerous personal donations for modern equipment at that center, Molasky was instrumental in building the Nathan Adelson Hospice, named for his associate's father, who died of cancer. "We heard of a program in England, at a place called St. Christopher's where they taught people who are dying how to live their last years in dignity," Molasky remembered. "So, the university gave us a lease for a dollar a year to build this kind of facility here." For the past quarter century, Nathan Adelson Hospice has accepted patients, regardless of their ability to pay, and the facility's home care service has helped thousands more Las Vegans cope with the stress of terminal illness.

Molasky's financial contributions to Las Vegas, such as the hospice, Sunrise Hospital, the Boulevard Mall, and a larger campus for UNLV, resulted from his early success in developing the lands south of Las Vegas in the Strip suburbs. While he developed some projects in the city, like Valley Bank (today the Bank of America) Plaza downtown, he kept returning to the suburbs, where in the twenty-first century he built luxury high-rise apartments in the Howard Hughes Center. In this respect, Molasky, like many of his counterparts in 1950s local development, recognized that the building trend in Las Vegas was southward—and he did what he could to reinforce the trend.

Much to the city's dismay, the Las Vegas Strip acted like a magnet for population after 1950. The Strip's burgeoning development caused the metropolitan area's growth southward, just as defense spending spurred growth northward. Still, Fremont Street welcomed important new hotel-casinos of its own in the 1960s. The 1962 debut of the high-rise Mint Hotel above its 1950s namesake casino was a major addition, as was the Four Queens. Opening in 1966, just a few months before Caesars Palace, the Four Queens was the eight million–dollar brainchild of former Riviera executive Ben Goffstein. The new hotel, named for his wife and three daughters, anchored the southeast corner of Fremont and Second (later Casino Center Boulevard) Streets, which, with the Horseshoe, Fremont, and Golden Nugget already facing one another, was fast becoming the major intersection of the downtown's casino core. But despite its new resorts, downtown was slowly losing its battle for customers with the Strip.

It was not so much the number of new resorts built on or near Las Vegas Boulevard South in the sixties, but their size and quality. Jay Sarno,

In 1965, the "four corners"—the Strip and Flamingo—looked vastly different than it does today. Caesars Palace and the MGM Grand (today's Bally's) were not yet built. The Dunes and its country club have given way to the Bellagio, the Flamingo has added towers, and Michael Gaughan built the Barbary Coast on the street corner. Looking north, the Landmark is still under construction. Nevada State Museum and Historical Society

a builder, designer, and operator of the Cabana Motel chain, longed to build a sumptuous resort. He chose the Strip, with its still relatively cheap land compared to California resort areas, as the place for his Greco-Roman gambling palace. Sarno leased the land from Kirk Kerkorian (who later owned the Flamingo across the street). Using Melvin Grossman (whose firm designed the impressive Acapulco Princess Hotel) as his architect, he built Caesars Palace. Caesars represented a marked departure from all the other properties in the valley, including the Fabulous Flamingo and Tropicana Hotels. Sarno spared no expense in lavishing his resort with tons of imported marble, Romanesque fountains, statuary, Roman friezes, and other antiquities. With its elegant gardens and pricey gourmet rooms, Caesars was a step above places like the Desert Inn and Hacienda. Its fourteen-story tower of elegantly appointed rooms and the low-rise wings around the pool made Caesars the first major resort in the valley. While not a destination resort in the true sense of the term, it was a "must-see," and clearly helped to draw curious tourists to town.

Kirk Kerkorian, who eventually sold the site to Caesars, imitated Sarno and built the International in 1969 just north of the convention center on Paradise Road. With 1,568 elegant rooms, the International was the world's largest resort and briefly the state's tallest building. Its numerous restaurants, featuring Chinese, Japanese, Italian, Mexican, German, and other cuisines, set a precedent for today's megaresorts. However, with Nevada's corporate gaming law in 1969, Kerkorian sold the International and the Flamingo to Hilton and used these profits to build a still grander resort that set a new standard for size and elegance in the Las Vegas Valley, the first MGM Grand (today's Bally's).

While residents across the valley took pride in the exciting new resorts that Sarno and Kerkorian planted on the Strip, Caesars, the International, and even Howard Hughes's Landmark Hotel (today the parking lot west of the convention center's pedestrian bridge) were bad news for the city. For the hotels and casinos on Glitter Gulch, these towering new resorts were impressive monuments to the county's growing dominance of the local tourist industry.

To be sure, downtown also claimed its share of talented casino operators. Benny Binion, Sam Boyd, and Jackie Gaughan were three of the major operators downtown in the years after 1950. Binion, a former Texas bootlegger and gambler, came to Las Vegas in 1946 as part-owner (with

In the 1960s, Jay Sarno's Caesars Palace featured unique statuary. Victor Borge's brilliant piano playing and phonetic punctuation drew crowds to the showroom. In the lounge, Tony Sandler and Ralph Young were Las Vegas mainstays. Special Collections, UNLV Libraries

J. Kell Houssels Sr.) of the Las Vegas Club. In 1951, he opened his own place, the Horseshoe, although he lost his gaming license a few years later when he was convicted of income tax evasion and sent to the Leavenworth federal penitentiary for more than three years. After Binion returned, he and his sons regained control of the Horseshoe, although he never got his gaming license back. The innovative Binion filled the casino nightly by giving gamblers what they wanted: higher house limits on table games than elsewhere, $3.95 premium steak dinners (supported by meat from his Montana ranch), and prestigious events like the annual World Series of Poker. Until his death in 1989, Binion refused to build a hotel above his casino or even consider selling to corporate interests. His sons insisted on purchasing Del Webb's Mint Hotel next door and breaking through the walls to double the size of the Horseshoe's casino. Not until 2003 did his daughter, who forced out his sons, even begin negotiations to sell the property. But it was not in time: federal agents closed the place in

For proof of how the Las Vegas Valley has developed, consider how lonely the now-departed Landmark Hotel and Convention Center rotunda look. Nevada State Museum and Historical Society

In 1968, the land east and west of the Strip was barely occupied. Nevada State Museum and Historical Society

January 2004 for nonpayment of almost $2 million to union pension funds and taxes. The Horseshoe reopened in April after a complicated deal in which the new owner, MTR, allowed gaming giant Harrah's, which had earlier purchased the Horseshoe's out-of-state casinos, to retain rights to the brand name and the famous World Series of Poker, in addition to managing the casino for two years.

Sam Boyd came to Las Vegas in 1941. Formerly a dealer on cruise ships and in Hawaii, Boyd dealt roulette and other games before going off to war. He returned in 1946 and headed not downtown but to the Strip,

(*Right*) Kirk Kerkorian stands in front of the International, which he opened on Paradise Road in 1969. Special Collections, UNLV Libraries

(*Below*) Looking west, at the bottom is the Convention Center rotunda, and on the Strip is the Stardust. To the right, the Thunderbird Downs racetrack, built by Joe Smoot, is just behind the hotel. Next to it is the high-rise Riviera. Special Collections, UNLV Libraries

where he dealt cards at the El Rancho before moving to the Flamingo as a shift boss. Boyd's engaging personality and grasp of the business attracted the attention of managers like Charles Resnik, who recommended Boyd for increasingly important positions. Boyd served as a floor man, pit boss, and shift boss, and in other capacities at several Strip resorts before purchasing a 1 percent share of the Sahara, where he worked as a shift boss

Downtown in the 1960s. Next to the Mint was Binion's Horseshoe, which took over the property in the 1990s. Much more than today, downtown boasted entertainment (singer Joni James, singer-songwriter Brook Benton, and comedian Buddy Lester at the Fremont, with Judy Lynn reflecting the Golden Nugget's emphasis on country music). The Four Queens is under construction. Special Collections, UNLV Libraries

When the Mint opened an addition to the hotel-casino, Las Vegans celebrated with a giant cake. Wielding the knife was Mayor Oran Gragson, for whom part of U.S. 95 is named. To his left, in the cowboy hat, was the Mint's general manager, Sam Boyd, who had come there from the Sahara and would later build several other hotel-casinos in southern Nevada. Special Collections, UNLV Libraries

in the 1950s. When the Sahara Nevada Corporation, headed by Milton Prell and his associates, opened the Mint Casino on Fremont Street in the mid-1950s, they sent Boyd there to serve as vice president and general manager.

But unlike Binion, Boyd had worked on the Strip and recognized that the suburbanization of gambling held untold profits. In 1962, Boyd and his son Bill, who practiced law for fifteen years, built the Eldorado Club in the growing city of Henderson, far from the Strip and Fremont Street. Boyd left the Mint after Del Webb bought it and, with several investors, built the Union Plaza Hotel at the head of Fremont Street on the site of Senator Clark's old railroad depot. Ever the innovator, Boyd hired women dealers. While women dealers were relatively common in Reno, they were few and far between in southern Nevada, except during the labor shortages of World War II. Boyd's action represented a major breakthrough for women in the profession, because in 1958 male dealers had convinced city commissioners in Las Vegas to pass an ordinance banning the few women dealers working in town.

The Boyds further reinforced downtown's vitality by opening the California Hotel on North Main and First Streets in 1975. This resort, catering primarily to a Hawaiian clientele, created a new northern extension for the downtown's casino core. Four years later, as the metropolitan area exploded outward, Boyd exploited the east-side suburban market (just three years after the Palace Station exploited the west valley market) with Sam's Town on Boulder Highway. In the early 1980s, the Boyd company gave a boost to border-town gambling by building another Sam's Town in Laughlin to grab a share of the Arizona market, whose profitability the elder Boyd had come to appreciate from his earlier association with Del Webb's organization at the Sahara and Mint. But like Kell Houssels, who eventually owned a large share of the Tropicana, Boyd knew no borders between the city and county. In the 1980s, Boyd's company bought the Stardust on the Strip to go along with its properties downtown, in the suburbs, and on the Arizona border.

The third major figure downtown in the postwar years, Jackie Gaughan, had come to Las Vegas frequently while assigned to the gunnery school during World War II. The son of a bookmaker and nephew of a gambling hall operator, Gaughan learned the business early. Like the others, he began modestly before purchasing a small share of the Boulder Club, where he learned the art of casino management in the 1950s, and later invested in the Showboat. In 1963, Gaughan bought the El Cortez from Houssels and kept it profitable with cheap food, penny slots, and promotions that appealed to low-end gamblers. Over the decades, he acquired full or controlling interests in the Union Plaza, Western, Gold Spike, and other downtown clubs, most of which he sold in 2003 at the age of eighty-two. In the 1970s, he helped his son Michael launch the Coast hotel chain by purchasing the future site of the Barbary Coast from right under Baron Hilton's nose.

Binion, Gaughan, and other operators certainly strengthened the downtown casino core after 1950. But by the mid-1960s, despite these efforts, the city could no longer match the county in resort development or gross casino winnings. Nevertheless, the city continued to grow, both with new construction inside its borders and by annexation of adjacent subdivisions. While the creation of Winchester and Paradise Townships in the early 1950s blocked the city from annexing the county's Strip suburbs, there were few obstacles to expanding east or west. Las Vegas annexed lands, but the process was not haphazard.

Under Mayor Gragson's able leadership, the city expanded its borders in an orderly manner. For example, in 1964, when Las Vegas began its

A gathering of elites. *From left to right:* Moe Dalitz, builder of several hotels, housing developments, country clubs, and shopping centers; Elvis Presley; dancer Juliet Prowse; Wilbur and Toni Clark of the Desert Inn, with Cecil Simmons, a Desert Inn shareholder; and Joe Franks in back. Special Collections, UNLV Libraries

effort to annex Vegas Heights on the northwest edge of town, city planning director Don Saylor first identified the key problems in this sixteen-acre parcel of mostly ramshackle homes and trailers. Undeveloped streets, overloaded septic tanks, and bare electrical wires headed the list. Saylor responded by drafting a development plan, forming an assessment district to help fund improvements, and using his staff to bring the neighborhood's housing up to code. In contrast to the aggressive annexation policies of North Las Vegas, Las Vegas's approach to growth in the early 1960s was, for the most part, reasonable and well planned. Indeed, thanks to Saylor's efforts, the eighteen hundred residents of Vegas Heights benefited greatly from joining Las Vegas.

Of course, Clark County and North Las Vegas hardly stood by quietly. Throughout the early 1960s, Las Vegas, North Las Vegas, Henderson, and Clark County struggled with each other to obtain once vacant lands that valuable subdivisions were filling. Sometimes the struggle was over an existing development, while at other times it was an effort to leapfrog semi-vacant land to be positioned to snatch more valuable land ripe for potential growth.

In 1962, the city and county competition came to a head. Both Las Vegas and Clark County objected to North Las Vegas's effort to annex twelve square miles of a mostly barren floodplain to extend its boundaries eastward over to Sunrise Manor, a location below Sunrise Mountain that obviously would develop into a medium- to upper-income suburb someday. North Las Vegas city manager Clay Lynch used the approval of 58 percent of affected residents, most of whom lived in the area's extreme western portions near the current North Las Vegas boundary, to justify his action. Lynch wanted all of this sparsely populated ranchette land so that he could extend his city's sewer lines to the edge of Sunrise Manor. Lynch knew that once that area began to develop, home owners would rather hook up to the North Las Vegas sewer system than rely on cesspools and septic tanks. The sewers would automatically raise property values and allow North Las Vegas to grab a valuable new tax base. Clark County commissioners, shocked by the annexation of a largely barren desert that suddenly tripled the size of North Las Vegas, responded with a lawsuit to stop Lynch. The commissioners then planned to establish the unincorporated township of Thunderbird Field and connect it to county sewer lines.

This was the problem that Las Vegas faced on its southern and eastern fronts. Clark County had already blocked annexation of the Strip and its increasingly valuable suburbs by creating the unincorporated towns of Paradise and Winchester. Now, ten years later, both North Las Vegas (which Las Vegas could have easily annexed in the 1930s) and Clark County were trying to block growth to the east. With North Las Vegas also blocking Las Vegas to the northeast, something had to be done. Neither North Las Vegas nor the county had consulted with Las Vegas on this matter, so Las Vegas announced its intention of taking about one-third of the area that Lynch and the county commissioners wanted. In the end, the county did not create Thunderbird Field, nor did North Las Vegas acquire Sunrise Manor. But Las Vegas also found its expansion restricted in the zone. Having waited for too long to expand southward, Las Vegas's only remaining growth corridors were northwest up the Tonopah Highway and due west. It would exploit these options in the 1960s and even more so after 1970.

Into the 1970s, Las Vegas still tried to exert some control over the Strip suburbs. The new ploy mixed annexation and consolidation in the name of good government. The construction of such major resorts as Caesars Palace, the International, and the impending arrival of the first MGM Grand only heightened the city's fervor to at least capture some of the revenues of its wealthy progeny. Beginning in the late 1960s, one of Las Vegas's representatives on the county commission (and future Las Vegas mayor), Bill Briare, proposed a reform that would have brought the city and Strip together.

As a county commissioner, Briare fought for eight years to consolidate government services and even formed the League of Elected City and County Officials as a vehicle to do it. He devised a consolidation plan and sent it to the Clark County delegation in the state legislature for consideration. The goal, Briare claimed, was not annexation but efficiency. Specifically, he wanted to join the unincorporated Strip townships of Paradise and Winchester to Las Vegas. As Briare argued, "[T]here is no justifiable reason to continue to deny citizens of Las Vegas the tremendous additional tax revenue which would come with the annexation as well as the reduced costs and increased efficiency of public services which would come with consolidation." He also reasoned, somewhat tongue in cheek, that it was "unfair" for township residents to pay a half-cent sales tax, which, under current law, went only to the cities.

Briare's grander dream was to consolidate Las Vegas, North Las Vegas, Henderson, and the county into one government, much like the mergers of Indianapolis, Nashville, and Jacksonville with their county suburbs. He then secured funding to hire a prominent Chicago consulting firm, which, after months of study, prepared a report supporting the measure. In the end, this idea, too, failed for lack of support in the county. The merger of the Las Vegas Police Department and the county sheriff's office into Metro in 1973 was the only major fruit this effort bore. Even then, North Las Vegas and Henderson refused to give up their police departments, and much to Briare's chagrin no one agreed to consolidate fire departments, even though it would have made sense from the perspective of insurance companies.

Briare's idea never died. In 2003, Mayor Oscar Goodman once again suggested a valleywide consolidation of city and county governments to save money and streamline overlapping bureaucracies. One need only look at New York City, larger in size than the built-up portions of the Las Vegas metropolitan area with six times the population, where everyone has the same police and fire departments and most other municipal services. But the Las Vegas Valley is politically fragmented, even more than the Phoenix, Albuquerque, and El Paso metropolitan areas, and far more than San Antonio's, where the city annexed most of its suburbs.

Historically, valley residents have resisted consolidation for a variety of reasons. Money has always been an issue. Thomas Hull, William Moore, Cliff Jones, and the other early Strip operators wanted to avoid paying higher city taxes. For the same reason, the Basic Magnesium factory never joined Henderson, the city it created. To this day, it remains a county island surrounded by a city. Over the past sixty years, generation after generation of county commissioners played the same game that county leaders played in the Los Angeles Basin and all across suburban America, catering to anti–central city prejudices and emphasizing the tax savings by not joining cities. Indeed, the Strip suburbs today still pay considerably lower property taxes than those in Las Vegas, because the Strip hotels, with the millions they contribute annually in taxes to county coffers, in effect subsidize all property owners in the county. The creation of special service districts in the valley to provide schools, water, flood control, and libraries has eliminated the need to do what Roxbury, Brooklyn, and other suburban cities had to do in earlier centuries: join Boston, New York, or some other central city to get access to their water systems and their school construction funds.

More of a local reason also explains why the dream of consolidation may never come true: parochialism. While Las Vegas could have annexed Valle Verde (North Las Vegas) anytime in the thirty years after rancher Thomas Williams laid out this subdivision in 1917, Las Vegas had little chance to obtain the Strip, much less Henderson or Boulder City. Rather than growing slowly outward from a central core like many cities do, Las Vegas experienced a different fate. The federal government altered the process in 1931 and again in 1941 by suddenly creating substantial urban centers at Boulder City and Henderson. These places were simply too far away for Las Vegas to annex. Besides, Boulder City was a federal reservation that did not join the State of Nevada until 1960. Furthermore, in the 1930s and 1940s, Las Vegas lacked the revenue to govern these places anyway.

So residents of Boulder City, Henderson, and North Las Vegas, like those in the county, grew accustomed to ruling themselves and became fiercely independent over the years. They virtually prided themselves in not being part of Las Vegas. They ignored the creation of Metro in 1973, fearing they would be taxed to put more cops on the Strip and downtown Las Vegas instead of in their cities. For the same reason, they never embraced a valleywide fire department, fearing a lack of stations, equipment, and manpower. The same has been true of city planning. While one comprehensive plan for the region (as New York and other cities have) would make sense, five plans were created. Each government drew up a plan (they are periodically revised) for growth independent of each other: Las Vegas in 1959, Boulder City in 1964, North Las Vegas in 1965, Clark County in 1966, and Henderson in 1968. When cooperation is absolutely required, as with flood control or highway planning, a regional commission serves the purpose. However, in the case of valleywide social issues such as poverty or homelessness, the suburbs, like their counterparts across the county, have been content to leave the responsibility to the central city that helped create them and encouraged their growth—the same central city they have proudly never joined.

Despite all of their political differences, leaders from all four cities and the county worked together for the valley's modern jetport. Discussions about it in the 1950s turned into action in the 1960s. With the development of the commercial jetliner, a major opportunity that no city could afford to ignore, residents had no choice but to close ranks behind this project. The first test flight of the Boeing 707 over the skies of Renton, Washington, in 1957 meant that southern Nevadans had to act fast if they wanted to attract more visitors in the 1960s.

In August 1960, United Airlines began advertising its new, faster service to McCarran Airport. "Now for the first time, jet service to Las Vegas," the headline blared. The flight schedule printed below told the real story. Beginning on September 5, Chicago tourists could fly to Las Vegas in three hours, roughly half the time of a propeller-driven plane. Everyone knew that faster and safer jets could eventually bring millions more visitors to Las Vegas. But jets would require more space, gates, and baggage facilities that only a large airport could provide. Building a new facility would cost millions, but city, county, and business leaders agreed that the expense was worth it. Their only problem was convincing voters to approve a new airport just twelve years after building the existing one south of the Strip. Another bond election would be a hard sell, especially in a state noted for low taxes. But Las Vegas needed the jet plane. The increased tourism would benefit the resort industry, which in turn meant an expanded tax base and more jobs for the community. So, with the support of political leaders, the Chamber of Commerce, and both city newspapers, county commissioners scheduled the bond election for March 8, 1960.

Just a few weeks before the special election, promoters and government officials still worried that voters would turn down a new airport, especially since a six million–dollar school bond issue had barely passed the previous November. Furthermore, conservatives like popular radio personality Joe Julian openly rallied the city's perennial antitax faction once led by John Russell and Charles Pipkin. The business community worked overtime to counter this influence. On March 3, five days before the bond election, the Las Vegas Chamber of Commerce executive board endorsed the new airport by a twelve-to-one margin in an effort to give the campaign momentum. Members were no doubt pleased on election night that, with only 12 percent of eligible voters turning out, the bond issue passed by a two-to-one majority. County commissioners then rushed to build the facility. Construction took less than three years, and, from the day it opened in 1963, the new McCarran (later "International") Airport delivered more tourists to Las Vegas than ever before.

While Las Vegas's jetport opened ahead of schedule in 1963, the new freeway crept toward downtown for the rest of the decade. This was a problem for the city: Fremont Street's casinos relied heavily on cars and buses to deliver tourists from southern California. Although Interstate 15 raced across the desert lands between the California line and Sloan, its progress slowed remarkably as it approached the metropolitan area's outskirts. Disputes between federal and state public works officials were a major reason. In 1960, Governor Grant Sawyer met with Ellis Armstrong, the U.S. commissioner of public roads, after the latter rejected three proposed interchanges for I-15 at Spring Mountain and Flamingo Roads near the Strip and at Gass and Alta streets in the city due to high costs. In the end, the Strip was again the big winner, capturing more freeway on- and off-ramps than the city.

Six years later, downtown faced an even worse problem. All of the Strip interchanges were open, but the freeway was still years away from giving cars direct access to Glitter Gulch. By April 1966, Interstate 15 ran to Sahara Avenue, and the state's Department of Highways began condemnation proceedings for the lands along the route between West Charleston and Bonanza for the downtown interchange. But trouble loomed with the Union Pacific, which wanted nine million dollars for its lands, seven million dollars more than the state had budgeted for the acquisition. By late 1967, Interstate 15 had reached West Charleston. Here it ended, while conflicts over planning, funding, and rights-of-way delayed construction through downtown for another four years.

Like the freeway, street improvements also posed a challenge. Las Vegas's unabated growth in the 1960s forced the city to remain proactive with its public works programs. This was especially true of road building, which included the construction of new arteries and the widening of older ones to maintain traffic flow between downtown and the ever retreating suburbs. While the city completed many of the projects on schedule, some roads experienced the same type of delays that plagued freeway construction. For example, as Las Vegas's western suburbs grew, municipal officials scrambled to widen the two-lane Bonanza Underpass originally built under the Union Pacific tracks in the 1930s. But the state highway department and federal engineers balked at the plan, asserting that the new Interstate 15 downtown interchange would provide enough relief, a position rejected by the city.

Fortunately, federal officials were more enthusiastic about widening the road to Mercury, making it easier for Test Site personnel to live in Las Vegas and commute to work. In 1962, U.S. Senator Alan Bible announced that the new atomic energy bill in Congress contained twenty-five million dollars to widen the fifty-eight-mile highway between Las Vegas and the Test Site at Mercury to four lanes. This improvement and President John Kennedy's expansion of the facility's workforce stretched Las Vegas to the northwest, as developers built new subdivisions near the highway to house employees and their families. In late 1965, federal contractors finally completed the widening project, allowing Test Site commuters to drive at speeds of seventy miles per hour, cutting the one-way trip to forty-five minutes. This allowed hundreds of scientists and engineers to live in Las Vegas and encouraged the construction of still more housing subdivisions in Las Vegas's western suburbs.

Part of the problem with expanding the city by extending suburban roads outward was that more floodplains had to be crossed. Smoothing out the desert with paved streets, sidewalks, and subdivisions only increased storm runoff and created more property for the water to destroy. But city leaders had trouble convincing voters to approve funding to fight this problem. Only residents directly affected by the rains seemed concerned. Within days of the airport bond election in March 1960, metropolitan leaders tried to rally support for flood-control projects with a promise from Senator Howard Cannon that the federal government would pay two-thirds of the cost. Voters were unimpressed. After approving school and airport bond issues, they rejected the flood-control measure and delayed building an effective system of detention basins until 1986, when they finally approved the creation of the Clark County Regional Flood Control District.

An even more serious problem was the periodic flooding of the road from Los Angeles. The need for the new interstate highway and jetport became even more obvious in September 1960 when storms closed Highway 91 for several days, putting a major dent in Labor Day tourism. Both city and county leaders looked to the approaching Interstate 15 for permanent relief from this flooding problem. For their part, federal engineers assured everyone that they built the new highway on a high-enough grade to protect traffic from washouts and lengthy traffic delays. Fortunately, flood downpours were relatively rare.

Voters were reluctant to approve flood-control bonds while inundated with other important projects in need of funding. Despite Las Vegas's expanded tax base from earlier population gains, mushrooming growth in the 1960s was very expensive. Faced with a need for more schools or more detention basins, voters chose the former and rejected flood-control bonds by a substantial majority. However, in that same election, after local newspapers warned that "defeat of the bonds would strike the area with a water shortage next summer and cripple new construction at the height of the Las Vegas population explosion," voters responded positively by sanctioning millions of dollars in bonds to build new water pipes and pumping stations by a margin of three to one. Then in 1961, city and county voters endorsed still another school bond issue. They had no choice: overcrowding had forced almost four thousand of the district's twenty-nine thousand students into half-day schedules.

The late 1960s brought no relief from the barrage of growth-related bond issues. Still more money was needed, because the city had yet to undertake all the public works projects necessary to maintain public health in the face of rapid urbanization. In 1969, engineering consultants advised Las Vegas to expand its sewage treatment plant, warning that if the county's facility continued to malfunction, Las Vegas could not handle the overflow.

But this was not the only project the municipality needed. In June 1969, city manager Art Trelease urged voters to authorize more bonds to build a new city hall. Trelease wanted to raze the old 1935 War Memorial Building to clear the site. He explained how, over the years, city departments had taken over the auditorium (once the Las Vegas Convention Center opened in 1959) as well as new wings. Even with trailers parked on adjoining land, the old building was bursting at the seams. Thirty-five years of growth had so expanded municipal services that a new city hall had become a necessity. Voters supported the measure, and work soon began on the modern-looking city hall that stands today at Las Vegas Boulevard and Stewart.

All of these projects strained municipal finances. As budget estimates for new construction and municipal services increased, the city tried to curb spending by holding down employee salaries despite Vietnam War–era inflation. In 1969, frustrated Las Vegas firemen actually took the city to court to get a promised forty-four dollars a month raise and retroactive pay. They won. However, as one columnist observed, while this court action as well as pay increases for police and other municipal workers "put a crimp in the city's treasury, . . . the dire pre-raise predictions of financial disaster were never realized." Instead, the city raised user fees and other levies to support the rapid extension of municipal services into old and new suburbs. In a typical move, Public Works director Dick Sauer implemented sweeping sewer- and water-rate increases in 1969. Residents howled in protest, but as one reporter noted, it was "an absolute must if the city [was] to stay ahead in the race to provide adequate sewer disposal service."

Increased water rates also drew complaints. However, the water district's board of directors had no choice. The vital prerequisite for continued growth in the valley was an adequate water supply. Without it, Las Vegas had no hope of developing into a major metropolitan area. The key was to build large-diameter mains to tap Lake Mead's vast capacity. The water district's purchase of Senator Clark's water system, the construction of a line to Basic Magnesium, and the building of new mains cost millions of dollars that users had to pay. In 1953, the railroad's old utility had charged a $2.70 monthly flat rate for a single-family home. A year later, the water district raised the rate to $6.50, and, in a controversial 1957 move, began putting meters in some homes in the valley. By December 1958, all commercial and residential customers were on meters. Despite the imposition of metered billing, water use still rose dramatically in the decade. In 1954–1955, Las Vegas's population used 13.3 million gallons daily. Four years later, the figure soared to 20 million, going as high as 34 million gallons alone for just one day in July.

Growth was again the culprit. Numerous forces drove the urbanization of Las Vegas, especially the Strip's rapid development. Indeed, many in the growing army of Strip workers still preferred living in the city, because, until the 1970s, the Strip suburbs lacked enough houses and apartments. These new residents needed stores, doctors, and other services, and before 1970, the city still had more of them. The job-multiplier effect of each new hotel and motel room, as well as the expansion of Nellis and its payroll and supply requisitions, also increased population and water use. Given the single water pipe to Basic Magnesium, it was no wonder that demand still exceeded supply. Only six years after completing the line to BMI, a crisis loomed. In 1961, the water district had to stop construction of an apartment complex on Sahara Avenue east of Paradise Road "until it [could] be determined if there will be sufficient water to support the project."

By 1961, 15,000 water users in the valley were almost double the number of 1954. State engineer Ed Muth angered city and county commissioners in 1961 when he ordered a halt to well drilling for new subdivisions. But the issue was clear. Las Vegas and the Strip needed more and larger mains to Lake Mead. Accusations flew back and forth over why some golf courses received water approvals while new housing did not. But something had to be done—and fast. In the 1950s, the water district had embarked upon an ambitious program of extending mains to every community in the city served by well water. But pipes were needed in all directions, as the Strip and Las Vegas both underwent furious suburban development. Only Lake Mead could supply these areas and the desert flats beyond. The valley's diminishing artesian wells could no longer handle the task.

This was a matter of concern. In 1960, although only 127,000 residents lived in the area, water district officials predicted a metropolitan population of 600,000 by the new millennium, with the city accounting for 250,000 of the total. Even this bold prediction proved to be less than half the valley's population by 2000. In 1960, no one's crystal ball could have projected 1.5 million residents by century's end, or how large the county suburbs, Henderson or North Las Vegas, would become.

In May 1963, Stanford University consultants warned Las Vegas leaders that by 1980, the valley's population would consume most of Nevada's share of Colorado River water. Some in town even suggested building desalination plants for some coastal California communities in return for their share of Lake Mead water. At the same time, the Desert Research Institute proposed a study of whether Las Vegas sewer effluent could be treated and used for drinking water.

The first step, however, was to build a water project capable of delivering all of Nevada's share of Lake Mead under the Colorado River Compact of 1922. This was the only way to obtain enough water to support a population of 2 million. To this end, Senator Alan Bible introduced legislation in 1965 to build the Southern Nevada Water Project "to fill the needs of a rapidly increasing population." After a year of debate, the loyalty of Nevada's two senators, Bible and Cannon, to Lyndon Johnson paid off when the president pressured Congress into approving the expensive project as part of his Great Society programs. Costing almost $600 million in federal loans and state bonds, the project, begun in 1966, delivered the first large-diameter water line from Lake Mead in June 1971. Workers finished the final phase in April 1982. The Las Vegas Valley now had a delivery system capable of providing the valley with Nevada's full share of Lake Mead water under the 1922 compact, enough water to supply a city of almost 2 million.

As in earlier decades, all of these public works projects, as well as other issues and controversies, revolved around politics. For the most part, the 1950s and 1960s were a stable period in city government. Under the able leadership of Oran Gragson, Las Vegas took forthright steps to accommodate the rapid growth it was experiencing. In reviewing Gragson's first-term accomplishments as mayor, the *Las Vegas Review-Journal,* now edited by Gragson's fellow Republican Bob Brown, credited him with paving, guttering, and curbing more streets than any previous time in the city's history. The newspaper also emphasized Gragson's $2 million improvement district, which "revitalized the downtown area by widening streets and easing traffic congestion" and resulted in the expansion and remodeling of "numerous downtown firms." Gragson also expanded municipal services, increasing police and fire personnel by more than 80 percent compared to a 40 percent population increase during the same period. Even more important, he presided over the drafting of the city's first comprehensive master plan. Finally, like his predecessor, C. D. Baker, Gragson fought the "creeping favoritism" in city government that had been a continuing problem during the Cragin administration.

Of course, Gragson was not the only one responsible for the strong leadership at city hall. He was fortunate to work with a talented group of commissioners in the early 1960s, led by Reed Whipple and Ed Fountain. Both were successful businessmen who understood that even in a tax-conscious city like Las Vegas, public works required large sums of money to meet growth-related needs. Fountain's 1967 campaign for reelection illustrates the pressures that he and other commissioners faced. The *Review-Journal* once again endorsed Fountain, who held office during the period when Las Vegas grew from a city of 30,000 to 130,000. Obviously, he had managed growth problems well. His support for street construction and improvements, land acquisitions for parks, more stringent liquor laws, and better health codes reinforced his image as a capable leader.

In 1967, however, Fountain faced a formidable threat in Wes Howery, a Strip executive. His election, the newspaper warned, would "open the door of city government to the influence of the Strip." At the time, Strip executives were still locked in a fierce battle with their downtown counterparts for business, and would have preferred that city development policies not become too aggressive or threatening. "As a strip executive," Howery "would serve as a vehicle for the expression of Strip desires in the city. The city commission is no place for the expression of such interests."

Noting that he had been "a steadying influence at City Hall for the past twenty years," the newspaper also endorsed Whipple for reelection. A respected bank executive, Whipple first took office in the late 1940s "when the city treasury was in such bad shape" that payrolls were funded by bank loans. As one editorial put it, "the city was living from hand to mouth and living in the shadow of Reno." No wonder the early Strip wanted no part of joining the city. Despite support from Gragson and many members of the business community, both Whipple and Fountain went down to defeat, as restless voters opted for new blood on the city commission. Whipple also lost because he voted to modernize streets connecting Las Vegas with the booming Strip suburbs to the south. Many affected property owners hated to see their narrow, countrylike residential lanes of the 1940s and 1950s widened to accommodate 1960s traffic. As Gragson noted in a reminiscence, "if there was any single cause for Reed's defeat [in 1967], it was the widening of Maryland Parkway and Eastern Avenue."

While good government was more the norm than the exception in the sixties, major problems remained. For one, the city police department continued to be saddled with a corrupt image, something it had struggled with, off and on, for decades. A department investigation in 1960 revealed what many residents already suspected: a small ring of policemen was burglarizing local businesses. Indeed, this corruption helped inspire Gragson to run in the first place. Even worse, some officers higher up the chain of command were covering it up. These revelations did little to reassure the community about the integrity and effectiveness of the city police. As the Clark County grand jury pursued its investigation, fired police officer Al Mazzura only intensified public suspicion by seeking immunity from arson and burglary charges in return for testifying against some of his fellow officers. After a series of new police commanders, the city department

When this photo of Reed Whipple was taken in 1980, he could look back on considerable success as a banker, city commissioner, and leader of the Mormon community. The city's cultural arts center on Las Vegas Boulevard North near Washington
bears his name. Special Collections, UNLV Libraries

was cleaned up. In the long run, however, these and other events gave
weight to those who supported the creation of the new Metropolitan
Police Department, merged with the county sheriff's force to provide the
valley with a more professional law enforcement agency.

Metro's creation in 1973 followed the violence and other protests that
resulted from the civil rights movement. These incidents greatly disturbed the business-as-usual atmosphere of Las Vegas in the 1960s. But
trouble had been brewing for decades within the community. The main
shortcoming of local and state government in the 1960s, as well as earlier
decades, was the failure to safeguard the civil rights of African American
and other minority residents and visitors. In Las Vegas, the first major bat-
tlefront was the campaign to open hotels and casinos to black patrons.

Ironically, early Las Vegas had been more integrated and racial discrimination had, for the most part, been minimal. True, the city's brothels and

the El Portal Theatre practiced segregation and only a smattering (fewer than sixty) of black workers could get jobs at Hoover Dam, but African Americans resided downtown, and black shops and businesses dotted the side streets. This changed in the early 1940s, as the growing number of white tourists expected a Jim Crow town. And they got it. In both the city and county, black residents and visitors soon discovered they were no longer welcome at any of the resorts on Fremont Street, the Strip, or the Boulder Highway. Even headliners like Nat King Cole and Lena Horne, who filled the showrooms at the El Rancho, Flamingo, and other venues, had to spend the night in Westside rooming houses. Into the 1950s, no African American could go to a hotel room, restaurant, casino, showroom, or even a pool—as black entertainer Dorothy Dandridge learned in 1953 when the Hotel Last Frontier drained the pool after she deliberately dipped her foot in it. Change came slowly. In 1955, the Sands agreed to allow Nat King Cole to become the first black entertainer to stay at the resort where he was headlining, but it was years before all of the resorts followed suit.

The Las Vegas civil rights movement certainly gained some impetus from the national movement, but there were local reasons for its success, too. By 1960, thanks to the growth of the resort industry and the thousands of low-paying service-sector jobs it created, the number of black Las Vegans had swelled to more than eleven thousand in the metropolitan area, more than enough of a base to support effective protests. Black leadership also grew with the addition of several new activists, especially Drs. James McMillan and Charles West. Of these, McMillan became the most prominent symbol of the movement in the early 1960s. Born in Mississippi and raised in a variety of northern cities, including New York, Philadelphia, and Detroit, McMillan graduated from dental school during World War II and served a stint in the army before setting up his practice in Detroit near his friend West. The latter married a showgirl, whose career kept her in the West. During one of his car trips to California, West stopped in Las Vegas, saw the opportunities for serving a growing black community, and moved to town in 1955. He soon convinced McMillan to come also.

When McMillan arrived, the civil rights movement was already well under way, spearheaded by a local NAACP chapter that had been active for years. David Hoggard, a truant officer and member of the police force;

Woodrow Wilson, a BMI worker and later Nevada's first black assemblyman; Lubertha Johnson, a nurse and president of the local NAACP in the mid-1950s; and others were already working to combat discrimination in the gaming industry. McMillan and Hoggard, whose wife, Mabel, was also an activist and one of the first African American teachers in the state, wrote to local companies like Highland Dairy urging them to hire blacks and organized boycotts of resorts like the Sands. Because Al Cahlan rarely covered these protests in the *Las Vegas Review-Journal,* McMillan and Hoggard started a black newspaper, the *Missile,* in 1957. The paper went through several owners, but today's *Las Vegas Sentinel Voice* traces its lineage directly back to the *Missile.* Because the NAACP charter banned formal political action, McMillan, West, and others formed the Negro Voters League (a similar organization formed in 1928 had disbanded) to begin pressuring local political candidates.

After years of protest, the local chapter of the NAACP, led by McMillan, West, Johnson, David and Mabel Hoggard, and a group of outspoken ministers, threatened a mass march down the Strip on March 26, 1960, as well as similar protests on Fremont Street if area resorts did not immediately open their properties to African American customers. Inspired by successful protests in Alabama, Georgia, and Mississippi, McMillan and West knew that a resort city could ill afford the potential bloodshed that this event could bring. Resort operators recognized the consequences of broadcasting television pictures of the violence to prospective vacationers and conventioneers across the nation. So, after a series of meetings (mediated by the *Las Vegas Sun*'s Hank Greenspun) involving Gragson, county commissioners, resort executives, and the NAACP representatives, the city and county resorts gave in. But not all of them: it took several more years and the federal Civil Rights Act of 1964 before the Horseshoe, Sal Sagev, and a few remaining properties went along.

Ironically, the first casino forced to close for discrimination against minorities was the Moulin Rouge. In 1961, city commissioners responded to charges that Moulin Rouge owner Leo Fry discriminated against black patrons by pulling his liquor license, forcing him to close his hotel. A desperate Fry insisted that he discriminated only against "certain persons," not all African Americans. But his protests were in vain; too many complaints had been lodged against him. While Fry rented rooms to all races, he admitted charging black customers more for drinks than whites paid.

At an NAACP dinner, *left to right:* the Reverend Marion Bennett, later an assemblyman; the Rev. Jesse Scott, a community activist; Eileen Brookman, a community
leader and legislator; Mayor Oran Gragson, who surprised many in the black community with his commitment to racial justice; Sarann Knight Preddy, the first African
American woman licensed to run her own casino in Nevada; her son, James Walker;
and Woodrow Wilson, Nevada's first black assemblyman and founder of the Westside Federal Credit Union. Special Collections, UNLV Libraries

He defended this policy by claiming it was a common practice in Las Vegas
bars and stores at the time—a statement that was not altogether false.

The struggle to end racial discrimination in public places was a major
victory for the local civil rights movement, but other battles remained to
be fought. Job discrimination as well as school and residential segregation
all thrived in Las Vegas. But not everyone agreed. At least one local newspaper saw the opening of public accommodations in 1960 as a giant step
forward and urged black residents and tourists to be patient, insisting that
Las Vegas was no less progressive on racial matters than other major cities.
As the *Las Vegas Review-Journal* editor declared, "We feel that as of today
Negro visitors will find a situation no better and no worse than San Fran-

cisco when it comes to public accommodations, hospitality, and welcome." He conceded that "certainly, the situation is far from ideal." But, he asked, "Is Chicago ideal, Detroit, Los Angeles?" Al Cahlan's steadfast loyalty to the city and his go-slow attitude toward racial equality were shared by many white residents, including his brother John.

For black Las Vegans this was not the issue. They had waited for years, expecting that a series of mayors, county commissioners, and governors would attack Jim Crow. But, aside from some forceful rhetoric, the white effort had been feeble at best. By 1960, local African Americans, led by McMillan, West, and a host of black ministers, teachers, and businesspeople, were prepared to vigorously support the local civil rights movement.

It was not just a matter of freedom; money was also an issue. In 1961, sympathetic governor Grant Sawyer appointed the Nevada Equal Rights Commission to act as a fact-finding body and make recommendations. The commission held meetings in Las Vegas and Reno to investigate employment practices. It found that black workers in the casino industry faced rampant job discrimination. In 1962, Strip and city casino executives explained the lack of black dealers, bellmen, waitresses, pit bosses, and office personnel by claiming that "non-Caucasians" rarely applied for those jobs. However, when commissioners asked for statistics, Sam Boyd of the Mint and Charles King of the Golden Nugget flatly refused to cooperate, and Ed Levinson of the Fremont and Sal Sagev executives even declined the invitation to appear.

While conceding that they employed few blacks and only a "scattering of Orientals" in those positions, other resort leaders at least agreed to gather some statistics. Major Riddle of the Dunes reassured frustrated commission members that "things are changing." Indeed, he noted that blacks comprised 10 to 20 percent of the workforce at most Strip hotels. This was an improvement, he insisted, because "four or five years ago, there would have been considerable opposition to Negroes in some of the positions."

The battle for fair employment dragged on for many years. After several failed attempts, civil rights advocates, including representatives from white Catholic and Protestant churches and members of Nevada's Jewish community, along with other groups, pressured lawmakers to approve a state civil rights act in 1965. The conservatives in rural counties and some suburban areas could no longer hold out, given the political climate generated by the Freedom Rides, the violence in Birmingham and Selma, the Civil Rights Act of 1964, the Voting Rights Act of 1965, Lyndon Johnson's Great Society, and a score of recent federal district court and Supreme Court (led by Chief Justice Earl Warren) decisions against discrimination and segregation.

Despite the new law, most Las Vegas casinos and unions continued to discriminate in hiring bartenders, dealers, casino managers, and hotel managers and in filling union apprentice positions. Charles Kellar, a determined and outspoken black attorney, filed numerous complaints with state courts and the gaming commission. Throughout the 1960s, civil rights leaders asked Governor Sawyer and his successor, Paul Laxalt, to pull the gaming and business licenses of any resort or casino that discriminated in hiring against black Americans—the same demand they had made in the earlier campaign for open accommodations. Both governors and state gaming commissioners sidestepped the issue, with the gaming commission claiming that it had no authority to pull a license for mere discrimination.

Ultimately, Kellar went to federal court where the runaround ended. In June 1971, U.S. District Court judge Roger D. Foley pressured Las Vegas resort operators as well as leaders of the culinary, bartender, stagehand, and other unions to sign a consent decree ending discrimination against minority workers. This victory by Las Vegas's African American community benefited not only that race, but Asian, Hispanic, and other minority Americans, too.

Of course, discrimination against women, white and nonwhite, in gaming continued at most properties. If industry executives were aware of women's liberation, they showed no signs of it. The 1958 city ban against women dealers had forced Sarann Knight, one of the town's few black female dealers, out of a job, as it did her white counterparts. Pressure from the national and local civil rights movements, as well as court rulings, had effectively made the ban unenforceable, but as late as 1971, women dealt only at the Union Plaza and perhaps a few other places. Unofficial discrimination within the industry was the reason. Female casino employees spoke bitterly of being relegated to the "girls' ghetto" of keno running and cocktail waitressing. Change came slowly. Although the casinos quickly learned that many male and female gamblers preferred women dealers, and hired more of them, women hit the "glass ceiling" when it came to being promoted to pit boss, shift boss, and other high-level casino and hotel management positions. A decade later, the federal courts once again intervened, issuing another consent decree that formally banned unfair employment practices based on gender in Nevada's gaming industry.

The two remaining areas of contention, school segregation and open housing, also required protracted campaigns. In a metropolitan area where most black and Hispanic residents lived in Westside or North Las Vegas and neighborhood schools were the rule, school segregation was rampant. Only the valley's high schools were integrated. As busing spread across the United States in the 1960s, black Las Vegans fought for integration against a white community that was determined to keep schools separate but equal. Frustration led to violence, first in the high schools and later in Westside. A series of incidents ignited racial tensions in 1969. On January 23, North Las Vegas police broke up a minor racial conflict at Rancho High. Four days later, another disturbance occurred at Las Vegas High when four white teens threw a black student through a trophy case. A few days later at Clark High, a wild melee involving one thousand students forced the shutdown of all the valley's high schools for the week. On Monday, February 3, they reopened with all but Valley High requesting a police presence to safeguard students. Continued segregation in area grade schools, coupled with a relative lack of city and state funding for Westside poverty programs, led to a full-scale riot on the Westside in October 1969. For two days, gangs and arsonists roamed the streets around the riot's epicenter, the Golden West Shopping Center on H and Owens Streets. Police patrolled the area, and Governor Paul Laxalt even mobilized the National Guard. While local black ministers and civil rights leaders worked to restore calm, they nevertheless reiterated to Mayor Gragson and other area leaders that discrimination remained the underlying problem and had to be eliminated.

Like cities, towns, and metropolitan areas across the country, Las Vegas had to face these problems head-on. Violence was particularly damaging to a resort city projecting the image of a fun-filled environment to attract vacationers. Finally, after disturbances at local high schools continued into May 1970, the Clark County School District, led by future Nevada governor Kenny Guinn, devised the sixth-grade plan by which black students would be bused to white schools for the first five grades, and all Las Vegas, North Las Vegas, and Strip suburban students would attend the sixth grade in Westside schools. To accomplish this, all Westside classrooms were converted to the sixth grade.

The underlying cause of school segregation, residential segregation, legally ended a year later. In 1971, new governor Mike O'Callaghan, himself a former teacher at Basic High School, pressured and even threatened conservative lawmakers into voting for an open housing bill with the aid of Assemblyman Woodrow Wilson, a longtime West Las Vegas leader. Restrictive deed covenants and overt methods of housing discrimination were now banned by law. Las Vegans of all races could live where they pleased in the metropolitan area—if they could afford it.

During World War II and the two decades thereafter, some popularly referred to Las Vegas as the "Mississippi of the West." This, however, is somewhat of an exaggeration. Certainly, Las Vegas was no bastion of racial equality, and most white residents gave in on civil rights only under pressure from federal courts and events nationwide. But Jim Crow reigned across the West. In some respects, cities like Albuquerque, Phoenix, Tucson, and many a rural and large town in California treated minorities far worse than Las Vegas. Even Los Angeles, with its largely Anglo police force, was hardly an enclave of liberalism for blacks and other minorities. Throughout the 1930s and 1940s, Filipinos and Mexicans were threatened, beaten, and even deported. In the Southwest, which contained thousands of white transplants from Dixie, local Klan chapters actively harassed black, Hispanic, and Asian residents and travelers. So the reference to Mississippi, while certainly understandable in view of Las Vegas's lame civil rights record, could just as easily be used to describe race relations in many of the West's larger and smaller towns. Las Vegas was hardly the worst Jim Crow city in the region; it was just typical of a region where Jim Crow pervaded the social landscape for Hispanic, black, brown, yellow, and red racial minorities.

In many ways, the 1960s were the best decade yet for the advancement of Las Vegas and the growing suburbs around it. The civil rights movement was particularly important, forcing white residents and the gaming industry to accept the fact that Las Vegas operated within a multiracial, multinational society. Moreover, as the twentieth century continued and more racial minorities rose above the poverty line, open accommodations and equality would result in more minority business for Las Vegas and an expanded pool of labor for its economy.

Unfortunately, political fragmentation worsened in the sixties, prompting more clashes between the county and its cities on a variety of fronts. Of course, the continued rise in population and tourists eased some of the frustration. Glitter Gulch grew larger than ever before, but the Strip began to pull steadily ahead in profits and visitors. Caesars Palace and the International, with their size and unprecedented splendor, created a new resort model that required a lot of space, something that the downtown area lacked. The trend toward expensive, must-see resorts would only contribute more to the Strip's tourist appeal. Nevertheless, Las Vegas continued its vibrant expansion as a city in the 1960s, attracting thousands of new residents to its suburbs while, at the same time, anchoring what soon became the Southwest's newest fast-growing metropolitan area.

GAMING AND WORLD RECOGNITION

WHILE LAS VEGAS ENJOYED SIGNIFICANT expansion in the years between 1930 and 1970, in the thirty-five years thereafter the valley underwent the kind of explosive growth that few American cities have ever experienced. For all of the 1990s and into the twenty-first century, Las Vegas was the fastest-growing metropolitan area in the nation. From 1970 to 2000, the population soared from 270,000 to more than 1.3 million, straining budgets and government services as never before.

The major force powering the valley's growth continued to be the Las Vegas Strip. After 1970, resort development along the old Los Angeles Highway reached new heights. By the 1990s, the Strip was more than a national must-see. It had become a world tourist destination.

The 1970s gave only a glimpse of the future. True, more new hotels sprang up in this decade than in the 1960s. The Holiday Inn–Harrah's (1973), the Marina (1974), the Maxim-Westin (1977), the Imperial Palace (1979), and the Barbary Coast (1979) all appeared on Las Vegas Boulevard. In addition, casino development veered off the Strip with the 1976 Bingo Palace (becoming the Palace Station in 1984) on Sahara Avenue and Sam's Town and the Nevada Palace (both 1979) on Boulder Highway.

However, the only major resort built in the sumptuous tradition of Caesars Palace was Kirk Kerkorian's first MGM Grand Hotel in 1973. Kerkorian, a former pilot who had flown California gamblers to Las Vegas in the 1940s and later formed his own airline, had witnessed the Strip's early prosperity and in the 1950s bought land at the intersection of Las Vegas Boulevard and Flamingo. He made a small fortune renting and then selling the site to Caesars Palace and later selling the Flamingo and International to Hilton. By 1971, after acquiring a controlling interest in MGM Studios,

Kerkorian decided to build a Hollywood-theme resort based on the movie *Grand Hotel* (1932). When it opened on December 5, 1973, the first MGM Grand (today's Bally's) was the largest hotel in the free world with twenty-two hundred rooms and suites, five restaurants, two showrooms, and even a jai alai pavilion. While it lacked the magnificent gardens of Caesars Palace, it rivaled or surpassed Sarno's resort in size, services, and appeal. Kerkorian later built New York–New York and the second MGM Grand. The International (1968), first MGM Grand (1973), and second MGM Grand (1993) gave him the distinction of being the only person to build the largest hotel in the world on three separate occasions.

But even as late as the 1970s, the Strip's remarkable future was not yet evident. When Atlantic City gambling began in 1978, it drained thousands of East Coast gamblers out of Las Vegas. Places like the MGM cut costs by closing gourmet rooms two nights a week, reducing the number of performances in their showrooms, and implementing other cutbacks. As the 1980s began, a series of disasters hurt Nevada and Las Vegas tourism. Following a disgruntled gambler's bombing of Harveys Wagon Wheel Hotel-Casino at Lake Tahoe in August 1980 (which required the complete rebuilding of that resort), the MGM Grand also closed for nine months following a huge fire in November 1980 that gutted the building and killed eighty-five people. Three months later, a spectacular fire at the Las Vegas Hilton burned on almost thirty floors of the resort's east wing near a bank of elevators. This fire closed the Hilton for almost two weeks. This event plus another blaze at Caesars a few weeks later raised serious concerns about the safety of Nevada's hotel rooms.

By the mid-1980s the state-mandated retrofitting of all high-rise buildings in Nevada had allayed tourist fears. But the fires and the bombing, coupled with the debut of Donald Trump's much ballyhooed resorts in Atlantic City, did little to help Las Vegas tourism. Nor did the return of a recession and double-digit inflation help the tourist economy.

However, this period of adjustment proved to be a prelude rather than an epilogue. Just as Thomas Hull, Jay Sarno, and Kirk Kerkorian came along in earlier decades to build a resort that took the valley's tourist industry to the next level, so too in the 1980s another dynamic figure took center stage. After a boyhood visit to Las Vegas with his father in 1952 to establish what ultimately became a failed bingo operation, Steve Wynn returned as an adult in 1967 as a minority owner of the Frontier Hotel.

While there, he served as slots manager and assistant credit manager, which, along with his bingo experience, taught him the rudiments of casino management.

After the Frontier's sale to Howard Hughes in 1967, Wynn, with financial help from Valley Bank's Thomas and Mack, bought a wholesale liquor business. His major customers were the hotels on the Strip and downtown. In this capacity, Wynn met all the gaming legends from the town's salad days: Benny Binion, Sam Boyd, Jackie Gaughan, Jay Sarno, and others, all of whom gave Wynn valuable insights on hotel and casino operations. In fact, Wynn is today the one figure whose knowledge bridges the past seven decades of Las Vegas gaming, because he knew all of the major people from the early days and knows all of the major people today.

After becoming president of the Golden Nugget in 1973, Wynn set out to revive the place. In a major coup, he convinced city officials to close Carson Street just behind the property to provide enough land to build a Strip-type resort in the narrow confines of downtown. In the 1980s, Wynn removed all of the blazing neon from the Nugget's exterior and spent millions refurbishing the old casino with plants, flowers, belt lighting, smoked mirrors, and gourmet restaurants. In the rear, he built a new high-rise hotel and a seven-story parking garage. He also added a luxurious pool and deck as well as a showroom where Frank Sinatra made the only downtown headliner appearances of his career.

Having resurrected the fading Golden Nugget and built in Atlantic City, Wynn next set his sights on the Strip. At several meetings in the early 1980s, Wynn had emphasized that Strip resorts were too small. His comments startled even seasoned hotel executives who thought that Caesars, the Hilton, MGM, and even the older properties were plenty big enough. But in 1989, Wynn made his point when he mesmerized a skeptical audience with The Mirage. True, the Flamingo, Sahara, Sands, and other Strip hotels of the 1940s and 1950s, built in the style of the spa resorts found in Scottsdale and Palm Springs, had drawn the early tourists to the valley. These resorts contained elegant, if not spectacular, casinos. Some, like the Tropicana, Dunes, and Desert Inn, even boasted golf courses. Together, these properties had established a firm foundation for the Strip's tourist industry in the 1940s and 1950s.

In the 1960s and early 1970s, however, Sarno and Kerkorian upped the ante by building the first major resorts. These were large facilities contain-

The Strip at night, north from the Foundation Room at Mandalay Bay. Celebrities and tourists from around the world check out this view regularly. Photograph by Clint Karlsen and copyright by Las Vegas Review-Journal

ing millions of dollars in extra spending for statuary, crystal chandeliers, wall tapestries, crown molding, coffered ceilings, and other extravagances that made Las Vegas a must-see for millions.

However, Wynn took tourism and resort making to the next level when he invented the megaresort. The Mirage boasted not only size and elegance, but also the special attractions that separated the Strip from Fremont Street, Reno, other Nevada resorts, and every gambling town, tribal casino, and Internet Web site in the world. When it opened in 1989, The Mirage set a new standard by which every future resort would be judged. Its flaming volcano, white tiger exhibit, and bottle-nosed dolphins (which arrived from the Atlantic in 1990) attracted so many visitors that in just one year the resort replaced Hoover Dam as the state's leading tourist attraction. In one stroke, Wynn raised the cost of building new competitive resorts from the millions to the billions of dollars. This factor, as much as the liberalization of corporate gambling, put the mob on the sidelines in Vegas.

The Mirage Revolution sparked a building boom down the south Strip, which resulted in operators like Kerkorian and Circus Circus's William Bennett responding with icons of their own. The Excalibur (1990), the second MGM Grand (1993), and places like New York–New York (1997), the Luxor (1993), Venetian (1999), and Paris (1999), whose "Disneyfied" and "event" architecture were major draws in themselves, made the Strip more popular than ever. Wynn contributed to his own revolution with Treasure Island (now T.I.) in 1993, Monte Carlo (in which he partnered with Mandalay Resorts) in 1996, and the magnificent Bellagio in 1998, before selling all of his properties to Kirk Kerkorian in 2000.

Having used the money from this sale as capital to buy the two hundred–plus acres of the Desert Inn Hotel and Country Club, Wynn went to work building his namesake hotel, which will no doubt become his next masterpiece of resort art. Located just across the street from the recently enlarged and beautified Fashion Show Mall, Wynn–Las Vegas may well spark another building boom, this time up the long-quiescent north Strip.

Despite the clean-cut corporate image that Las Vegas casinos began to project in the 1970s, the gaming industry continued to be tainted by charges of mob influence. Most of the action in the 1970s and 1980s centered on the Strip rather than Fremont Street. In 1979, for instance, the Gaming Commission, chaired by later U.S. senator Harry Reid, closed the

Aladdin Hotel because its owners concealed hidden underworld interests in the resort. The Tropicana, which in 1957 won notoriety for its connection to New York's Costello crime family, once again drew the interest of investigators. In 1978–1979, a series of FBI wiretaps revealed an organized crime effort to use entertainment director Joe Agosto, a front man for Kansas City boss Nick Civella, to skim money from the resort without the knowledge of majority owner Mitzi Stauffer Briggs.

In 1976, Allen Glick's Argent Corporation, which had purchased the Hacienda in 1971 before securing a seventy million–dollar loan from the Teamsters' pension fund to buy the Stardust, Fremont, and Marina, became the focus of another federal and state investigation. Gaming Control Board agents discovered a massive skimming operation at the Stardust in 1976, and the Justice Department's Organized Crime Strike Force in Las Vegas ultimately charged that bookmaker Frank Rosenthal was the Chicago underworld's director of operations at the resort. Supporting Rosenthal in his efforts was Anthony Spilotro, the mob's alleged enforcer in Las Vegas. Their stormy relationship became the subject of Martin Scorsese's film *Casino* (1995). Rosenthal's ouster from the Stardust in 1979 hardly ended the resort's problems. Another skimming operation by four executives in 1983 ultimately led to the Stardust's sale to the Boyd Group in 1985, which finally gave the resort respectability.

Even after Rosenthal's departure and Spilotro's murder, charges of street racketeering and other activities have continued. In the past twenty years, however, mob involvement in major hotel skimming operations has not been evident. But charges continue to fly regarding elected officials doing favors in return for bribes for Las Vegas's growing number of topless cabarets (both in the city and in the county), whose owners, according to law enforcement officials, have alleged mob ties.

The decline of the mob's presence within major resorts over the past two decades has only promoted the Strip's growth and the positive image of Las Vegas that resort executives want to project. This process has also benefited downtown, whose national image, like the Strip's, suffered for years from the publicity generated by mob convictions, Senate hearings, and FBI investigations.

To be sure, Fremont Street operators did not sit idly by while the Strip reinvented itself. The downtown casino core, seeking to revitalize its economy in response to the booming Strip, undertook a number of renovations, expansions, and new projects. In the 1980s, the Las Vegas Club, which had replaced the historic Overland Hotel, added a sixteen-story tower that doubled its room capacity besides giving the place a larger casino, a sports bar, and a small convention center. In addition, the Four Queens and Union Plaza were renovated and modernized. Owners of the Golden Gate, which had begun its life as a small casino underneath the Sal Sagev in 1955, bought the entire building in 1974, and it became the Golden Gate Hotel. Sam Boyd's company, under the leadership of his son Bill, not only put the Fremont through a facelift, but also purchased and revitalized what had been Major Riddle's Holiday Inn in the 1980s. In 1991, Bob Snow, who developed Orlando's popular Church Street Station, made an abortive effort to revive the property as Main Street Station, an antique-filled shrine to the golden age of railroads. But Boyd ultimately resuscitated the place. Today, the once dead section of Glitter Gulch on North Main is a busy tourist thoroughfare, thanks to the Boyd Group's investment, expertise, and link to its California Hotel, which itself became a lively retreat for Hawaiian gamblers.

There have also been other revitalization efforts on Fremont Street. Some of them have been wildly successful, others have failed, and still others have never gotten off the drawing board. In the latter category is Binion's Horseshoe, which in 1995 announced plans for a thirty-six-story, seventy million–dollar tower that would have doubled the property's room capacity. But it never happened. In January 2004, federal marshals closed the Horseshoe for debts owed to several union pension and welfare funds, as well as to the IRS. The taped-up doors and darkened neon, the signature look of a once lively casino now dead, were reminiscent of downtown Reno in the wake of California's tribal gaming boom. Fortunately for downtown, the Horseshoe came back to life a few months later.

On the brighter side, the new Fremont Street Experience matched Wynn's dramatic transformation of the Golden Nugget. For years, city leaders and hotel operators pondered what to do about revitalizing the casino corridor. Numerous plans got a hearing, including Wynn's suggestion to build a water feature of some kind, perhaps one similar to San Antonio's popular Riverwalk. In the end, leaders decided to build the seventy million–dollar Fremont Street Experience, an electronic canopy of lights, computerized animation, and music that opened in December 1995. The city closed Fremont Street to cars and converted the venerable old thoroughfare into a pedestrian mall, which served as an open-air theater in the early evening when adjacent casinos dimmed their lights on the hour for the show. The costly experiment worked, as gaming revenues on Glitter Gulch rose by 20 percent above previous levels by summer 1996. Doing so required the city to shut down and take over various Fremont Street businesses, prompting lawsuits that worked their way to the U.S. Supreme Court, which ultimately ruled in favor of the city.

Since 1970, the city's gaming industry has expanded in several ways. First, new construction and major renovations on Fremont Street have been significant. Aside from Boyd's California Hotel and Wynn's dramatic transformation of the old Golden Nugget, there have been other valuable contributions. In 1980, Fitzgeralds of Reno opened its casino on Fremont Street. Seven years later, it completed a thirty-four-story tower that briefly made it the state's tallest building. This soaring addition to the city's skyline provided visual confirmation of downtown's vitality, and Detroit businessman Don Barden's purchase of Fitzgeralds marked a historical turning point: the first downtown property owned by an African American.

In addition to gaming's vertical growth downtown, the city's industry also experienced horizontal growth outward. The rapid suburbanization of the city after 1970 encouraged the suburbanization of gambling. In 1976, the Bingo Palace (today's Palace Station) opened near Interstate 15 just across the city's southern limits. Then, in 1995, Stations Casinos unveiled its Texas Station just across the city line in North Las Vegas at Rancho and Lake Mead to serve Las Vegas's northern suburbs.

Other new resorts sprang up within the city. In 1979, Bob Stupak opened Vegas World just two blocks north of the city line at Sahara Avenue and the Strip. While the moonscaped high-rise, an eyesore by any community's standards, drew its share of gamblers, Stupak dreamed of something grander. In 1960, Oran Gragson had popularized the idea of building a tower that would allow tourists and residents to enjoy the valley's scenic splendor and perhaps catch a glimpse of Lake Mead. The opening of Howard Hughes's thirty-one-story Landmark Hotel in 1969 seemed a worthy response at the time. But Stupak envisioned a truly large structure, maybe even taller than New York's Empire State Building, with lounges, restaurants, observation decks, a wedding chapel, and perhaps even a ride or two on top. Stupak started the project in the mid-1990s, but

Las Vegas has become the place to be on New Year's Eve. Up to half-a-million visitors crowd the Strip and downtown to celebrate and watch fireworks shows like this one, which rang in 2004. Photograph by Clint Karlsen and copyright by Las Vegas Review-Journal

The Fremont Street Experience has contributed to tourist traffic downtown. The installation of the canopy required negotiations to get downtown casino operators to shut down their neon for the hourly light show each night. In 2004 officials modernized the lighting and the programs. Photograph by John Gurzinski and copyright by Las Vegas Review-Journal

lacked the capital to finish it. He took on partners with deeper pockets, and in 1996 the new hotel opened in the blare of a great fireworks display. At 1,141 feet (the Federal Aviation Administration would not allow it to be as tall as the Empire State Building) and boasting a roller-coaster and "Big Shot" ride, the Stratosphere became one of the city's star attractions, although its proximity to the Strip did little to lure visitors downtown.

Besides these resorts, other new ones opened farther out in the city's newer suburbs. In 1991, Paul Lowden used profits from his Sahara and Hacienda hotels on the Strip to build the Santa Fe (today a Stations Casinos resort) at U.S. 95 and Rancho in the city's western suburbs. In 1999, the elegantly landscaped Regent–Las Vegas, perhaps the most beautiful resort in the entire valley, opened amid the championship golf courses in Summerlin. Despite its appeal, the property went through bankruptcy and several ownership changes before it returned to life as the J. W. Marriott in 2001. Earlier, the Suncoast, catering to lower-end gamblers, debuted nearby. And more resorts are on the drawing board for developing lands on the far western edge of the city and valley, especially near the entrance to Red Rock Canyon. The long-dormant Moulin Rouge, which suffered a disastrous fire in 2003, may have been rescued in 2004 when a black-owned corporation bought the property and announced plans for constructing a new Moulin Rouge Hotel-Casino on the site.

The year 2004 also brought other problems. The old Showboat (Castaways) on the city's eastern edge closed its doors for the foreseeable future, the victim of changing neighborhood demographics. But the Horseshoe's temporary decline may indicate a more serious problem. As Becky Binion Behnen herself noted, downtown's gaming industry today faces two serious threats: the rise of Indian casinos and Las Vegas's own suburban casinos. Just as northern California's tribal casinos have hurt Reno-Tahoe, gaming centers in the Southland are taking a toll on downtown's tourism. Gamblers still come to Fremont Street, but less frequently than they used to. Adding to the problem, many locals in places like Summerlin come to Glitter Gulch less often because suburban casinos like the Suncoast and Texas Station give them all of the action and amenities they need.

Notwithstanding these problems, tourism continues to grow both downtown and on the Strip. While airports, freeways, and new resorts have all helped boost business, popular culture has also played a role. Hundreds of books and films have publicized Las Vegas to the world, portraying it as a maverick society—different from the rest of America—an intriguing and electric place worth experiencing.

Las Vegas's twenty-four-hour party atmosphere gradually captured America's attention and transformed the city into a trendy icon. After 1950, it was no longer a regional destination for the Los Angeles and Palm Springs crowd. Las Vegas regularly appeared in national magazines, portrayed in a variety of different images. Writers characterized the casino city as a "Klondike in the Desert," an "Atomic Boomtown in the Desert," a

"Hollywood Sandbox," "the town that gangsters built," a "divorce capital," and a "last frontier." The town's wedding chapel and church weddings, popularized by such notables as Elvis Presley, Paul Newman, and Bing Crosby, as well as its reputation for "quickie marriages" epitomized by Mickey Rooney (on numerous occasions), Dennis Rodman, Carmen Electra, Britney Spears, and thousands of starry-eyed couples, contributed further to Las Vegas's "sin city" image.

The advent of television and the jet plane allowed millions more Americans to experience Las Vegas's appeal. By day, visitors gambled and lounged around hotel pools, and by night they gambled, danced, and went to shows. In the 1930s, the Meadows featured such performers as the Gumm Sisters, one of whom changed her name to Judy Garland. As early as the 1940s, Las Vegas lounges and showrooms presented major performers. By the 1960s, however, the Strip garnered most of the publicity, as stars like Tony Bennett, Don Rickles, and Sammy Davis Jr. regularly plugged their showroom appearances on Johnny Carson's show (and he was a frequent headliner at the Sahara) and other TV talk shows. Over the past six decades, virtually every important show business personality from Liberace to Willie Nelson has appeared either on stage or in the audience, justifying Las Vegas's reputation as the "entertainment capital of the world."

Yet as Las Vegas changed, the form and style of its entertainment changed with it. Frank Sinatra, Dean Martin, Elvis Presley, and other headliners put on great shows, but what mattered most was whether they attracted gamblers to the casino. As Burton Cohen, the former president of Caesars Palace and the Desert Inn, once put it, "I'm not in show business; I'm in the people-moving business. My job is to move people through my casino." The trend of hiring big-name marquee acts survives, but with several twists. One is that prices today are much steeper than they were in the 1950s and 1960s, when the Sands charged less than twenty dollars to see the Rat Pack and their friends cavort on stage at the Copa Room. This change reflects the importance of entertainment itself, and the demands of a corporate structure for each department to make a profit. In addition, many Strip hotels have stuck with not only production shows like the Tropicana's Folies Bergere, but major headliners as well. For years, the first MGM Grand (today's Bally's) had two showrooms, one for its Hallelujah Hollywood stage show and the other for Dean Martin and fel-

Jim Cashman drove Liberace to the Riviera's opening in an older car he probably chose not to offer for sale on his car lot. This was a typical news bureau pose at the time, merging the old and new Las Vegas with a dash of celebrity thrown in. Special Collections, UNLV Libraries

low headliners. The Mirage blended a little of both, with Siegfried and Roy, formerly of the Stardust's Lido de Paris and their own Frontier production show. In recent years, Wayne Newton not only performs at the Stardust showroom, but also books other acts who appear there. Some superstars, who normally spent weeks on the road doing one-nighters, now spend much of their time in Las Vegas and let their fans come to them. This is the case at Caesars Palace, which built a magnificent showroom to accommodate Celine Dion's show, and, when she is away, Elton John performs, and even lives, at Caesars for a month or more.

Two other changes reflect the differences between the Strip and other venues. On the Strip, some of the hotels now boast large arenas that host major concerts. Paul McCartney, Mick Jagger, Barbra Streisand, and Bette Midler play Las Vegas, but not in the intimate or even large showrooms for a week or two; they appear in large venues and only for a night or two, which obviously increases the ticket prices. The smaller downtown properties can hardly compete—and do not. Indeed, this is another major change in how Las Vegas hotel-casinos provide entertainment: places like the Fremont and Golden Nugget, once known for their lounge performers, have moved away from that emphasis. The exceptions are the neighborhood casinos run by Stations Casinos, Michael Gaughan's Coast Resorts, and others, but they too tend to promote concerts rather than longer runs.

Aside from shows, showgirls, and nightlife, movies have also reinforced Las Vegas's glamorous image. As early as 1915, the filming of a serial, *The Hazards of Helen,* brought the railroad town some attention. The Rat Pack's classic *Ocean's Eleven* (1960, remade in 2002) and the James Bond thriller *Diamonds Are Forever* (1971) were two of many adventure and crime movies set in and around Las Vegas. These also included parts of the *Godfather* series (1972–1990) as well as *Bugsy* (1991) and Martin Scorsese's *Casino* (1995), in which now mayor Oscar Goodman played himself. These films contributed to the image of Las Vegas as a mob haven—an image that the city has alternately capitalized on and resented. Other films exploited a variety of themes for which Las Vegas also served as an appropriate setting. From the atomic bomb genre, films like *The Amazing Colossal Man* (1957) and *Desert Bloom* (1986); to edgier flicks like *Leaving Las Vegas* (1995), *Fear and Loathing in Las Vegas* (1998), *Con Air* (1997), *Virtual Vegas* (2001), and *The Cooler* (2003); westerns like *Heldorado* (1946); and lighter romances like Elvis Presley and Ann Margret's *Viva Las Vegas* (1964), the town provided an ideal stage. The only best-picture Oscar winner filmed at least partly in Las Vegas, *Rain Man* (1988), even suggested the town's possibilities when an autistic man triumphed in the end.

The town has also been the subject of hundreds of novels, television shows, documentaries, songs, and even rock videos. For years, the green felt ambience of the neon city that rules the night has drawn the interest of writers, filmmakers, and musicians from around the world. Not a few of these became residents. Indeed, the show business celebrities who have lived in the valley go far beyond Liberace, Robert Goulet, Wayne Newton, and other stage performers who played the showrooms. Hollywood actors such as Tony Curtis, Orson Welles, Pat Morita, and many others have called Las Vegas home. The same could also be said of those in other parts of the entertainment business, such as sports figures. This group of residents has included baseball players Jim Brosnan and Bo Belinsky, heavy-

The set for *The Hazards of Helen,* a serial filmed by Kalem Company in 1915. At right is Helen Holmes, the star. It was the first movie shot in Las Vegas. Special Collections, UNLV Libraries

This is not an average Las Vegas Strip sighting, contrary to popular belief. Filming *Elvis Has Left the Building,* a group of Elvis impersonators cross the Strip between Circus Circus and the Rivera. As their presence, and the popularity of Elvis imper-sonators in shows and at wedding chapels, demonstrate, the king of rock 'n' roll still matters to Las Vegas. Photography by K. M. Cannon and copyright Las Vegas Review-Journal

weight champions Sonny Liston (who is even buried in Las Vegas) and Mike Tyson, and many retired NFL greats, along with athletes from other sports.

In fact, Las Vegas has functioned not only as the "entertainment capital of the world," but as a sports center, too. It began in the 1930s when race books first appeared in downtown casinos, drawing horse-racing enthusi-asts. The trend intensified during the 1970s when the Union Plaza, the Stardust, and other casinos built sports books where gamblers and fans alike could bet on their favorite team and individual sports. A decade ear-lier, Las Vegas laid claim to being the "boxing capital of the world" when Caesars Palace and other resorts began staging world championship fights featuring the likes of Muhammad Ali and Floyd Patterson, and later Tyson, Sugar Ray Leonard, and Marvin Hagler.

Of course, Las Vegas's growing fame as a sports center was not just limited to the Strip and Fremont Street. Beginning in the 1970s, the local university gained national attention for its major athletic programs. Basketball was the most visible. The hiring of Jerry Tarkanian as coach in 1973 brought UNLV to national prominence over the next two decades during which the Runnin' Rebels secured numerous conference titles, went to the Final Four four times, and won the national championship in 1990. In the process, Larry Johnson, Reggie Theus, and other standouts graduated from these teams to successful NBA careers. At the same time, the university's other sports teams, while less well known, featured athletes like NCAA heptathlon champion Sheila Tarr-Smith and three-time Olympic gold medalist Lori Harrigan, who starred as amateurs, as well as Todd Stottlemyre, Matt Williams, Randall Cunningham, and others who went on to successful professional careers. In addition, local schools contributed their share of luminaries, including Andre Agassi, Greg Maddux, and PGA golfer Robert Gamez.

While Las Vegas has produced sports stars, it has yet to produce significant professional sports teams. The Las Vegas Wranglers, a Class C minor league baseball team, played downtown at Cashman Field in the 1940s and 1950s, but weeds sprouted there for more than twenty years until the AAA Las Vegas Stars arrived in 1983. Affiliated with the San Diego Padres, they gave Las Vegans a chance to see future Hall of Famers like Tony Gwynn. The team eventually switched affiliations (to the Los Angeles Dodgers, a more popular team with locals due to the city's long connection to that part of southern California) and names, becoming the 51s, in honor of Area 51, the supersecret land where federal weapons tests have been conducted and aliens are alleged to have dwelled.

With the exception of minor league baseball, sports franchises have had rough going in Las Vegas. An Arena League football team, the Wranglers, does well, and Las Vegas's XFL franchise did better than most in that short-lived league, but minor league football, hockey, and soccer have fared poorly in comparison with the town's one-time love affair with the Runnin' Rebels. And that affair ended when coach Jerry Tarkanian departed after the 1991–1992 season. UNLV continues to draw, but not the consistently large crowds that used to fill the Thomas & Mack Center. Mayor Oscar Goodman has promoted the idea of a major league sports franchise, especially a National Basketball Association team. But casino owners have shown little interest in a sports attraction (except for the National Finals Rodeo) that would divert gamblers from the tables and require the sports books to take any team's games off the betting boards. The issue goes deeper than that, though. It reflects the amazing expansion of the gaming industry—and how the city of Las Vegas has both benefited and suffered from it.

Whether or not major sports teams someday come to Las Vegas, there is little doubt that the Strip and downtown will continue to grow, albeit at different rates. Las Vegas will also maintain its magnetic appeal and continue to be the subject of numerous books, films, and other expressions of popular culture.

10 SUBURBANIZATION AND DIVERSITY, 1970–2005

FOR MILLIONS, LAS VEGAS IS an entertainment capital, a weekend getaway, a setting for popular films, and a place to get married fast and divorced easily. But it is also a metropolis, experiencing virtually all of the problems afflicting New York, Los Angeles, and other large cities. Over the past thirty-five years, Las Vegas has undergone a suburban boom whose sprawl now threatens to envelop the entire valley.

In the years after 1970, the city of Las Vegas continued to grow, especially in population, but so did surrounding areas. It was not just the Strip suburbs east of the resorts that expanded, but also sections that had experienced little if any previous development. This area included not only the lands west of Interstate 15 out to the mountains, but also the Henderson and North Las Vegas areas.

Helped by the construction of Green Valley, Henderson made the unlikely transition from a blue-collar factory town to a modern "edge city" like those found on the periphery of large metropolitan areas. Office centers, resort complexes, shopping centers (including the enclosed Galleria Mall), along with miles of middle- and high-end subdivisions and gated communities have largely transformed the old magnesium town. Henderson's population of 16,000 in 1970 roared past 150,000 in 1999. In 1997, Henderson became the nation's fastest-growing city and continues to rank in the top three. Once a ramshackle community of demountable homes, trailers, and old concrete buildings, Henderson today claims some of the valley's most fashionable addresses. On its eastern edge lies Lake Las Vegas, an upscale resort community boasting two Jack Nicklaus golf courses, the Hyatt and Ritz Carlton hotels, fashionable shops, and hundreds of pricey condominiums, mansions, and villas.

An aerial view of downtown Las Vegas in the 1970s, looking northwest, with the Union Plaza Hotel and Fremont Street at the lower left. Special Collections, UNLV Libraries

Creating the momentum for Henderson's metamorphosis has been the development of Green Valley. Its origins lie in the land acquisitions of *Las Vegas Sun* editor Hank Greenspun in the southeastern portion of the valley, west of Henderson. Between 1956 and 1971, he bought eight thousand acres of land with the intention of bringing in large developers to build residential communities that the City of Henderson would eventually annex. After several abortive attempts to develop the land, Greenspun himself took control of the American Nevada Corporation and put his then son-in-law Mark Fine in charge.

Fine had only a few years of experience in the land development section of New York's Chemical Bank, but he proved to be an astute corporate president. As head of American Nevada, Fine divided one thousand acres of Greenspun's holdings into ten-acre parcels and then sold them to developers for the discount price of twenty-five thousand dollars each. Fine marketed the Green Valley (as Greenspun called it) project as a master-planned enterprise, and published a map outlining the plan in 1972. These actions attracted Pardee, which was building homes in Spring Valley. US Home, Collins Brothers, and other builders followed, knowing that many home buyers preferred living in master-planned communities.

Still, there was no rush to Green Valley until the 1980s. Most builders were convinced that development would veer west of Interstate 15 toward

This aerial view of Green Valley, looking northwest, suggests both the growth that has led to Henderson's ranking as the nation's fastest-growing community, and the views offered by parts of the Las Vegas Valley, 1997. Photograph by Gary Thompson and copyright Las Vegas Review-Journal

higher, cooler, and more scenic land approaching the mountains. In the 1970s, they were also convinced that Spring Valley and neighboring areas would sell faster because of their proximity to the major resorts and their superior road connections. Green Valley was lower, more subject to flooding, and uncomfortably close to Basic Magnesium and the "Henderson cloud," a polluted mass of air that periodically hung over the city until the 1990s.

But the developers were wrong. Green Valley grew simultaneously with Spring Valley and sooner than Summerlin. Of course, it needed help. Fine convinced county commissioners to rename Lamb Boulevard Green Valley Parkway, which he connected to Patrick Lane. This gave residents in the Strip suburbs another route to Green Valley's model homes until Sunset Road, Warm Springs, and Eastern Avenue could be widened or extended. With Fine releasing new parcels every few months, developers built additional subdivisions featuring homes, and later condominiums, and apartments in all price ranges, including half-acre semicustom home sites.

To be sure, the process was never smooth. The local recession caused by a national downturn, Atlantic City's gambling debut, a lack of roads, and other factors limited sales in the early 1980s. But construction of the east leg (U.S. 93 and 95) of the freeway that will someday connect to the beltway, and completion in the 1990s of the 215 freeway to the airport and Strip, opened the area to thousands of newcomers as well as current residents. White families, in particular, flocked to the area, some undoubtedly because mandated school busing to sixth grade centers to achieve racial integration did not apply to Henderson. Fine presided successfully over the first phase of Green Valley's development, overseeing construction of the early "villages" with their walking trails, libraries, schools, and miniparks. In the process, Fine sharpened his skills for what would be his next venture, the development of Summerlin in the western part of the valley for the Howard Hughes Corporation.

After Fine's departure, American Nevada executives implemented some new policies in the 1990s that Fine had resisted. First was approval of the Stations Casino at Green Valley Ranch. Fine had fought gambling in Green Valley because he thought it conflicted with the community atmosphere American Nevada was trying to create. The company also initiated the use of special improvement districts to pay more easily for infrastructure costs and maintenance for the last village to be built in Green

This is a combination of three people who greatly influenced Las Vegas: Alan Bible, Gus Guiffre, and Judy Bayley in 1971. Bible was the driving force behind the Southern Nevada Water Project. Guiffre was a popular longtime television host and announcer who was part of many civic and charitable activities. And Bayley was the first major woman executive on the Strip. The Judy Bayley Theatre at UNLV is named for her. Special Collections, UNLV Libraries

Valley, Green Valley Ranch, and assessed home owners until the bonds were paid off. The device, though expensive, will help Green Valley Ranch residents finance the upkeep of their infrastructure more easily as it ages than their counterparts in the older villages.

By the late 1990s, as developers began running out of affordable land, the city began annexing more vacant land. But Henderson's growth has been an expensive undertaking that significantly raised property taxes and use fees, just as it has in Las Vegas. At the same time, Henderson's aggressive growth policy has frightened its neighbor to the south, Boulder City. The latter's slow-growth approach to urbanization results, on the average, in the construction of less than forty new homes annually. In 2003, Boulder City's leaders became so concerned about Henderson leapfrogging Railroad Pass and annexing land for light industry in the dry lake valley south of their city that they reluctantly annexed the tract just to keep Henderson out.

Henderson's rapid growth also influenced another traditional backwater in the metropolitan area, North Las Vegas. By the 1990s, this old bootleg suburb of Las Vegas, a comparatively poor and crime-ridden place for most of its history, contained miles of vacant and relatively cheap land close to Fremont Street and the Strip. Builders began invading in the 1990s. In 2003, Del Webb executives, who had virtually filled their original Sun City Summerlin retirement community and were approaching the final stage of sales in Henderson's Sun City Anthem, announced plans to break ground for a new seniors-only development in North Las Vegas, Sun City Aliante.

Thanks to this project, along with the city's first major hotel-casino at Texas Station and other factors, North Las Vegas in 2003 became the fastest-growing city in the United States. In the late 1990s, Henderson passed Reno to become the second-largest city in Nevada behind Las Vegas. Demographers now predict that by 2010, North Las Vegas will also pass Reno. By late 2003, the city of Las Vegas claimed 528,617 residents (of a metropolitan population of approximately 1.7 million), while Henderson counted 217,448, Reno 195,727, and North Las Vegas 146,005. In 2005, with the growth of Henderson, North Las Vegas, and other minidowntowns in the Strip suburbs and in Summerlin, the Las Vegas metropolitan area is beginning to resemble the multicentered metropolitan areas in California, Texas, and elsewhere.

Of course, some of the most dramatic development has occurred in the valley areas west of Interstate 15 in the county and west of Decatur Boulevard and the black Westside in the city of Las Vegas. In these new tracts stretching from Decatur Boulevard to the beltway and beyond, master-planned communities have been the device that developers have used, as they have in Green Valley, to attract builders and home owners.

The western side of the valley was largely empty until the 1970s, because Las Vegas first grew to the east and south, away from the railroad tracks that served as the town's original baseline for growth. Once the Strip became the metropolitan area's major job zone, it became the new baseline for growth. During the 1950s, new housing and commercial center construction began heading eastward along a broad corridor between the Strip, where thousands worked, and Lake Mead, where they obtained

LAS VEGAS METROPOLITAN AREA, 2000

their water and sent their sewage. In the 1950s and 1960s, many resort workers and other commuters drove to work along Sahara Avenue, Vegas Valley Drive, East Desert Inn Road, East Flamingo, East Tropicana, and other newly extended east-west arterials. Developers preferred filling in the lots bordering these roads initially, because it was more practical to build the needed sewer and water mains under them first. In later decades, if the population continued to grow, the western valley could then be used. And this is what happened after 1970.

In the 1970s, developers and builders moved even farther out from existing suburbs, as Henderson served as a base for significant growth of new communities in what became Green Valley. At the same time, Las Vegas and the Strip also served as a dynamic base for major suburbanization to the west. While small subdivisions and shopping centers dotted West Tropicana, Spring Mountain Road, West Sahara, and other roads in the 1970s, these arteries would speed the march of population westward after 1980.

Four new master-planned communities keyed this growth. Beginning in 1984, Collins Brothers developed the Lakes. Tied closely to Citibank's massive credit card processing facility, the residential area gradually emerged along Sahara and Buffalo Drive. Then in 1987, Richmond American Homes began work on Desert Shores, a second master-planned community just north of today's Summerlin. Taking a cue from Collins Brothers, this one thousand–acre project featured four small lakes and even some beach areas. Both Desert Shores and the Lakes were under way before water waste became the burning issue it is today. In the 1990s, builders also filled in much of the seven hundred–acre Peccole Ranch development between West Charleston Boulevard and Sahara with medium-priced and high-end homes. In the 1980s, these three master-planned communities in the city of Las Vegas complemented other large subdivision projects built in the county, such as the upscale Spanish Trail community and numerous home and condominium complexes north and east of it.

For the most part, these new developments in the county were too far away for the City of Las Vegas to annex. Many were located in Spring Valley, an unincorporated town. Like the Strip towns of Paradise and Winchester, the city could not annex it without the approval of county commissioners.

But Summerlin was the real jewel in the crown, and the city would add much of this community to the municipal tax base after 1990. Actually, the Lakes and Desert Shores could have been in Summerlin, since they lie mostly on Howard Hughes Corporation land. But company executives, anxious to finance the enormous road and park projects that have attracted thousands of home buyers to their development, sold these lands to meet Summerlin's enormous start-up costs.

Summerlin and Peccole Ranch were similar in that they were built partly (in the former's case) or totally (in the latter's case) on land swapped with the federal government for other land that Hughes and Peccole had acquired in the 1940s. In Summerlin's case, the Hughes Corporation gave up parcels that could have been sold as high-end custom home sites in the scenic Red Rock Canyon area for tracts closer to the built-up periphery of Las Vegas.

Hughes executives decided to allow Las Vegas to annex Summerlin North for a variety of reasons. The key one was the proximity of the city's sewer and sewage treatment systems, which meant huge savings for developers and home owners. The benefit to Las Vegas has been not just the expanded tax base, but also the accelerated pace of construction, which will result in Summerlin's being sold out by 2015, not 2030 as originally projected.

Three years of planning and Summerlin's innovative design contributed mightily to its perennial number-one national ranking in new home sales. First announced in 1987, Del Webb's Sun City Summerlin got Hughes's master-planned community off to a fast start in 1990 with brisk home sales to seniors. But the rest of Summerlin was intended for residents of all ages. Planners divided the 36-square-mile property (22,500 acres) into a series of villages containing different "neighborhoods" of mostly single-family homes, with some medium- to high-priced multioccupancy condominiums begun in the 1990s. One of Summerlin's main selling points has been the numerous parks the Hughes Corporation built to beautify its villages. These recreational spaces in turn have been connected by more than one hundred miles of landscaped trails. Company planners also reserved land for schools, retail shopping, and Summerlin Center, a large office-mall-gaming complex near the western beltway. By 2002, eight golf courses and more than twenty schools (including such elite institutions as the Meadows School, the Hebrew Academy, and Faith Lutheran) enhanced Summerlin's appeal to prospective home buyers.

For its part, the City of Las Vegas, having failed for years to snare its southern Strip suburbs, made no such mistake in the west. From the beginning, Oran Gragson's mayoral successor, Bill Briare (1975–1987), and city commissioners worked to obtain this valuable tax base. The group included future mayor Ron Lurie, who sat as the city's representative on the Regional Transportation Commission. Lurie made sure there were no snags in the construction of roads connecting the city's existing street system with Summerlin's major thoroughfares. This required delicate negotiations with the Hughes Corporation over construction of Summerlin Parkway, the vital four-mile extension of u.s. 95 from the Rainbow Curve to Summerlin.

Summerlin continues to grow, covering much of the western valley on land still owned by The Howard Hughes Corporation, 2002. Photograph by Jeff Scheid and copyright Las Vegas Review-Journal

Mayor Bill Briare shakes hands with an officer from Nellis Air Force Base in 1983. At the time, Briare was seeking his third term as mayor, having already served as a state assemblyman and county commissioner. Nellis Air Force Base was, and remains, a major influence in the metropolitan economy as an employer and contributor to residential building in North Las Vegas and northeast Las Vegas. Special Collections, UNLV Libraries

In addition, working with Hughes executives, the City of Las Vegas in 1989 approved the first-ever special improvement district for a developer in which the municipality agreed to issue bonds to reimburse the Hughes Corporation for millions of dollars in public improvements to sell the homes. Summerlin North residents are paying off the bonds over a twenty-year period to defray the costs of building Summerlin Parkway and thirty miles of water, sewer, power, gas, telephone, and cable lines, all of which were needed before home construction could begin.

While Summerlin, Peccole Ranch, Desert Shores, and the Lakes in the City of Las Vegas were master-planned communities, the disconnected subdivisions built by Pardee and other developers in Spring Valley were not. Finally, in 2003, Clark County commissioners scheduled public meetings to draw up a master plan for Spring Valley. But in this case, residents were not potential home buyers who could select the best plan and then move into that community. Instead, they already owned their home and now had to joust with influential developers trying to shape the plan to their liking, whether or not it conflicted with the existing community's interests.

This issue is becoming important as valley residents begin to debate the kind of development they want as never before. Unlike Atlantic City and Miami Beach, whose fragile wetland ecosystems often suffered in the mad rush to build resorts, golf courses, and other tourist-related businesses, during the first five decades of Las Vegas's postwar growth, residents showed little concern for the environmental implications of the area's frantic urbanization. True, they debated water quality and protection of the desert tortoise and other endangered species from the developer's spade, but in the early twenty-first century opposition became more pronounced. Typical was the movement led by Blue Diamond residents in early 2003 to oppose developer Jim Rhodes's plans for building thousands of homes near scenic Red Rock Canyon. Clark County commissioners, impressed by the size and intensity of the public clamor, voted not to rezone Rhodes's tract to allow the denser building pattern he preferred. Later that year, the commissioners faced another tough decision. This time, Summerlin residents, environmental advocates, and other citizens joined forces to oppose Stations Casinos's plan to build a 300-foot, 23-story hotel tower at Summerlin Center near West Charleston and the beltway. For residents and environmental advocates like Jeff Van Ee of the Sierra Club, these buildings in effect put a minidowntown on the edge of the metropolis virtually at the entrance to the scenic Red Rock Canyon National Recreation Area. As Van Ee glumly noted, "Red Rock Canyon is sort of dying from a thousand cuts"—with Summerlin Center one of the largest.

Summerlin residents accused the Hughes Corporation and Stations Casinos of deceiving them into believing that Summerlin Center would contain no tall buildings. Home owners had known that Summerlin Center would include a casino-resort since 1996 when county commissioners approved Summerlin's master plan. But everyone expected a low-rise Green Valley Ranch type of resort, not a 23-story tower. Stations Casinos consultant Jeff Rhoades, however, explained that since Hughes executives planned to erect two 200-foot office towers nearby, Stations Casinos had to construct its tower higher than originally planned to give penthouse-suite customers a valley view. Rhodes insisted that only with a 23-story hotel could the resort's suites and high-rise gourmet restaurant make money. County commissioners again sided with the public. In December 2003, the board decided not to approve the higher tower, but delayed a final vote to give residents and resort executives more time to work out a compromise. In January 2004, they did when Stations Casinos settled for a 198-foot tower.

Although developers like Irwin Molasky, whose own plans for offices in the west valley faced some opposition, saw these protests as antigrowth movements, they were really more about the kind of development that builders would pursue. While some environmentalists like Van Ee oppose, for example, the northwest beltway that Las Vegas city planners proposed in 2004 to run through empty desert, they are a distinct minority and do not yet constitute a broad-based pressure group. To date, the only valley-wide opposition to growth is in Red Rock Canyon itself, a place that, virtually everyone agrees, should retain its pristine beauty. Opposition to growth itself in the past decade or so involves a different set of issues than the Red Rock–Stations Casinos protest. Obviously, air pollution, crowded schools, snarled traffic, and strained government services have worsened over the past twenty years. However, this is nothing new in the history of Las Vegas. Although residents have been struggling with a variety of growth-related problems for years, they have not supported the kind of growth restrictions that Boulder City enacted years ago.

Nevertheless, pressures to slow down come not so much from powerful community groups as from economic forces that exert themselves when certain thresholds of growth are met. In the Las Vegas Valley's case, once population reached a million back in the early 1990s, residents willingly footed the bill for an expensive beltway to bind the outer suburbs more closely to core areas and improve east-west traffic. In the early 1990s, the valley finally got a reliable Citizen Area Transit (CAT) bus system. In 2004, the initial leg of an elevated train system opened between the Sahara and MGM Grand hotels. This monorail will eventually whisk passengers down both sides of the Strip, connect to the airport and downtown, and perhaps continue along such key east-west arterials as Sahara Avenue. But Las Vegans will never build a monorail system from one end of the valley to the other, because it would be prohibitively expensive and the metropolitan area's population will never get that dense completely across.

Population, now at 1.7 million, will not go much past 2 million because of a lack of water. Already in the face of drought, *and to allow for more growth,* the water district has raised water rates, implemented year-round lawn-watering restrictions, and threatened other drastic measures. The district is also working feverishly to purchase more water from other states, but there are limits even to this in the arid West.

The Southern Nevada Water Project began pumping water throughout the Las Vegas Valley in the early 1970s. Without it, Las Vegas could not have become a metropolis of 1.7 million residents. Special Collections, UNLV Libraries

A second restraining factor is taxes. In the 2003 legislative session, Republican governor Kenny Guinn convinced lawmakers to raise taxes by an estimated $836 million and warned that future spending will require even more revenue. Conservatives and Libertarians howled in protest just as California voters were recalling newly reelected governor Gray Davis, whose policies had helped drive that state into spiraling debt. Ironically, the very group that championed uncontrolled growth in Las Vegas was the one group that did not want to be taxed for it: business. Even as the legislature debated a business payroll tax, the Clark County School District had to wait until the state tax increase had passed to hire the new teachers it desperately needed to handle skyrocketing enrollments.

Officials in Las Vegas, Henderson, and North Las Vegas still favor unregulated growth, although some are more cautious than others. But as the mayors of both Henderson and North Las Vegas conceded in 2002, growth does not pay for itself—at least not in the short run. In 1997, state senator Dina Titus (D–Las Vegas) proposed her "ring around the valley" bill to limit growth in the metropolitan area. City and county politicians, with the exception of Las Vegas mayor Jan Jones, as well as developers and the conservative media opposed it. Valley leaders remain unwilling to adopt anything resembling Portland's strict growth controls. And while county commissioners later agreed to establish a regional planning board to make recommendations concerning new development projects on the urban periphery, no one was ready to put the "fastest-growing" reputation of their metropolis behind them. It is noteworthy that in 2004, county commissioner Bruce Woodbury and new colleagues Rory Reid and Mark James (who has since resigned) proposed a task force to study growth problems and consider policy changes. But inevitably, in the long run, lack of water, rising taxes, higher utility costs, and shortages of cheap land will force growth controls.

Of course, the struggle over the size and direction of growth has not just pitted residents against developers or local politicians against the state. Local politicians have also battled each other, just as they have for decades. In the politically fragmented valley, Las Vegas and Clark County leaders clashed again in the 1990s over highway construction policies.

The last portion of the fifty-three-mile beltway around the metropolitan area finally opened for traffic in November 2003. Unsurprisingly, this stretch of road lay in the northwest portion of the valley, mostly within the Las Vegas city limits. In the mid-1990s, Clark County constructed a large section of the beltway from Green Valley and McCarran Airport over to the then largely empty southwestern part of the valley. Over the next ten years, this action supplemented the county's already large tax base with new commercial and residential developments spawned by beltway interchanges at Rainbow, Jones, and other key thoroughfares. Las Vegas leaders protested in vain. Mayor Jan Jones and city councilmen, most notably Matthew Callister, correctly pointed out that the heavily populated Summerlin area needed relief from the snarled traffic on U.S. 95–395. This issue, however, was just another example of how the political fragmentation of the valley into multiple jurisdictions worked to the county's advantage. It would be more than a decade before beleaguered city residents in Las Vegas's northwestern suburbs would benefit from the widening of U.S. 95–395.

Valley governments and community institutions have been strained by the size and direction of the metropolitan area's growth and by the diversity of the new migrants, many of whom are not the WASP residents the valley has traditionally lured. Indeed, since 1970, the metropolitan population has not only grown exponentially, but has also become more diversified racially and ethnically. In 1950, even with Basic Magnesium's wartime recruitment, only 3,174 blacks resided in the valley. They composed just 6.6 percent of the metropolitan area's total population. However, the availability of custodial, room maid, porter, and other low-end service jobs created by the tourist industry increased the number of black residents to more than 11,000 (8.7 percent) by 1960 and almost 25,000 (9.1 percent) in 1970. Of course, the staggering increase of resort properties and hotel rooms in the three cities and county, coupled with the success of the civil rights movement in opening up more higher-paying jobs to minorities, helped drive the black population to 46,000 (9.5 percent) in 1980 and to more than 120,000 by 2000.

Ironically, while the African American population increased, its percentage of the total population began to drop after 1990, a phenomenon also typical of California, Arizona, and other southwestern areas. The enormous influx of Hispanic migrants is responsible. In 1910, Las Vegas had only a handful of Spanish-speaking residents, all Mexicans, who worked on the railroad. Even the 1960 figure was only 578, but it would soon grow, thanks to an influx of Cubans who came to Nevada after Fidel

Castro closed Havana's casinos. However, the 1980 number for the metropolitan area was 35,000, or 7.2 percent of the total population, 83,000 in 1990 (11.2 percent), and 302,000 (21.9 percent) in 2000.

The reasons for this trend are numerous. Certainly, the growth of low-paying service-sector positions (including landscaping jobs created by the enlarged Anglo population of affluent home owners), the creation of a good CAT bus system, a lower cost of living compared to California, and a growing Hispanic home community are all factors.

This recent migration is more ethnically diverse than Las Vegas's early Hispanic population. Today, individuals from every nation in Central and South America, as well as many Caribbean islands, are represented in the valley. While this diversity has enriched the metropolitan area culturally with hundreds of new stores and services catering to Hispanic tastes and needs, the population influx has strained government services and forced the construction of many new schools.

At the same time, the migration has pressured other community institutions like the Catholic Church. The Las Vegas diocese, traditionally short of vocations due to the city's affluence and appealing secular culture, has seen its worship services suddenly flooded by thousands of new congregants. In a 2003 study, local Catholic officials reported that in contrast to the East and Midwest where churches are being closed by the hundreds, in Las Vegas the bishop cannot build them fast enough. It is not just the rapid leapfrog growth of local Germans, Irish, Italians, and Poles into tracts once inhabited by rattlesnakes and jackrabbits, but also the massive increase in the Hispanic population in and around the three cities that requires the planting of more parishes. But the problem is not just the construction of more churches; it involves personnel, too. Today, parishioners outnumber Las Vegas–area priests by as much as 18,000 to one, a ratio unmatched elsewhere. One Las Vegas parish has two priests for almost 40,000 parishioners. And Latinos go to Mass more than Anglos. In a city where the usual attendance is 14 percent of census Catholics, the Hispanic percentage of actual worshipers is much higher. Unsurprisingly, Las Vegas has become the fastest-growing Catholic diocese in the United States, and one of the fastest in the world.

However, it is not just the Hispanic population that is growing in the valley, but the Asian–Pacific Islander group, too. Only a handful of Chinese and Japanese residents called Las Vegas home in its early railroad decades. As late as 1980, the group's 9,207 people accounted for less than 2 percent of all residents. But in 1990, the figure jumped to 25,153 (3.4 percent), and in 2000 it soared again to 78,959 (5.7 percent). In fact, demographers predict that this group will eventually pass local African Americans in total numbers. Like the Hispanic population, the Las Vegas area's Asians are more ethnically diverse than their predecessors. The Filipinos, not the Chinese or Japanese, are the largest contingent, constituting more than 40 percent of the group's local population.

The explanation for this influx is similar to the one for Asians and Hispanics. Of special importance was the shift in U.S. immigration policy away from the traditional European groups. New regulations, adopted in 1965 by President Lyndon Johnson, favored non-European groups from Africa, the Middle East, Central and South America, the Caribbean, Asia, and Micronesia. The chief point of entry began to shift from New York and the Northeast to port and border cities in the South and West. This pulling factor helped create the vast pools of immigrants that have moved into Texas, New Mexico, Arizona, and California, and from these states eventually into Nevada.

Unlike New York, Chicago, San Francisco, and other traditional cities, there is no Chinatown or specific Hispanic enclave where the group lives. Las Vegas has no "South Central." In Las Vegas, the racial and ethnic populations have scattered all over the metropolitan area since open housing began in 1971. While some Hispanics prefer to cluster residentially together and others must settle for low-income areas that whites and wealthier African Americans have fled—especially eastern Las Vegas and downtown North Las Vegas—Hispanic communities exist in all three cities and the county. Dispersal, rather than segregation or ghettoization, has been the norm since 1970.

Like Las Vegas's African American community, all of these groups have formed organizations to pursue their interests. For example, the Latin Chamber of Commerce promotes Hispanic-owned businesses. The United Latin Americans, Hispanics in Politics, and other groups have been formed to address issues of significance to their community and support candidates for political office. Much of this activity is based in the cities of Las Vegas and North Las Vegas. But the situation varies with other groups. While the Filipino population is more city-based, the Chinese, Japanese, and Koreans tend to conduct their activities south of Las Vegas's borders.

Indeed, the massive "Chinatown" shopping complex of Asian businesses resides on Spring Mountain Road west of the Strip in the county. Despite their varying approach to life in Las Vegas, these groups have contributed mightily to the valley's diverse retail sector. They have also supplemented the usual fare of Anglo publications with foreign language newspapers of their own that examine local issues and world events from differing cultural perspectives.

The valley also contains a substantial Mormon community. While Mormons had settled in Las Vegas in 1855, their speedy departure gave them no foothold in the community, and their influence grew only with the World War II and postwar booms. Numbering an estimated 10 percent of the population, they became prominent in the business community, especially in banking, led by Reed Whipple and E. Parry Thomas. As noted earlier, Thomas became the first banker to make and arrange loans for casinos. Teaming with partners Nate and Jerry Mack, Thomas became one of the most important figures in Las Vegas history. In politics the most important was Harry Reid, a convert to the church who has risen from Henderson city attorney to U.S. senator—a position previously held by another Mormon who began his career as Las Vegas city attorney, Howard Cannon. Families like the Christensens, Gibsons, Woodburys, Lambs, and Ashworths have made their mark in state and local politics, while the judiciary has included such prominent Mormons as federal judges Lloyd George, Clive Jones, and Roger Hunt. The church's expansion with Las Vegas's growth also was evident in the opening of a temple at the base of Sunrise Mountain in 1989.

The Las Vegas Jewish community likewise has been limited in size but is important to the area. From the founding of its first synagogue, Temple Beth Shalom, in 1943, it has reflected and helped shape Las Vegas's growth. From its original location in the city at Thirteenth and Carson, the temple moved to Seventeenth and Oakey, a more elite residential area, in 1957. Then, at the end of the twentieth century, it moved to a new facility far outside the original city and its earlier suburban offshoots, in Summerlin. Another twenty congregations have joined it, ranging across the spectrum from Orthodox to Reform, and meeting in their own buildings or in community centers.

While the Jewish community never seems to have exceeded an estimated 5 percent of the population, its influence has been considerable.

Many of the Strip and downtown casinos were run by Jews who had operated illegal casinos elsewhere, making their expertise crucial to the city's biggest industry—from Moe Dalitz at the Desert Inn, Showboat, Stardust, and Sundance to Eddie Levinson at the Sands and Fremont. Lawyers such as Louis Wiener, George Rudiak, David Goldwater, and Sam Lionel represented many leading individuals and corporations. Lloyd Katz operated several theaters, including the Huntridge, and played an active role in the civil rights movement. He and his wife, Edythe, involved themselves in numerous community activities. Hank Greenspun was not only the crusading publisher of the *Las Vegas Sun,* but also a businessman and land developer whose family developed Green Valley, owned Channel 8, and invested early in cable television, with son Brian selling the family's share of Prime Cable in 1998 for $1.3 billion. And Jews enjoyed considerable political success: Chic Hecht, whose family long had owned a downtown department store, became a U.S. senator; Shelley Berkley served in the legislature, on the board of regents, and in the House of Representatives; and longtime defense attorney Oscar Goodman became mayor in 1999. Controversial and colorful, Goodman became one of the most popular politicians ever, attracting token opposition to his reelection in 2003 while garnering 86 percent of the vote.

Considering the challenges posed by the growing diversity and size of the local population, the amazing growth of Summerlin, and the need to maintain a strong gaming industry in the face of Strip competition and rapid suburban development, Las Vegas has been fortunate to be led by two vibrant mayors since 1990. Two-term mayor Jan Jones—Las Vegas's first woman mayor—brought a fresh perspective to city hall when she arrived in 1991. A Stanford graduate and business executive, Jones energized city government with more community outreach, bureaucratic reorganization, a significant development effort, and a greater flair for publicity than her predecessors. Following Jones was the flamboyant and ever astute Goodman, who made his reputation in the early 1970s as a high-priced defense attorney for Caesars Palace and Circus Circus developer Jay Sarno when the latter faced federal tax evasion charges. Goodman later defended noted oddsmaker and Stardust Hotel executive Frank Rosenthal, one of the mob principals later depicted by Robert de Niro in Martin Scorsese's film *Casino.* Rosenthal was an associate of Chicago mob enforcer Anthony Spilotro, who also retained Goodman's services during various bouts with the law. In 1999, after three decades of building a reputation as the mob's chief defense attorney in Las Vegas, Goodman shocked everyone by announcing that he would run for mayor of Las Vegas and, if elected, put his legal career on the shelf. His easy victory over veteran city councilman Arnie Adamsen reflected not only Goodman's overwhelming popularity, but also voter displeasure with business as usual.

Both Jones and Goodman faced their share of problems regarding the city's future direction. Downtown redevelopment and tourism were major issues. During her tenure, Jones pushed hard to revitalize downtown with a new federal court building (which opened in 2000) and other projects funded partially by the city. In an effort to revive downtown tourism, Jones was instrumental in convincing the major casinos in Glitter Gulch to support construction of the Fremont Street Experience and championed what became the Neonopolis Mall.

Both, however, have had their problems. The mall has limped along since its staggered opening in 2002. And even the Fremont Street Experience showed signs of weakness in the new century. During its first five years of operation, the experience drew increased crowds every year and helped Fremont Street's casinos to win back a small percentage of the tourist play they had lost to the Strip. But the light-show attraction drew few repeat visitors. By 2002, annual attendance fell to 15.4 million, its lowest figure ever. In that year, the ten adjoining hotels that jointly own the experience hired Joe Schillaci as CEO to restore the attraction's glitter. Schillaci, who had competed for customers with Disneyland and Universal Studios as president of Six Flags Magic Mountain, immediately began a $17 million renovation to install a new light-emitting diode system designed to energize the show with a wider range of images.

Aside from maintaining a healthy tourist industry downtown, Jones and Goodman, like their counterparts in older cities across the nation, have also struggled with the problem of downtown revitalization. The trick has been not to waste money and make mistakes. But even with the best consultants, this is no easy task. The land is available, because the old railroad yards built by Senator Clark behind his depot at the head of Fremont Street were removed by Union Pacific in the early 1990s. Under both Jones and Goodman, the city moved to develop this strategic land behind the Plaza Hotel.

In the decade since the Union Pacific sold the site, a number of development schemes have been proposed to use the location for transforming downtown into something more than a tourist center. While new management in 2004 promised to reinvigorate the Neonopolis Mall, the latter's failure to reinforce the Fremont Street Experience from 2002 to 2004 has made the larger downtown redevelopment project all the more important. During Jones's tenure, a domed stadium was the popular concept. Texas entrepreneur Paul Tanner bought the railroad's sixty-one-acre parcel with a $48 million note from Lehman Brothers, and promised to build the $750 million multipurpose facility. But unable to obtain the financing, he later declared bankruptcy. Saddled with this unwanted property, Lehman Brothers was happy to sell Tanner's parcel to the City of Las Vegas in exchange for suburban land that municipal officials once intended to be the Las Vegas Technology Center.

Mayor Goodman, who made downtown redevelopment one of his priorities, orchestrated this deal. While the old Technology Center land has undergone a dramatic increase in value, thanks to new buildings, since the city owned it, most observers agree that municipal leaders have wisely delayed the development of the old railroad yards. Mayor Goodman envisions using this land to diversify downtown's economy with a prestigious academic medical center, a performing arts facility, and other buildings. Already, Goodman's enthusiasm for the project, his determination to avoid costly mistakes, and his direct control over the process have prompted developers like Irwin Molasky and Summerlin's Mark Fine to build office buildings adjoining the site. Moreover, the success of Las Vegas Premium Outlets, the arrival of a large-scale furniture mart, and other businesses have convinced Goodman and other city officials to take their time and develop the former railroad property correctly.

Today, as the city of Las Vegas embarks upon its second century, the prospects are bright for the metropolitan area as a whole. The city has undergone a shift in the past twenty years. Gaming and tourism, while as vibrant as ever, will never compete with the Strip. The industry that has really expanded and enriched the city of Las Vegas over the past two decades has been real estate, not gaming. Both Mayors Jones and Goodman are therefore correct in emphasizing the development of Senator Clark's old railroad yards behind the Plaza Hotel.

The city will continue to expand outward until developers reach the mountains. The city and county will still tussle over new lands in the

This was the new post office and courthouse at Third and Stewart, built in the early 1930s with federal help. As part of the city's centennial celebration, it is being turned into a museum. Special Collections, UNLV Libraries

northwest valley along the road to the nation's nuclear storage facility. But Mayor Goodman is right. The city must continue to diversify its economy with a prestigious medical center if possible. It must also work in the coming years with UNLV and other entities to develop a science and technology center to attract more research and information-based industries to Las Vegas. Even though tourism is at an all-time high, and even though the county has greatly expanded the 1963 jetport with "McCarran 2000" and the convention authority has greatly enlarged the Las Vegas Convention Center to make it the second largest in the nation, the Strip is benefiting more from these improvements than the city. In the new millennium, the

City of Las Vegas can no longer afford to rely so heavily on gaming and tourism for its future. As Reno has learned, diversification is crucial lest the economy become a house of cards.

Las Vegas should succeed in this effort, because it has been a flexible, resilient community throughout its history. Like a chameleon, it has been able to change colors as the need arose: beginning as a ranch area, it became a railroad town, then a dam gateway, then a recreation center for troops and defense workers, and now a mecca for world tourism. The pioneer residents of 1905 would not recognize their valley today. Eiffel Towers and glass pyramids symbolize the dramatic transformation that has remade Las Vegas. Gone are the icehouse, the repair shops, the water tower, and the other railroad signatures of a bygone era—replaced by Roman palaces, medieval castles, Venetian canals, and other structures celebrating Las Vegas's modern commitment to illusion, escapism, and leisure.

In less than a century, Senator Clark's sleepy little railroad town has become a metropolis of nearly two million people. It should never have happened, given the valley's lack of a lake, an ocean, rich mines, or productive farmlands, but it did. One hundred years of leadership, perseverance, hard work, and imagination have created the world's most visited city in a most unlikely place, the Mojave Desert. The dream of the city's pioneers and five generations of promoters has come true. Today's metropolis is more than they ever hoped for. But it did not happen the way they expected. Las Vegas did not become a railroad hub like Chicago, or a mineral processing point like El Paso, or an agricultural center like Omaha. It became something else—a festival city built on dreams, chance, and self-indulgence where America and the world came to play.

(Facing page) Seventy years after its completion, Hoover Dam remains central to Las Vegas. Still a major tourist attraction, its water and power are vital to the Southwest. Without the dam's water supply, growth and master-planned communities like Summerlin and Green Valley would still be on the drawing board. Special Collections, UNLV Libraries

BIBLIOGRAPHY

BOOKS

Abbott, Carl. *The New Urban America: Growth and Politics in Sunbelt Cities.* Chapel Hill: University of North Carolina Press, 1981.

Allen, Marion. *Hoover Dam and Boulder City.* Redding, Calif.: C.P. Printing and Publishing, 1983.

Balboni, Alan. *Beyond the Mafia: Italian-Americans and the Development of Las Vegas.* Reno: University of Nevada Press, 1996.

Barlett, Donald L., and James B. Steele. *Empire: Life, Legend, and Madness of Howard Hughes.* New York: Norton, 1979.

Berman, Susan. *Easy Street.* New York: Dial Press, 1981.

———. *Lady Las Vegas: The Inside Story behind America's Neon Oasis.* New York: TV Books, distributed by Penguin, 1996.

Bernard, Richard, and Bradley Rice, eds. *Sunbelt Cities: Politics and Growth since World War II.* Austin: University of Texas Press, 1983.

Best, Katharine, and Katharine Hillyer. *Las Vegas, Playtown U.S.A.* New York: D. McKay, 1955.

Brill, Steven. *The Teamsters.* New York: Simon and Schuster, 1978.

Brooker, Angela, and Dennis McBride. *Boulder City: Passages in Time.* Boulder City: Boulder City Library, 1981.

Burbank, Jeff. *License to Steal: Nevada's Gaming Control System in the Megaresort Age.* Reno: University of Nevada Press, 2000.

Chung, Su Kim. *Las Vegas: Then & Now.* San Diego: Thunder Bay Press, 2002.

Dahl, Albion. *Nevada's Southern Economy.* Carson City: University of Nevada Bureau of Business and Economic Research, 1969.

Davies, Richard O., ed. *The Maverick Spirit: Building the New Nevada.* Reno: University of Nevada Press, 1998.

Demaris, Ovid. *The Last Mafioso.* New York: Bantam, 1981.

Denton, Ralph, and Michael S. Green. *A Liberal Conscience: Ralph Denton, Nevadan.* Reno: University of Nevada Oral History Project, 2001.

Denton, Sally, and Roger Morris. *The Money and the Power: The Making of Las Vegas and Its Hold on America, 1947–2000.* New York: Alfred A. Knopf, 2001.

Dondero, Harvey N. *History of Clark County Schools.* Las Vegas: n.p., 1987.

Driggs, Don W., and Leonard E. Goodall. *Nevada Politics and Government: Conservatism in an Open Society.* Lincoln: University of Nebraska Press, 1996.

Dunar, Andrew J., and Dennis McBride. *Building Hoover Dam: An Oral History of the Great Depression.* 1993. Reprint, Reno: University of Nevada Press, 2001.

Edwards, Jerome. *Pat McCarran: Political Boss of Nevada.* Reno: University of Nevada Press, 1982.

Elliott, Gary E. *The New Western Frontier: An Illustrated History of Greater Las Vegas.* Carlsbad, Calif.: Heritage Media, 1999.

———. *Senator Alan Bible and the Politics of the New West.* Reno: University of Nevada Press, 1994.

Findlay, John M. *People of Chance: Gambling in American Society from Jamestown to Las Vegas.* New York: Oxford University Press, 1986.

Fisher, Charles W., and Raymond J. Wells. *Living in Las Vegas: Some Social Characteristics, Behavior Patterns, and Values of Local Residents.* Las Vegas: n.p., 1967.

Fogelson, Robert. *The Fragmented Metropolis: Los Angeles, 1850–1930.* Cambridge: Harvard University Press, 1967.

Garreau, Joel. *Edge City: Life on the New Frontier.* New York: Doubleday, 1991.

Garrison, Omar. *Howard Hughes in Las Vegas.* New York: Dell Publishing, 1971.

Gottdiener, M., Claudia C. Collins, and David R. Dickens. *Las Vegas: The Social Production of an All-American City.* Malden, Mass.: Blackwell Publishers, 1999.

Greenspun, Hank, with Alex Pelle. *Where I Stand.* New York: D. McKay, 1966.

Hanna, David. *Bugsy Siegel: The Man Who Invented Murder.* New York: Belmont Tower Books, 1974.

Hartigan, Francis X., ed. *History and Humanities: Essays in Honor of Wilbur S. Shepperson.* Reno: University of Nevada Press, 1989.

Hess, Alan. *Viva Las Vegas: After Hours Architecture.* San Francisco: Chronicle Books, 1993.

Hinds, James. *Epitome of the History of Nellis Air Force Base.* Las Vegas: Nellis Air Force Base, 1977.

Hopkins, A. D., and K. J. Evans, eds. *The First 100: Portraits of the Men and Women Who Shaped Southern Nevada.* Las Vegas: Huntington Press, 1999.

Hulse, James W. *Lincoln County, Nevada, 1864–1909: History of a Mining Region.* Reno: University of Nevada Press, 1971.

———. *The University of Nevada: A Centennial History.* Reno: University of Nevada Press, 1974.

Hulse, James W., with Leonard Goodall and Jackie Allen. *Reinventing the System: Higher Education in Nevada, 1968–2000.* Reno: University of Nevada Press, 2002.

Hundley, Norris. *Water and the West: The Colorado River Compact and the Politics of Water in the American West.* Berkeley and Los Angeles: University of California Press, 1975.

Jaschke, Karin, and Silke Otsch, eds. *Stripping Las Vegas: A Contextual Review of Casino Resort Architecture.* London: Verso, 2003.

Jones, Florence Lee, and John F. Cahlan. *Water: A History of Las Vegas: History of the Las Vegas Land and Water Company.* 2 vols. Las Vegas: Las Vegas Valley Water District, 1975.

Kefauver, Estes. *Crime in America.* Garden City, N.Y.: Doubleday, 1951.

Land, Barbara, and Myrick Land. *A Short History of Las Vegas.* Reno: University of Nevada Press, 1999.

Lauritzen, Jonreed. *Las Vegas, Nevada for Fun in the Sun.* Las Vegas: n.p., 1947.

Luckingham, Bradford. *The Urban Southwest: A Profile History of Albuquerque–El Paso–Phoenix-Tucson.* El Paso: Texas Western Press, 1982.

Maggio, Frank. *Las Vegas Calling.* Las Vegas: TAD Publishing, 1972.

McBride, Dennis. *In the Beginning: A History of Boulder City, Nevada.* Boulder City: Boulder City Chamber of Commerce, 1981.

McMillan, James Bates, Gary E. Elliott, and R. T. King. *Fighting Back: A Life in the Struggle for Civil Rights.* Reno: University of Nevada Oral History Project, 1997.

Meyers, Sid. *The Great Las Vegas Fraud.* Chicago: Mayflower Press, 1958.

Miranda, M. L. *A History of Hispanics in Southern Nevada.* Reno: University of Nevada Press, 1997.

Moehring, Eugene P. *Resort City in the Sunbelt: Las Vegas, 1930–2000.* Reno: University of Nevada Press, 2000.

Murray, Jack. *Las Vegas: Boomtown U.S.A.* Phoenix: Lebeau Printing, 1962.

Nash, Gerald. *The American West Transformed: The Impact of the Second World War.* Bloomington: Indiana University Press, 1985.

Paher, Stanley. *Las Vegas: As It Began—As It Grew.* Las Vegas: Nevada Publications, 1971.

Perry, David C., and Alfred J. Watkins. *The Rise of the Sunbelt Cities.* Beverly Hills: Sage Publications, 1977.

Pomeroy, Earl. *In Search of the Golden West: The Tourist in Western America.* New York: Alfred A. Knopf, 1957.

Ralli, Paul. *Nevada Lawyer: A Story of Life and Love in Las Vegas.* Dallas: Mathis Van Nort, 1946.

Ray, Clarence, Helen Blue, and Jamie Coughtry. *Black Politics and Gaming in Las Vegas, 1920s–1980s.* Reno: University of Nevada Oral History Project, 1991.

Reid, Ed. *Las Vegas: City without Clocks.* Englewood Cliffs, N.J.: Prentice-Hall, 1961.

Reid, Ed, and Ovid Demaris. *The Green Felt Jungle.* New York: Pocket Books, 1963.

Reisner, Marc. *Cadillac Desert: The American West and Its Disappearing Water.* New York: Viking, 1986.

Roske, Ralph. *Las Vegas: A Desert Paradise.* Tulsa: Continental Heritage Press, 1986.

Rothman, Hal K. *Devil's Bargains: Tourism in the Twentieth-Century American West.* Lawrence: University Press of Kansas, 1998.

———. *Neon Metropolis: How Las Vegas Started the Twenty-first Century.* London: Routledge, 2002.

Rothman, Hal K., and Mike Davis, eds. *The Grit beneath the Glitter: Tales from the Real Las Vegas.* Berkeley and Los Angeles: University of California Press, 2002.

Schumacher, Geoff. *Sun, Sin and Suburbia: An Essential History of Modern Las Vegas.* Las Vegas: Stephens Press, 2004.

Schwartz, David G. *Suburban Xanadu: The Casino Resort on the Las Vegas Strip and Beyond.* New York: Routledge, 2003.

Sheehan, Jack E., ed. *The Players: The Men Who Made Las Vegas.* Reno: University of Nevada Press, 1997.

Smith, John L. *No Limit: The Rise and Fall of Bob Stupak and Las Vegas' Stratosphere Tower.* Las Vegas: Huntington Press, 1997.

———. *Of Rats and Men: Oscar Goodman's Life from Mob Mouthpiece to Mayor of Las Vegas.* Las Vegas: Huntington Press, 2003.

———. *Running Scared: The Life and Treacherous Times of Las Vegas Casino King Steve Wynn.* New York: Barricade Books, 1995.

Squires, Charles P. *Las Vegas, Nevada: Its Romance and History.* 2 vols. Las Vegas: n.p., 1955.

Sternlieb, George, and James W. Hughes. *The Atlantic City Gamble.* Cambridge: Harvard University Press, 1983.

Stevens, Joseph. *Hoover Dam: An American Adventure.* Norman: University of Oklahoma Press, 1988.

Teaford, Jon. *City and Suburb: The Political Fragmentation of Metropolitan America, 1850–1970.* Baltimore: Johns Hopkins University Press, 1979.

Thompson, Hunter. *Fear and Loathing in Las Vegas.* New York: Random House, 1971.

Titus, A. Costandina. *Bombs in the Backyard: Atomic Testing and American Politics.* Rev. ed., Reno: University of Nevada Press, 2001.

Venturi, Robert, Denise Scott Brown, and Steven Izenour. *Learning from Las Vegas: The Forgotten Symbolism of Architectural Form.* Cambridge: Harvard University Press, 1977.

White, William T., Bernard Malamud, and John E. Nixon. *Socioeconomic Characteristics of Las Vegas, Nevada.* Las Vegas: UNLV Center for Business and Economic Research, 1975.

Wiley, Peter, and Robert Gottlieb. *Empires in the Sun: The Rise of the New American West.* New York: G. P. Putnam & Sons, 1982.

Wolfe, Tom. *The Kandy-Kolored Tangerine-Flake Streamline Baby.* New York: Farrar, Straus, and Giroux, 1965.

Wright, Frank. *Clark County: The Changing Face of Southern Nevada.* Reno: Nevada Historical Society, n.d.

Yantis, Betty. *Desert Airways: A Short History of Clark County Aviation.* Henderson: Clark County Heritage Museum, 1993.

———. *Fact Book for Las Vegas and Clark County.* Las Vegas: UNLV Center for Business and Economic Research, 1977.

ARTICLES

Adams, Charles. L. "Las Vegas as Border Town: An Interpretive Essay." *Nevada Historical Society Quarterly* 21 (summer 1978): 51–55.

Balboni, Alan. "Southern Italians and Eastern European Jews: Cautious Cooperation in Las Vegas Casinos." *Nevada Historical Society Quarterly* 38 (fall 1995): 153–73.

Beebe, Lucius. "Las Vegas." *Holiday* 12 (December 1952): 106–8, 132–37.

Beville, John M. "How Las Vegas Pioneered a Rotary Club." *Nevada Historical Society Quarterly* 10 (fall 1967): 29–34.

Bracey, Earnest N. "Anatomy of Second Baptist Church: The First Black Baptist Church in Las Vegas." *Nevada Historical Society Quarterly* 43 (fall 2000): 201–13.

———. "The Moulin Rouge Mystique: Blacks and Equal Rights in Las Vegas." *Nevada Historical Society Quarterly* 39 (winter 1996): 272–88.

Davenport, Robert W. "Early Years, Early Workers: The Genesis of the University of Nevada." *Nevada Historical Society Quarterly* 35 (spring 1992): 1–20.

Dobbs, William T. "Southern Nevada and the Legacy of Basic Magnesium, Incorporated." *Nevada Historical Society Quarterly* 34 (spring 1991): 273–303.

Elliott, Gary E. "Senator Alan Bible and the Southern Nevada Water Project, 1954–1971." *Nevada Historical Society Quarterly* 32 (fall 1989): 181–97.

Findlay, John M. "Suckers and Escapists? Interpreting Las Vegas and Postwar America." *Nevada Historical Society Quarterly* 33 (spring 1990): 1–15.

Fitzgerald, Roosevelt. "Blacks and the Boulder Dam Project." *Nevada Historical Society Quarterly* 24 (fall 1981): 255–60.

French, William. "Don't Say Las Vegas Is Short of Suckers." *Saturday Evening Post* 228 (November 5, 1955): 12.

Friedman, Robert. "The Air-Conditioned Century." *American Heritage* (1984): 20–33.

Green, Michael S. "The Las Vegas Newspaper War of the 1950s." *Nevada Historical Society Quarterly* 31 (fall 1988): 155–82.

Grose, Andrew. "Las Vegas–Clark County Consolidation: A Unique Event in Search of a Theory." *Nevada Public Affairs* 14, no. 14 (1976).

Hill, Gladwin. "Atomic Boomtown in the Desert." *New York Times Magazine* (February 11, 1951): 14.

———. "Klondike in the Desert." *New York Times Magazine* (June 7, 1953): 14, 65, 67.

———. "Las Vegas Is More than the 'Strip.'" *New York Times Magazine* (March 16, 1958): 18, 31–32.

Jones, Florence Lee. "Las Vegas: Golden Anniversary Edition." *Las Vegas Review-Journal* (February 28, 1955).

"Las Vegas: 'It Just Couldn't Happen.'" *Time* (November 23, 1953): 30–34.

"Las Vegas Hedges Its Bets." *Business Week* (August 11, 1956): 157–58.

Moehring, Eugene P. "Las Vegas: Growth and Infrastructure: A Legacy of Poor Planning." *Western Planner* 18 (December 1997): 12–14.

———. "Las Vegas and the Second World War." *Nevada Historical Society Quarterly* 29 (spring 1986): 1–30.

———. "Profile of a Railroad Town: Las Vegas in 1910." *Nevada Historical Society Quarterly* 34 (winter 1991): 466–87.

———. "Public Works and the New Deal in Las Vegas." *Nevada Historical Society Quarterly* 24 (summer 1981): 107–29.

Nystrom, Eric. "Labor Strife in Las Vegas: The Union Pacific Shopmen's Strike of 1922." *Nevada Historical Society Quarterly* 44 (winter 2001): 313–32.

Pasquale, Verona, and Cheryl Rose Crockett. "The End of the Line? The Railroad Cottages of Las Vegas: Then and Now." *Nevada Historical Society Quarterly* 27 (winter 1984): 268–77.

Pastier, John. "The Architecture of Escapism: Disney World and Las Vegas." *American Institute of Architects Journal* 67 (December 1978): 26–37.

Patrick, Elizabeth Nelson. "The Black Experience in Southern Nevada." *Nevada Historical Society Quarterly* 22 (summer 1979): 128–40.

Rocha, Guy Louis. "The I.W.W. and the Boulder Canyon Project: The Final Death Throes of American Syndicalism." *Nevada Historical Society Quarterly* 21 (spring 1978): 3–24.

Stabler, Charles. "Fades and Factories: Las Vegas and Reno Want More Industry to Back Dice Tables." *Wall Street Journal* (January 22, 1957): 1, 12.

Swallow, Craig F. "The Ku Klux Klan in Nevada during the 1920s." *Nevada Historical Society Quarterly* 24 (fall 1981): 204–20.

Townley, Carrie Miller. "Helen J. Stewart: First Lady of Las Vegas." Parts 1 and 2. *Nevada Historical Society Quarterly* 16 (winter 1973): 214–44; 17 (spring 1974): 2–32.

Wild, Roland. "Las Vegas." *New Yorker* (April 1953): 39–44.

GOVERNMENT DOCUMENTS AND REPORTS

C. B. McClelland Co. *Report of Las Vegas, Nevada Housing Survey.* December 1947. Riverside, Calif., 1948.

City of Henderson. *Henderson: An American Journey.* Henderson, 2004.

Clark County Board of Commissioners. *A Workable Blueprint for Local Government in Clark County, Nevada.* Las Vegas, March 1969.

———. *Clark County Road and Flood Control Needs Assessments.* Las Vegas, April 1981.

Clark County Planning Commission. *Comprehensive Plan: Clark County, Nevada.* 6 vols. Las Vegas, 1981.

Clark County School District. *An Action Plan for Integration of Six Westside Elementary Schools . . . Prepared by Superintendent James I. Mason.* Las Vegas, 1969.

Cohen, Burrell. *An Action Plan for Downtown Las Vegas.* Las Vegas, 1975.

Duff, Anderson, and Clark. *Las Vegas and Clark County, Nevada: An Economic and Industrial Analysis.* Chicago, 1956.

Edgerton, Germeshansen, and Grier, Inc. *The Nevada Test Site and Southern Nevada.* Las Vegas, 1961.

Eisner-Stewart and Associates. *Land Use Inventory and Analysis.* South Pasadena, 1966.

———. *Proposed General Plan: Las Vegas Valley.* South Pasadena, 1966.

Henderson City Planning Commission. *General Master Plan of the City of Henderson, Nevada.* Henderson, 1969.

Las Vegas Chamber of Commerce. *Where Is Las Vegas Going? Get the Full Facts on the Present and Future Economy of Las Vegas.* Las Vegas, 1974.

Las Vegas Chamber of Commerce Industrial Committee. *Story of Southern Nevada.* Las Vegas, 1948.

Las Vegas Chamber of Commerce Research and Statistical Bureau. *A Compendium of Statistics and Social Facts of Las Vegas, 1952–1975.* Las Vegas.

Las Vegas City Planning Commission. *Capital Improvement Program, 1969–1974.* Las Vegas.

Las Vegas Valley Water District. *Master Water Plan, Las Vegas Valley.* Las Vegas: Boyle Engineering, 1970.

Local Government Study Committee. *Report on Local Governments in Clark County.* Las Vegas, 1973.

Los Angeles Bureau of Municipal Research. *Economic Base Study—Las Vegas, Nevada.* Los Angeles, 1958.

Metcalf & Eddy Engineers—Montgomery Engineers. *Facility Plan Las Vegas Valley Regional Secondary Treatment Facilities: Clark County, Nevada.* Las Vegas, 1976.

North Las Vegas City Council. *City of North Las Vegas: Community Renewal Plan.* Vol. 1. North Las Vegas, 1972.

Peabody College for Teachers. *Public Education in Nevada: A Digest of the Survey Report.* Nashville, 1954.

U.S. Atomic Energy Commission. *The Story of the Nevada Test Site.* Washington, D.C., 1963.

NEWSPAPERS

Clark County Review. 1909–1922.

Las Vegas Age. 1905–1947.

Las Vegas (Evening) Review-Journal. 1929–present.

Las Vegas Sun. 1950–present.

Las Vegas Times. 1905–1906.

North Las Vegas Valley Times. 1964–1984.

Pioche Record. 1905–1909.

MANUSCRIPT COLLECTIONS (Lied Library, Department of Special Collections, University of Nevada, Las Vegas, unless otherwise noted)

Aplin, Charles. Papers. 1907–1960.

Baker, Charles Duncan. Papers. 1926–1972.

Cahlan, Albert E. Papers. 1930–1968.

Cahlan, John. Papers.

Cashman, James. Family Papers. 1901–1961.

Economic Opportunity Board of Clark County. Archives. 1963–1970.

Franklin, George E. Manuscripts.

Grant, Archie. Family Papers. 1918–1973.

Las Vegas Land and Water Company.

Squires, Charles Pemberton. Papers. 1893–1958.

Union Pacific Railroad Collection.

UNPUBLISHED MATERIALS

Baldwin, Edward E. "Las Vegas in Popular Culture." Ph.D. diss., University of Nevada, Las Vegas, 1997.

Elliott, Gary E. "The Moulin Rouge Hotel: A Critical Appraisal of a Las Vegas Legend." Paper. Lied Library, Department of Special Collections, University of Nevada, Las Vegas.

Fitzgerald, Roosevelt. "Black Entertainers in Las Vegas, 1940–1960." Paper. Lied Library, Department of Special Collections, University of Nevada, Las Vegas.

———. "The Evolution of a Black Community in Las Vegas, 1905–1940." Paper. Lied Library, Department of Special Collections, University of Nevada, Las Vegas.

———. "The Impact of the Hoover Dam Project on Race Relations in Southern Nevada." Paper. Lied Library, Department of Special Collections, University of Nevada, Las Vegas.

Gray, Raymond Guild. "The Organization of a County School District: A Case Study of District Consolidation and Administrative Organization." Ph.D. diss., Stanford University, 1958.

Green, Michael S. "A Partisan Press: The Las Vegas Newspapers and the 1932 Election." Paper. Lied Library, Department of Special Collections, University of Nevada, Las Vegas.

Gubler, Ward H. "Las Vegas: An International Recreation Center." Master's thesis, University of Utah, 1967.

Kaufman, Perry. "The Best City of Them All: A History of Las Vegas, 1930–1960." Ph.D. diss., University of California, Santa Barbara, 1974.

Kieser, Mary. "A History of Las Vegas Schools, 1905–1956." Professional paper, University of Nevada, Las Vegas, 1977.

Lay, Matt. "Narrative History of the History of Henderson." Paper. Lied Library, Department of Special Collections, University of Nevada, Las Vegas.

Murphy, Don. "The Role of Changing External Relations in the Growth of Las Vegas." Ph.D. diss., University of Nebraska, 1969.

Sadovich, Maryellen. "Basic Magnesium, Incorporated and the Industrialization of Southern Nevada." Master's thesis, University of Nevada, Las Vegas, 1971.

Swallow, Craig F. "The Ku Klux Klan in Nevada during the 1920's." Master's thesis, University of Nevada, Las Vegas, 1978.

ORAL HISTORIES

Aplin, Charles. *An Oldtimer in Las Vegas.* University of Nevada Oral History Project, 1969.

Binion, Lester Ben. *Some Recollections of a Texas and Las Vegas Gaming Operator.* University of Nevada Oral History Project, 1973.

Boyer, Florence. *Las Vegas, Nevada: My Home for Sixty Years.* University of Nevada Oral History Project, 1967.

Cahill, Robbins. *Recollections of Work in State Politics, Government, Taxation, Gaming Control, Clark County Administration and Nevada Resort Association.* University of Nevada Oral History Project, 1973.

Cahlan, John. *Reminiscences of a Reno and Las Vegas, Nevada Newspaperman, University Regent, and Public-Spirited Citizen.* University of Nevada Oral History Project, 1970.

Coughtry, Jamie, ed. *Lubertha Johnson: Civil Rights Efforts in Las Vegas, 1940s–1960s.* Reno: University of Nevada Oral History Project, 1988.

Edwards, Elbert. *Memoirs of a Southern Nevada Educator.* University of Nevada Oral History Project, 1968.

Godbey, Erma. *Pioneering in Boulder City.* University of Nevada Oral History Project, 1967.

Patrick, Elizabeth Nelson. *Oral Interview of Coral Williams.* Las Vegas, 1978.

———. *Oral Interview of Lubertha Johnson.* Las Vegas, 1978.

———. *Oral Interview of Reverend Prentiss Walker.* Las Vegas, 1978.

Patrick, Elizabeth Nelson, and Rita O'Brien, eds. *The Black Experience in Southern Nevada.* Las Vegas, 1978.

Rockwell, Leon. *Recollections of Las Vegas, Nevada, 1906–1968.* University of Nevada Oral History Project, 1969.

INDEX

Note: Italic page numbers refer to illustrations.

Block & Botkin's store, 21
Blue Diamond, 50, 236
board of trade, 20
Boggs, Benjamin, 21, 29, 36
Bolshevik revolution, 38
Bonanza Airlines, 145, 146–47
Bonanza Underpass, 189
Boone, Pat, 142
Borge, Victor, 176
Boston, Mass., 186
Boulder Addition, 83
Boulder Canyon Project Act of 1928, 84, 92
Boulder City: and agriculture, 51; and an-
    nexation, 187, 229–30; and Boulder Dam
    construction, 90, 99; and growth restric-
    tions, 237; as neighboring city, xiv; and
    politics, xvi, 187; and railroad industry,
    77; and Six Companies, 80–82, 86; slow-
    growth approach, 229; and tourism, 1
Boulder Club, 87, 182
Boulder Dam. See Hoover Dam
Boulder Dam Stage Office, 75
Boulder Drug Company, 75
Boulder Highway: and casinos, 87, 139, 165,
    182, 205; completion of, 81; and prostitu-
    tion, 117; and segregation, 197; and Six
    Companies, 86; and suburban growth,
    99, 111; and urbanization, 136
Boulder Lake Regatta, 91
Boulder Station, 140
Bow, Clara, 68
bowling, 140
boxing matches, 29, 32, 222
Boyd, Bill, 181, 212
Boyd, Sam: career of, 131, 175, 178, 180–82,
    207; and civil rights, 200; photograph of,
    181; and revitalization of Fremont Street,
    212, 213
Boyd Group, 211, 212
Boyle, Emmet, 47, 58, 61
Bracken, Anna, 14, 53
Bracken, Walter: club activities of, 53; and
    Las Vegas Land & Water Company

(LVL&W), 43, 62; and Lincoln County
    Division Club, 25; as Mason, 29; and
    McWilliams, 43–44, 45, 62; photographs
    of, 14, 35; as railroad agent, 11, 14, 18; and
    social class, 34; and Union Pacific, 59–
    60, 61; and water company, 19; Williams
    compared to, 49
Breakenridge, William, 92
Breeze, Clarence D., 59, 63, 70
Brennan (judge), 35
Briare, Bill, 185–86, 234, 235
Briggs, Mitzi Stauffer, 211
Brigham Young University, 159
Bringhurst, William, 4, 5
Brookman, Eileen, 199
Brosnan, Jim, 221
Brown, Bob, 194
Brown, James, 33
Brown, Joe W., 146–47
Brown, Mahlon, 159
Brown, T. A., 27
Brown v. Board of Education (1954), 164
Buck's Addition, 19, 45, 62
Bugsy (film), 220
Bullfrog district, 46
Bunker, Berkeley, 66
Bunker, Bryan, 68
Bunker, John, 27, 55
Bunker, Wayne, 66
Bunker, Wendell, 66, 169
Bunker family, 53, 66
Bunkerville, 68
Buol, Frank, 29
Buol, Peter: and agriculture, 41, 42; and
    artesian springs, 19; and business inter-
    ests of, 51; Swiss heritage of, 34; and
    Levy, 53; photograph of, 42; and politics,
    25, 39, 54, 55; and Scottish investors, 49
Bureau of Reclamation, 38, 58, 77, 80, 86

Cabana Motel chain, 175
Caesars Palace, 173, 175, 176, 185, 204–7, 220,
    222

Cahill, Robbins, 119

Cahlan, Al: and Baker, 169; and Basic Magnesium, Inc., 102–3; and civil rights, 198, 200; and community conflicts, 149–50; and convention center, 147; and Cragin, 125; and development, 96, 142; as editor, 68–69, 78, 79; and Gay, 67; and Greenspun, 168–69; and legalized prostitution, 118; and politics, 64, 70; and water shortage, 116

Cahlan, John, 45, 69, 74, 200

Caliente, 24, 25, 60, 61, 72

California: and civil rights, 203; and electric power, 157; and federal government, 135; and gambling, 90–91; and highway construction, 46, 47, 74, 85, 147, 189; Las Vegas compared to, 1; Las Vegas's connections with, 2; military bases/defense plants of, xiv; and mining industry, 21, 46; and Old Spanish Trail, 2; population of, 58; and railroad industry, 10, 16; tribal gaming boom, 212, 217; U.S. acquisition of, 4; water needs of, 89; and World War II, 101

California Edison, 157

California Hotel, 182, 212, 213

Callister, Matthew, 240

Campbell, Thomas, 156

Camp Pendleton, 104

Camp Sibert, 104

Cannon, Howard, 165, 171, 190, 193, 243

Capone, Al, 78, 150, 151

Capone-Siegel mob, 150

Carey, Raymond, 167

Carlson, William, 160

Carnegie, Andrew, 29

Carnival Lounge, 142

Carroll, Thomas, 78–79

Carson, Johnny, 218

Carson City, 47

Carver Park, 103, 162

Cashman, James, 66, 70, 74, 109, 126, 152, *219*

Casino (film), 211, 220, 244

casinos: and banking, 134, 243; and Basic Magnesium, Inc., 102; and Boulder Highway, 87, 139, 165, 182, 205; and civil rights, 165–67, 197–201; and entertainment, 218, 220; on Fremont Street, xiv, 87–88, 111, 115; and Gragson, 170; growth of, 171; and highway construction, 147; Indian casinos, 217; and *Las Vegas Sun,* 168; and the mob, 119–21, 127, 129, 131, 150–52, 210–11; and politics, 128–30; proposed federal taxes on, 144; and sports, 223–224; and tax evasion, 91, 176, 178; and tourism, 100, 115; and World War II, 104

Castro, Fidel, 240–41

Catholic Church, 71, 241

cemeteries, 53

Central Labor Council, 92

Chamber of Commerce: and airport, 188; and Cashman, 66; and community conflicts, 149; formation of, 41; and Griffith, 23; and higher education, 160; and highway construction, 46–47; and Hull, 109; and Las Vegas Land and Water Company (LVL&W), 63; and legalization of prostitution, 117–18; and sanitation, 117; and Test Site, 136; and tourism, 75, 115; and water use, 39. *See also* Las Vegas Promotion Society

Charleston, S.C., 3

Charleston range, 3, 36, 144

Charleston Underpass, 122–23

Chicago, 146, 162, 242

Chief Hotel, 108

China, 135

Chinese immigrants, 241–42

Chop House Bill's, 27

Christ Church Episcopal Church, 29

Church of Jesus Christ of Latter-day Saints, 4

Circus Circus, 138, 210

Citibank, 232

Citizen Area Transit (CAT) bus system, 237, 241

City Beautiful Movement, 84

city planning, 187, 237. *See also* master-planned communities

Civella, Nick, 211

civic improvements, 40, 52, 53. *See also* municipal services; public works

Civil Aeronautics Board (CAB), 145

civil rights: and African American population, 240; and casinos, 165–67, 197–201; and cold war, 164–65; and gaming industry, xv, 196–98, 201–2, 203; and Gragson, 170; and Jewish community, 244; and Metro, 196; public debate over, 165; and public works, 164; and racial violence, 165, 196, 198, 202

Civil Rights Act of 1964, 198, 201

Clark, Ed W.: and agriculture, 41–42; businesses of, 22–23; and Colorado River Commission, 58; and founding of Clark County, 25, 26, 27; and highway construction, 47; and politics, 55; and water use, 20

Clark, J. Ross, 10, 13, 16, 22, 59

Clark, Pat, 128–29

Clark, Ramsey, 151

Clark, Toni, *183*

Clark, Wilbur, 119, 151, *183*

Clark, William Andrews: background of, 9–10, 34; and development of Las Vegas, 16; and founding of Clark County, 26, 27; and founding of Las Vegas, xiii, 11–13, 15, 246; and ice plant construction, 17–18; and John T. McWilliams, 11, 17, 20; and railroad industry, 145; and sale of holdings to Union Pacific, 59; and Helen Stewart, 9; and water use, 162, 192

Clark County: and airport, 145; and annexation, 148–49, 184, 185, 186; buildings of, 134; and El Rancho Vegas, xv; and environmental concerns, 236; founding of, 24–26, 32; and higher education, 160;

and highway construction, 47, 239–40; and hospital, 86; offices of, 42–43; and Pahrump Highway, 144; and political fragmentation, 239; and prostitution, 117, 118; and the Strip, 145

Clark County Courthouse, 12, 43, *44,* 134–35

Clark County Defense Council, 50

Clark County Hospital, 172

Clark County Museum, Henderson, 24

Clark County Regional Flood Control District, 190

Clark County Review, 33, 41–42, 61, 68

Clark County School District, 123, 157–58, 202, 239

Clark County Wholesale, 23

Clark High School, 202

Clark Inn Motel, 108

Clark Townsite, 11–13, 15, 23, 45, 49, 59, 80, 111, 116, 162

Club Alabam, 164

coal mining towns, 15

Coast Resorts, 182, 220

Cohen, Burton, 218

cold war, 106, 112, 135, 164–65

Cole, Nat King, 197

Collins, J. L., 52

Collins Brothers, 227, 232

Colonial House, 172

Colorado River: dam on, 49, 57–59, 76. *See also* Hoover Dam

Colorado River Commission, 58, 116

Colorado River Compact, 59, 193

Colorado River Hydro-Electric Company, 49

Colored Democratic Club, 52

Colored Progressive Club, 52

Colossal Circus, 53

Colton, Rodney, 119

communism, 38, 39, 135

Community Chest, 149

Community College of Southern Nevada, 159

and operation of Clark Townsite, 12, 13; role in social life, 53; Union Pacific's ownership of, 59; and water district, 117, 161–62; and water use, 13, 18–19, 20, 26, 43, 53, 116

Las Vegas Mormon Fort State Park, 6

Las Vegas Pharmacy, *100*

Las Vegas Post Office, 40, 82, *247*

Las Vegas Premium Outlets, 246

Las Vegas Promotion Society, 20, 21, 28, 34, 41. *See also* Chamber of Commerce

Las Vegas Ranch, 6–7, *6,* 43–44, 45

Las Vegas Review, 57, 68–69, 72

Las Vegas Review-Journal: and airport, 145–46; and Basic Magnesium, Inc., 102–3; and city manager position, 167; and civil rights, 198, 199–200; and community conflicts, 149; and convention center, 147; and Ernie Cragin, 96, 125; and development, 78, 79; and Oran Gragson, 194; and *Las Vegas Sun,* 168–69; and sanitation, 117; and tourism, 107, 115

Las Vegas Sanitary Committee, 28

Las Vegas Sentinel Voice, 198

Las Vegas Spring Ranch, 6

Las Vegas Springs Preserve, 2–3, 17

Las Vegas Stars (baseball team), 223

Las Vegas Sun: and convention center, 147; and local government, 167–69; and the mob, 150, 151; and prostitution, 118–19; and Charles P. "Pop" Squires, 22

Las Vegas Taxpayer's Association, 128, 153

Las Vegas Taxpayer's League, 98

Las Vegas Times, 11, 20–21, 30, 34

Las Vegas Union School District, 63

Las Vegas Valley, 2–4, 91, 101, 103, 156, 237. *See also* metropolitan area

Las Vegas Valley Water District, 116–17, 126, 156, 161–62, 192–93, 238

Las Vegas Wranglers, 23

Latin Chamber of Commerce, 242

Laubenheimers family, 49

Laughlin, 182

law enforcement: development of, 32; and gambling, 48, 71, 78, 90, 91; and Ku Klux Klan, 71; and Las Vegas's image, 90; and the mob, 150; and Prohibition, 48–49, 59, 70–71, 78, 88, 90; and prostitution, 118–19; and railroad strike, 60. *See also* police

Lawson, Samuel, 153, 157

Laxalt, Paul, 120, 201, 202

lead mining, 5

League of Elected City and County Officials, 185

Leaving Las Vegas (film), 220

Leavitt, Newell, 53

Lee, Henry, 25, 26

Lee Canyon, 20

legal community, 66

Lehman Brothers, 246

LeRoy Corporation, 167

Lester, Buddy, 180

Levinson, Eddie, 143, 200, 244

Levy, Adolph, 21, 36, 53

Lewis, Maxine, 112

Liberace, 218, *219,* 221

Liberty Loan Drive, 50

libraries, 29, 43, 52, 157

Lido de Paris Revue, 137, 138, 220

Lillis, Henry, 27, 29, 34, 45, 55

Lincoln County, 10, 24–25, 43

Lincoln County Division Club, 25–26

Lincoln Hotel, 21

Lionel, Sam, 244

Lion's Club, 115

liquor licenses: and Block 16, 12, 13, 30, 31–32; and Block 17, 12, 13; and civil rights, 198; and prostitution, 118

liquor sales: limiting hours of, 144; stringent laws concerning, 194; and tourism, 92; and Steve Wynn, 207

Liston, Sonny, 222

Little Church of the West, *113*

Live Wire Fund, 115–16, 149

local government: and airport, 84, 103, 114,

Nuclear Test Site, xiv
Nye County, 144

Oakey, 49
Oasis (restaurant), 67
O'Callaghan, Mike, 203
Ocean's Eleven (film), 220
Oddie, Tasker, 39, 74
Ogden Tower, 142
Old Mormon Fort, 77
Old Spanish Trail, xiii, 2
On the Waterfront (film), 151
opera house, 29, 39, 41
Organized Crime Strike Force, 211
Organized Crime Treaty of 1977, 151
Orr, William, 43
Overland Hotel, 21, 39, *40,* 66, 75, *99,* 212
Overton, 25, 61

Pacific Fruit Express Company, 23
Pacific Islanders, 241–42
Pahrump Highway, 144
Pair-O-Dice Club, 87, *88,* 106
Paiutes, 2, *3,* 4, 5, 6, 8
Palace Hotel, 21, 54
Palace Station, 182, 205, 213
Palms (store), 51
Palm Springs, Calif., 100, 207, 217
Panaca, 25
Panama-California Exposition, 41
panic of 1907, 22, 28
Paradise (as unincorporated township), xiv, 128, 170, 183, 185, 232
Paradise Development Company, 172
Paradise Grove, 158
Pardee, 227, 236
Paris, the, 210
Park, John S., 14–15, 22, 24, 28, 29, 51, 67, 75, 133
Park, William S., 22
parks, 126, 194, 233. *See also* state parks
Parks, Anna Roberts, 24
Parks, Rosa, 164

partnerships, 21–22
Patterson, Floyd, 222
Peabody Teacher's College, 157
Peccole, William, 129, 154, 169
Peccole Ranch, 232, 233, 235
Pecetto, Domenic, 36, 51
penicillin, 117
Pentagon, 132
Philadelphia, Penn., 146
Phoenix, Ariz., 100, 101, 122, 135, 142, 156, 186, 203
Phoenix Open, 91
Pike, William, 51, 67
Pine, Fred, *35*
Pioche, 24, 25, 72
Pioche Manganese, 106
Pioche Record, 25
Pioneer Heights, 45
Pipkin, Charles, 128–29, 153, 188
Pittman, Key, 69, 70, 93, 95, *98,* 101
Pittman, Vail, 150, 153, 168
police: and corruption, 195–96; and Oran Gragson, 194; and local government, 124; and Metro, 186, 187, 196; and population growth, 162, 163; and racial policies, 164; and school violence, 202. *See also* law enforcement
polio, 117
politics: and civil rights, 198; and corruption, 96; and elite, 22, 66–67, 69–70, 74; and formation of state of Nevada, 5; and founding of Clark County, 24–26; fragmentation of, xv–xvi, 170, 186–87, 204, 239, 240; and highway construction, 148; and Hispanics, 242; and Jewish community, 244; and Ku Klux Klan, 70–71; and mining industry, 9, 10; and the mob, 150; and Mormons, 243; and population growth, 144, 239; and post–World War II era, 112; and the press, 33–34, 69, 78, 96; and public works, 95–96, 121–24, 129, 194; and right-to-work law, 152–53; and sanitation, 117; and tourism, 109, 114;

trends in, 54–55; and unions, 1, 92–93. *See also* Democratic Party; Republican Party

popular culture, 217, 224

population, characteristics of, 34–36

population growth: and banking, 134; and Basic Magnesium, Inc., 101–2; and Boulder Dam construction, 88; and competition for county seat, 26; and diversity, 240–44; and education, 1, 37, 85, 123, 157, 158, 191, 239, 241; expenses related to, xv, 1, 37, 116, 121–23, 155, 191; and Ed Fountain, 194; from 1910 to 1920, 37; from 1920 to 1930, 57; from 1930 to 1940, 84, 88–89; and opposition to growth, 237, 239; and politics, 144, 204; and Strip, 173, 205; and tourism, 123, 132; and water use, 1, 37, 83, 116, 192–93; and World War II, 107, 116

Porchlight Campaign, 160

Portland, Ore., 239

Powell, John Wesley, 6

Preddy, Sarann Knight, *199*, 201

Prell, Milton, 181

Presbyterian Church, 29

Presley, Elvis, *183*, 218, 221

press: and airport, 115, 188; and annexation of the Strip, 126; and city manager position, 167; and Charles C. Corkhill, 32–33; and economics, 114; and education, 158; and ethnicity, 34–35; and growth limits, 239; and growth of Las Vegas, 68–69, 78; and Wes Howery, 195; and the mob, 150, 168; and politics, 33–34, 69, 78, 96; and public works, 123; and railroad strike, 61; and sanitation, 28, 117; and sewer system, 95, 192; and suburban development, 172; and tourism, 115; and water supply, 116, 191. *See also specific newspapers*

Princess Theatre, 53

Progressive Era, 37–39, 41, 49, 57, 84

property valuations, 122

prostitution: and Block 16, 31, 32, 104, 118;

elimination of, 104, 117, 121; and Ku Klux Klan, 71; legalization of, 117–18

Prowse, Juliet, *183*

Prudential Homes, 136

Public Service Commission, 59, 62

public works: and C. D. Baker, 170; and federal government, 96, 156; and the New Deal, 93, 95; and politics, 95–96, 121–24, 129, 194; and population growth, 232; and road building, 189–91; and taxation, 121, 122, 191, 194

Purple Gang, 151

race and race relations: and bigotry, 144; and Walter Bracken, 34; and civil rights, xv; and public works, 164; racial violence, 165, 196, 198, 202; and segregation, 52, 68, 130, 164–67, 196–203

radioactivity, 136

KENO (radio station), 115

Ragtown, 11, 13, *81*

railroad cottages, 16–17, *17*

railroad industry: and Chamber of Commerce, 41; and William Andrews Clark, 9–10; and county building, 42; and economics, 10–11, 13, 16, 36, 45–46, 57, 61–62, 84; and electrical service, 54; as employer and builder, 15–18; and entrepreneurs, 7, 8; Las Vegas as railroad town, 15; and mining industry, 16, 46; railroad repair shops, xiv, 61; and Helen Stewart, 9; and strikes, xiv, 42, 60–61, 84; and tourism, 82, 100; and track problems, 16–17; and waste removal, 28; and water use, 43

Railroad Pass Casino, 87, 88

Rain Man (film), 221

Rancho Circle, 148

Rancho High School, 158, 202

Rancho Hotel, 217

Ray, Clarence, 52

Reber, Frank, 33

Spring Mountain Ranch, 6
Spring Mountains, 20
Spring Valley, xiv, 137, 227, 228, 232, 236
Squires, Charles P. "Pop": and air service,
72; and annexation of the Strip, 127;
business interests of, 22, 28, 33; and city
government, 39; and Colorado River
Commission, 58; and Fremont Street
residence, 14; and *Las Vegas Age,* 33; and
Lincoln County Division Club, 25; pho-
tographs of, *15, 35*; and politics, 22, 27, 33,
124; and public works, 121–22; and rail-
road routes, 46; and railroad strike, 61;
and the Republican Party, 22, 33; and
sewer system, 95
Squires, Delphine, *15*
Squires, James, 33
Stalin, Josef, 114
Standard Metropolitan Statistical Area, xiv
Stardust, the, 120, 137, *138,* 140, 151, *179,* 182,
211, 220, 222
Star Saloon, 31
state parks, 58
Stations Casinos, 213, 216–17, 220, 228,
236–37
Stauffer Chemical, 106
Stewart, Archibald, 6–7
Stewart, Archibald (son), 7
Stewart, Helen, 3, 7–9, *8,* 11, 13, 44, 52, 55–56
Stewart, William J., 7, 26, 27, 39, 70
Stewart Ranch, 9, 11, 28
Stocker, Harold, 48
Stocker, Mayme, 48, 53
Stottlemyre, Todd, 223
Stratosphere, the, 158, 216
Streisand, Barbra, 220
Strip, the: and African American employ-
ees, 164; architecture of, xv, 110, 175, 210;
attempts to annex, 126–29, 148, 170, 183,
185, 186, 187, 234; and banking, 134;
boundaries of, xiv; building boom on,
210; and civil rights, 198, 200; and com-
munity conflicts, 149–50; development

of, xv, xvi, 84, 87, 106, 108, 109–11, 116,
136–37, 145, 157, 173, 175, 224, 230; and
entertainment, 220; and family-friendly
campaign, 138; and infrastructure, 170;
and Interstate 15, 189; and legalization of
prostitution, 118; and the mob, 119–21,
210–11; neon of, 1; overbuilding on, 137;
and population growth, 173, 205; and
segregation, 197; and Southern Nevada
Telephone Company, 153; and suburbs,
142, 171–73, 181, 185, 186, 192, 193, 225,
230, 232; success of, 142, 204; and taxation, 122, 127, 186; and tourism, 1, 112, 115,
137, 149, 150, 173, 175, 204, 205, 207, 210,
217; views of, *110, 174, 177, 178, 179, 208–9;*
and water use, 162; and wedding chapels,
113; and Steve Wynn, 207
Stupak, Bob, 213, 216
suburbs: and casinos, 165–66, 182; and community conflicts, 149; development of,
xv, 111, 132, 136, 172, 173, 183–84, 193, 225;
and education, 158; and gambling, xv, 131,
213, 216–17; and population growth, 132,
232; and public works, 122; and resorts,
109–11; and retail sector, 172; and sewer
system, 95; and social issues, 187; and
Southern Nevada Telephone Company,
153; and street improvements, 189–90;
and the Strip, 142, 171–73, 181, 185, 186,
192, 193, 225, 230, 232; and tourism, 114;
and water use, 162
Sullivan, Maurice, 69
Summerlin, 1, 217, 228, 233, *234, 235,* 240, 244
Summerlin Center, 233, 236
Summerlin North, 233, 235
Sun City Aliante, 230
Sun City Anthem, 230
Sun City Summerlin, 230, 233
Suncoast, the, 217
Sunrise Hospital, 172, 173
Sunrise Manor, 149, 184, 185
Sunrise Mountain, 184
Sunrise Park Division, 88

Ullom, James, 54
Union Hotel, 51
Union Pacific Railroad (UP): and Boulder
Dam, 58, 77; William Andrews Clark's
sale of holdings to, 59; depot of, 84; and
founding of Las Vegas, xiii, xv, 10–11, 13;
and Edward Henry Harriman, 10; and
highway construction, 189; and railroad
yards, 245–46; service cuts of, 146; strike
of 1920s, xiv, 60–61, 84; and *Sunset Magazine,* 41; and tourism, 82
Union Plaza Hotel, 146, 182, 201, 212, 222,
226
unions: and Benny Binion, 178; and Boulder
Dam construction, 92; and civil rights,
201; and Great Red Scare, 39; and the
mob, 151; and politics, 1, 92–93; and
right-to-work law, 152; and strikes, xiv,
42, 60–61, 84
United Airlines, 145, 188
United Latin Americans, 242
United States Air Force, 106
University Medical Center, 172
University of Nevada, Las Vegas (UNLV),
108, 159–60, 173, 223, 247
University of Nevada, Reno, 158–59
University of Southern California, 159
urbanization: and Boulder Dam construc-
tion, 99; and city deficit, 129; and education, 157; and environmental concerns,
236; and Oran Gragson, 170; and health
issues, 93, 95, 191; and metropolitan area,
84; and public works, 121, 122, 163; and
the Strip, 136, 192; and tourism, 171; and
water supply, 116; and Westside, 163
U.S. Army Topographical Corps, 2
U.S. Bureau of Public Roads, 74
U.S. Congress, 4, 5
US Home, 227
U.S. Home and Housing Administration,
156
U.S. Justice Department, 90, 211
U.S. Senate, 10, 38

U.S. Supreme Court, 160, 201, 213
Utah, 46, 47, 85
Utah Territory, 4

Valley Bank, 134, 160, 173, 207
Valley High School, 202
Valley of Fire, 1
Valley of the Sun, 91
Van Ee, Jeff, 236, 237
Vegas Artesian Water Syndicate, 19
Vegas Heights, 184
Vegas World, 213
venereal disease, and prostitution, 104, 118
Venetian, the, 152, 210
Vietnam War, 135, 171, 191
Virginia City, 5
Virginia Hotel Corporation, 85
Virgin Valley, 25
Virtual Vegas (film), 220
Viva Las Vegas (film), 221
Volstead Act, 49, 90
volunteer fire companies, 27–28, 29, 39
Von Tobel, Ed, 20, 21, 27, 32, 34, *35,* 39, 54
Von Tobel, Ed, Jr., 21, 66
Von Tobel, George, 144
Von Tobel, Jake, 54
voting rights, 38
Voting Rights Act of 1965, 201

Wagner Act, 93
Waldman (neighborhood), 49
Waldman family, 66
Wakara (Ute chief), 2
Walker, James, *199*
Wall Street crash of 1929, 77
Wanniski, Jude, 167
Warren, Earl, 201
WASP society, 37, 38
water rates, 26, 192
water rights, 11, 18
water use: and Hoover Dam, 91; and Las
Vegas Land & Water Company (LVL&W),
18–19, 20, 26, 43, 53; and master-planned

communities, 232; and pollution, 43–45; and population growth, 1, 37, 83, 116, 121, 156, 161–62, 192, 238, 239; problems with, 114

Watson, Harry, 124

Watters, J. T., 63

Webb, Del, 133, 177, 181, 182, 230, 233

wedding chapels, 108, 113, 213, 218

Welles, Orson, 221

Wells Fargo, 133

Wengert, Cyril, 23–24, 85

Wengert, Frank, 23–24

Wengert family, 23–24

West, Charles, 197, 198, 200

West, the: and civil rights, 203; and William Andrews Clark's ambitions, 16; and federal government, 4; and irrigation, 38; and railroad industry, 10

Western, the, 182

Western Air Express (WAE), 72, 73, 85–86, 103–4, 128, 145

Western Douglas M-2 biplane, 73

West Las Vegas, 11, 45, 63, 137, 162, 163, 203

West-Marquis firm, 115

Westside neighborhood: and African American businesses, 130; and African American entertainers, 197; and C. D. Baker, 154; and Basic Magnesium employees, 162; development of, 230; and education, 84; and Interstate 15, 148; and Moulin Rouge, 165–67; and public works, 122, 164; and school segregation, 202–3; and urbanization, 163

Whipple, Reed, 65, 154, 155, 165, 194, 195, 196, 243

Whittemore, C. O., 12, 13, 18, 43, 74–75

Wiener, Louis, 244

Wiener family, 66

Wilbourn, Estelle, 159

Wilbur, Ray Lyman, 90, 91

Wilkerson, Billy, 111

Williams, Bill, 2

Williams, Frank, 55

Williams, Franklin, 165

Williams, Matt, 223

Williams, Thomas, 49, 187

Williamsville, 81

Willis, Vern, 136

Wilson, Woodrow (first black assemblyman), 164, 198, 199, 203

Wilson, Woodrow (president), 37

Wilson family, 6

Winchester (as unincorporated township), xiv, 128, 170, 183, 185, 232

Wingfield, George, 19, 37–38, 69, 91

Wisner, John, 21

Wolfskill, William, 2

woman suffrage, 38, 55

women: African American women, 164; and American Legion women's auxiliary, 50; as dealers, 182, 201; discrimination against, 201–2; and the Roaring Twenties, 57; and social organizations, 29, 52; and World War I, 50

Woodbury, Bruce, 239

Woolworths, 132

Works Progress Administration, 96

World Congress of Flight, 147

World Series of Poker, 177, 178

World War I, 38, 46, 49–50

World War I soldiers, 47

World War II: and airport, 103–4; and magnesium industry, 101–3, 104; and military bases, xiv, 104, 106, 108, 125; and residential development, 108; and tourism, 84, 107, 116

Wynn, Steve, 206–7, 210, 212, 213

Wynn–Las Vegas, 210

Yablonsky, Joe, 119

Young, Brigham, 4, 5

Young, Ralph, 176

Yount, George, 2

Yousen, Philip, 158

Zion Methodist Church, 52